Personality, Situation, and Persistence

NORWEGIAN STUDIES IN EDUCATION

No. 6

EDITOR

JOHS. SANDVEN
Professor of Education
University of Oslo

MANAGING EDITOR

PER RAND
Professor of Education
University of Oslo

CONSULTING EDITOR

ÅSMUND L. STRØMNES
Professor of Education
University of Tromsö

ROALD NYGÅRD

Personality, Situation, and Persistence

*A study with emphasis
on achievement motivation*

Universitetsforlaget

Oslo – Bergen – Tromsö

102515

© The Norwegian Research Council for Science and the Humanities 1977
(Norges almenvitenskapelige forskningsråd)

Section B.70.10–020T

ISBN 82-00-01563-7

Cover design by Per Syversen

Distribution offices:
NORWAY
Universitetsforlaget
Box 6589, Rodeløkka
Oslo 5
UNITED KINGDOM
Global Book Resources Ltd.
37, Queen Street
Henley on Thames
Oxon RG9 1AJ
UNITED STATES and CANADA
Columbia University Press
136 South Broadway
Irvington-on-Hudson
New York 10533

Printed in Norway by
Edgar Høgfeldt A/S, Kristiansand S.

CONTENTS

PREFACE

The kind of problems dealt with in this report first caught my interest while I was studying for my final examinations in education. In particular, my interest developed as a result of my friend John Johnsgard's calling my attention to the area of achievement motivation research, and of my subsequent participation in a project on achievement motivation in junior high school children, directed by Mrs. Lise Vislie, now associate professor, Mr. Edvard Befring, now professor, and Professor Per Rand. After initial concentration on the relationship between social background and achievement motivation (Nygård, 1967), I have in recent years been absorbed in the study of the effect of achievement-related motives on behaviour.

The present work deals primarily with one aspect of behaviour, that of persistence. This aspect was focused upon because persistence is assumed to be both a key factor in the level of performance at the particular tasks with which an individual is confronted, and, through its cumulative effect, a significant determinator of the individual's general course of development.

As will be obvious to the reader, the present work has been particularly influenced by that of Norman T. Feather on persistence problems. In his work two important circumstances have been stressed. Firstly, persistence should neither be regarded as an effect of personality characteristics alone nor of situation characteristics alone, but has to be understood as the result of personality characteristics in interaction with situation characteristics. The interaction viewpoint has found its clear expression through his application of achievement motivation theory on problems of persistence. Secondly, it has been underscored that persistence at a given task cannot be accounted for without taking into consideration the motivation for possible alternative tasks too. These two basic viewpoints are reflected in the theoretical approach to the problem area presented in Part 1, as well as in the plan of the empirical investigation of persistence accounted for in Part 2.

The distinction made by Feather between a personality-oriented, a situation-oriented, and an interaction-oriented approach to problems of persistence is reflected in the general plan of Chapter 1, where some background theory and re-

search along these lines are discussed. The essentials of the achievement motivation theory as initially set forth by David C. McClelland and his co-workers
and as further elaborated to a clear personality by situation interaction theory by
John W. Atkinson are presented in Chapter 2. The persistence research based on
this theory is discussed in Chapter 3. Some of the results from this research indicated that the personality by situation interaction might be even stronger than
that which was hypothesized by Atkinson. Thus, his theory assumes the motivation difference between achievement-oriented and failure-threatened individuals
to be strongest where the task is of some moderate difficulty, and to decrease
towards zero as difficulty approaches a very high or a very low level, while some
of the results indicated that achievement-oriented individuals are possibly less
motivated than the failure-threatened ones for very easy and very difficult tasks.
This question is further discussed in Chapter 4, where the integration of optimal
stimulation viewpoints from Daniel E. Berlyne, among others, has resulted in a
proposal for a revised, more strongly interaction-oriented theory of achievement
motivation. I hope that I have not distorted their intent by this integration. Some
indications of the validity of this revised theory from research on differences in
performance level are also presented in this chapter. This theory also provides
the basis for the guiding hypotheses, presented in Chapter 5, for the empirical
investigation of persistence in three different situational settings, according to
the difficulty level of an initial and an alternative task. Chapter 6 contains general
information concerning the empirical investigation. Measuring instruments, material, subjects, and methods of analysis are accounted for, and some of the practical difficulties encountered in connection with the investigation are discussed.
The results are presented in Chapter 7. Since the guiding hypotheses set forth in
Chapter 5 could also, albeit for different reasons, be set forth on the basis of the
achievement motivation theory as presented by Atkinson, this chapter also contains a section where a further examination of the alternative viewpoints offered
by the revised theory of achievement motivation is undertaken.

I am indebted to many institutions and private persons for their contributions
to this work. The project has been financially supported by scholarships, first
from the Norwegian Research Council for Science and the Humanities during the
years 1970-72, and next by the University of Oslo from 1973 on. During these
years I have had the opportunity to work and study at the Institute for Educational
Research, University of Oslo, and for this I offer thanks to the directors of the
Institute during these years, Professors Johs. Sandven and Anders Lysne, and
Associate Professor Bjarne Bjørndal. Further, my thanks are extended to the
then consultant, Bård Harboe, at the National Council for Innovation in Education

(Forsøksrådet for skoleverket), who helped me obtain permission to carry out the investigation among pupils participating in the IMU project; to the headmasters and the teachers involved at the Junior High Schools of Bingsfoss, Bråte, Fjellsrud, Gjerdrum, Kjellervolla, Skedsmovollen, Stav, and Vesong, who gave the final permission, and to the pupils for their co-operation.

Thanks are due to Leif Arne Dybdal and Ole Arne Mellingsæther, who assisted at the initial treatment of the data, to Odd Karlberg, who drew some of the figures, and to Karl Jan Solstad and Hans-Magne Eikeland for clarifying discussion on methodological problems. The latter has also through his teaching stimulated my interest in personality by situation interaction problems.

There are some people to whom I owe special thanks: To Professor Per Rand for his continuous interest, advice and encouragement during these years, and for having read the whole manuscript and suggested many improvements. To my friend, Torgrim Gjesme, who has also offered many critical and constructive comments on the manuscript. I can recall many stimulating discussions with him which have helped to clarify my thought. To Mrs. Betty Nicolaisen, who has typed the whole manuscript, and who has offered painstaking and high-level assistance both through her kind criticism of my phraseology and through her correction of grammatical errors.

Last, but not least, I am indebted to my wife, Kari Nygård, for her unfailing help and support, and for her great patience during the long period of work on this project. Her cheerful assistance in the final preparation of the manuscript, the proof-reading, and the bibliographic work has been of invaluable help in the recent busy weeks.

Although I have received great assistance from the persons mentioned above, I am, of course, entirely responsible for the final product.

Oslo, June 1974   Roald Nygård

PART 1

A THEORETICAL APPROACH TO THE PROBLEM OF
PERSISTENCE.

INTRODUCTION

Briefly the study of motivation can be said to cover the problems of selection, intensity, and persistence of behaviour (Bindra, 1959, p. 3; Birch & Veroff, 1966, p. 1; Hebb, 1949, p. 181; Jones, 1955, p. VII; Rethlingshafer, 1963, p. 2; Young, 1961, p. 24; among others). This means that motivational questions are of the utmost importance in connection with the problem of performance in the broadest sense of the word, whether we are concerned with this problem in schools, in daily work, or in leisure activities. The present study mainly focuses on one of the above-mentioned aspects, that of persistence in behaviour, which is dealt with from an achievement motivation point of view. The tasks which confront man during his lifetime are varied and numerous, ranging from simple routine tasks to those where a successful performance depends upon a maximum utilization of all his capacities. Differences in persistence are observed to occur both within the same individual from one kind of task to another and between individuals working at the same task. In a particular situation some individuals may appear strongly motivated to carry the tasks with which they are confronted to completion without regard to whether or not extrinsic rewards are offered, while others may refuse to exert themselves regardless of the efforts made to get them to work. Then, since performance level obviously depends very much on persistence in work, better insight into what causes such differences in persistence must be of central importance to all agents concerned with the arrangement of performance situations.

The importance of insight into the persistence problem should be even more clear when seen from a developmental or learning point of view. Thus, when faced with frustrations and failures in learning situations, some children return to these situations again, trying to master them, while others give up after the first failure. As strongly stressed by V. J. Crandall and Rabson (1960, p. 161), these two different modes of reaction should eventually affect the individual's general intellectual development. The consistently task-mastery-oriented individual is assumed to maximize his possibilities of developing greater problem-solving skills and freedom to use his abilities. In contrast, the consistently avoidance-oriented individual should minimize his possibilities of developing new methods of task solution, implying less utilization of his talents and abilities. An increased understanding of what lies behind these quite different persistence patterns is assumed to result in a better basis both for the child-rearing process and for the educational process more generally.

THE PERSISTENCE SITUATION

The concept of persistence has derived its meaning from that of its Latin cognate persistere, where per means by way of, and sistere to stand, and therefore carries the idea of remaining unchanged or fixed in a line of action (cf. Ryans, 1939b, p. 733). A theoretical distinction between the terms persistence and perseveration has been emphasized by Ryans (1938c, pp. 85 ff.), the first term referring to an active voluntary continuous response, the last one referring to a continuous repetition of the same response through inability to shift from one response to another. The present study is not aimed at enlightening typical perseveration problems, such as the difficulty of shifting set (e.g. in connection with alternatively adding and subtracting). On the other hand, the distinction between what is called voluntary and involuntary action is far from unproblematical, a circumstance which is revealed in the fact that the terms are to a large extent used interchangeably in the literature (cf. Ryans, 1938c, p. 85). Accordingly, although labelled a study of persistence, we may well come to touch, in the following, upon problems which are classified by some investigators as perseveration problems.

The problem area of this study is also very closely related to those listed under such terms as "resumption of interrupted activities" and "Zeigarnik effect". The first term refers to that type of situation described by Ovsiankina (1928), where subjects were set a task and then interrupted before it was completed, and where they later had the opportunity to resume the task without any obligation to do so (ibid., pp. 305 ff.). The latter term refers to a person's tendency to remember more about a task that was interrupted after he began working at it than about a task he was allowed to finish (Zeigarnik, 1927, pp. 4 ff.). Although both problem areas are aspects of persistence in a rather wide sense of the word, further attention will not be paid to them in the present study.

The exclusion of the fields of perseveration, resumption of interrupted activities, and the Zeigarnik effect considerably narrows down the field of investigation. Having said so much about what is not to be focused upon, we shall next turn to a more detailed description of what in the present study is to be meant by a persistence situation.

18

A persistence situation has been described by Norman T. Feather, one of the leading investigators within this area, as " ... that in which a person is confronted with a very difficult or insoluble task and is unrestricted in either the time or number of attempts he can work at it. He is unsuccessful at each of these attempts at the task, but can turn to an alternative activity whenever he wishes" (1962, p. 94). Thus, Feather is seen to restrict his attention to a very narrow range of situations, i. e. to those where the person is confronted with a task which he is unable to solve. However, as C. P. Smith (1964, p. 530) also points out, the general interest is in how long different persons persist at tasks of differing levels of difficulty before giving up or turning to alternative activities. Admittedly, Feather tried to throw some light upon this general question by creating different initial expectancies concerning the difficulty of the task through the use of false norms. However, to exemplify, even if the task is presented as a very easy one, the fact that the person works without success is presumed to cause a very rapid change in the perceived difficulty of the task. Accordingly, the results from such studies are held to offer very limited information about persistence at easy tasks.

The argument behind Feather's restriction probably is that it should be impossible to study persistence at a task which is soluble. This need not, however, be the case. As an example, the individual may be confronted with a pure routine task, such as drawing simple figures. The amount of figures drawn or the time spent in this activity is obviously a measure of persistence at that task. In a similar way, a set of moderately difficult tasks may be presented, and then the variation in time spent on the set is supposed to reflect differences in persistence at least for those subjects not solving all tasks in the set.

In other words, the study of persistence should not be restricted to situations involving insoluble tasks only. Within the present work a persistence situation is considered as one where the individual is confronted with a certain task and is unrestricted as to how much time or how many trials he can spend on it. This means that situations involving very difficult as well as moderately difficult and very easy tasks must be considered.

THREE POSSIBLE WAYS OF STUDYING THE PERSISTENCE PROBLEM

The fact that differences are observed to occur between individuals working at the same task as well as within the same individuals from one task to another indicates that the problem may be studied in at least three different ways. One possibility is to focus upon differences in persistence between individuals or between groups of individuals across a random sample of persistence tasks, or in other words to study what characterizes persistent individuals in contrast to the non-persistent ones. From this point of departure the characteristics of tasks or situations are of little or no interest, the problem being that of persistence regardless of task qualities. This may be characterized as a correlational or differential psychological approach to the problem (Cronbach, 1957, pp. 671 ff.). However, as Cronbach points out (ibid., p. 674), this approach in its pure form means neglecting that the same individuals may respond in a systematically different way to different situations, and the systematic variation from one situation or task to another is thus treated as error variation. Hence, a purely individual-oriented approach can at best give a very restricted insight into the persistence problem.

A second possibility is to make an experimental approach to the problem in terms of studying changes in persistence from one task or experimental condition to another in random samples of individuals. This, however, means neglecting the possibility that individuals may respond in a systematically different way to the same situation. In other words, it implies treating systematic individual variations as error variation (loc. cit.). Thus, both the situation-oriented and the individual-oriented approach in their pure form are burdened with serious weaknesses.

It should, however, be clear that the two methods for studying persistence considered above are in no way mutually exclusive. Experimental investigations may well take individual differences into account, in the same way as correlational investigations may be concerned with situational differences. When the two methods are integrated, we may talk about an interactional-psychological approach to the persistence problem. The main interest here is in this third way of studying the problem, and more specifically in studying persistence from an achievement motivation point of departure. A preliminary description of the achievement motivation concept is given below, while a more thorough examination of the concept is postponed to a later section.

ACHIEVEMENT MOTIVATION

According to John W. Atkinson, a distinguished investigator within the area of achievement motivation research, the motivation or tendency to undertake some activity is jointly determined by the relatively stable motives that characterize the personality and more spcific situation-related characteristics (1964, pp. 241 ff.). To focus upon the latter first, two characteristics are assumed to be important: expectancy and incentive value. The expectancy term covers the cognitive belief that engaging in an activity will lead to a particular consequence, and in the case of achievement motivation the relevant consequences are success or failure at the task in question. In this specific context the individual's expectancy may therefore also be thought of as his perceived possibility of success or failure at the task. The strength of this expectancy, which obviously must depend to a large extent upon the characteristics of the situation with which the individual is confronted, is one of the determinants of the motivation or tendency to act.

The incentive value represents the attractiveness or unattractiveness of the expected consequence of some act. Within the achievement motivation theory as developed by Atkinson the incentive value is directly related to the possibility of success. Thus, the attractiveness or incentive value of success is assumed to be higher the lower the possibility of success, and the unattractiveness or negative incentive value of failure is assumed to be higher the higher the possibility of success.

While the expectancy and the incentive value are important determinators of the motivation or tendency to act, they do not on their own cause any action. Thus, it is observed that some individuals engage more readily in achievement-oriented activities and derive more pleasure from success than others. The first group may be characterized as having a relatively strong motive to achieve success, the second one as having a relatively weak motive to achieve success. Some individuals resist achievement-oriented activities to a greater or lesser extent and are embarrassed when failing, while others do not worry at all about failure. The first group may then be thought of as having the stronger, the second one as having the weaker motive to avoid failure. It is therefore seen that the motives can in a way be said to be modifiers of the incentives, that is " ... if the incentive value of a given consequence is of a certain absolute strength, it will be more attractive to a person with a high motive for that consequence, and less attractive to a person with low motive for that consequence" (Birch & Veroff, 1966, p. 8). This quotation refers to positive incentives only, but the same line of thought may, of course, also be applied to negative incentives, such as failures. Thus, if the incentive value of a consequence is of a certain absolute negative strength, this consequence will be a greater deterrent to a person with a high motive to avoid that consequence than to one with a low motive.

Then, to sum up, the achievement motivation for a particular activity is the result of an interaction between the expected consequences of the activity in terms of success or failure and the incentive value of these consequences on the one hand, and on the other hand the strength of the individual's motive to achieve success and motive to avoid failure. If the individual does not expect to succeed at all, i. e. if he does not see any possibility of success, or if a success has no incentive value, then it does not matter how strong his motive to achieve is. In such a case there will be no motivation to achieve success. On the other hand, a certain possibility of success is of no significance unless there is a disposition in the individual to strive for success, i. e. unless he has a motive to achieve success. The same line of reasoning may be applied to the motivation to avoid failure. This means, as pointed out by Atkinson and Feather (1966, p. 5), that the theory of achievement motivation represents a step towards a conceptual integration of the two disciplines of scientific psychology (Cronbach, 1957), the one concerned with the study of individual differences, and the other with the effect of situation characteristics.

SUMMING UP: POINT OF DEPARTURE FOR THE STUDY

As pointed out in the foregoing, the persistence problem will in the present study be approached from the central interactional-psychological viewpoint represented in the theory of achievement motivation. This point of departure implies a consideration of persistence as the result of an interaction between personality characteristics and situation characteristics, and those to be focused upon in the present study are the motive to achieve success and the motive to avoid failure on the one hand, and the expectancy and incentive value of success and failure on the other. While this is judged to be a meaningful approach, the choice is made with full awareness that it does not represent the only possible interactional-psychological approach to the persistence problem. Thus, within the chosen frame of reference the only determinator of the incentive value is the expected possibility of success at the task in question (cf. Atkinson, 1964, pp. 242 ff.). However, it seems reasonable also to think of, for example, the individual's interests as important modifiers of the incentive value of success or failure at a task. In that case the relationship between motive strength and for example persistence should be different where the task is of central interest to the individuals and where it is of little or no interest. It is, however, outside the intentions of the study to discuss this and other similar problems.

Even if the preceding account has shown that the problem of persistence ought to be approached as an interaction phenomenon, it seems reasonable initially to pay some attention to the two more simple approaches, i. e. to that which is primarily individual-oriented and to that which is primarily situation-oriented. The results from these more extreme and restricted ways of studying persistence, although not considered as generally valid, are assumed to contribute at least something to the understanding of the problem. Maybe they can also provide a basis for further reasoning?

22

CHAPTER 1

THE PERSISTENCE PROBLEM: SOME BACKGROUND THEORY AND RESEARCH

In the introductory section three possible ways of studying the persistence problem were referred to: the individual-oriented, the situation-oriented, and the individual by situation interaction-oriented approach. The background theory and research along these lines have to a certain extent been reviewed by Feather (1962, pp. 95 ff.). His work therefore provides much of the basis for the first part of this chapter. However, since the problem area of the present work is considerably broader than that of Feather (cf. p. 19), the following discussion of theory and research has a somewhat wider scope.

First the individual-oriented way of studying the problem will be considered, since persistence is more directly discussed in that connection than in connection with primarily situation-oriented research. Since no typically individual-oriented persistence studies have been reported in recent years, the following is concerned with studies of a relatively early date.

PERSISTENCE CONSIDERED FROM AN INDIVIDUAL-ORIENTED POINT OF DEPARTURE

The underlying hypothesis for those who are most directly concerned with persistence from an individual-oriented point of view seems to be that a person who persists at one task will tend to persist at other tasks as well. This has directed interest towards differences between individuals in their tendency to continue in an activity once it is started, with relatively little regard to task characteristics, in other words, differences in underlying personality traits causing differences in the persistence of behaviour. Indeed, some of the researchers within this area designate the personality trait itself persistence.

Persistence regarded as an underlying personality trait

The consideration of persistence as an underlying personality trait has resulted in the construction of a great number of tests supposed to measure this trait. Further, stemming from the hypothesis of persistence as a trait manifesting itself rather independently of the task characteristics, the tasks in persistence tests have been extremely varied, ranging from such rather trivial performances as maintaining a handgrip (dynamometer task) or holding the breath (Thornton, 1939, pp. 6 f.) to more meaningful activities, such as word building and verbal recognition tasks (ibid., pp. 9 f.).

The investigations along these lines fall, as pointed out by Feather (1962, p. 96), into two sub-groups. The first contains studies concerned with correlations between persistence scores from a number of different tasks or correlations between persistence scores and scores on other variables. The second comprises studies where factor analysis has been used to account for the obtained correlations. Reviews of these studies are presented by Ryans (1939b), Feather (1962), and Eysenck (1970). Here we shall only consider some of these studies, to illustrate the individual-oriented approach to the problem of persistence.

The Nonfactorial Trait Investigations. Within this group the study by Porter (1933), although presented very shortly in terms of an abstract, serves as a good illustration of how bewildering the results from these studies are, at least so far as the question of the generality of persistence is concerned. Nine persistence tests, covering a wide variety of performances such as for example a dynamometer task and a word building task, were administered to 410 subjects, and the results are summarized in this way: "The picture revealed by some 350 coefficients of correlation, zero order, partial, and multiple, is one of almost complete lack of positive relationship among tests which have been considered valid tests of persistence" (ibid., p. 664). Thus, the results do not at all support the apprehension of persistence as a personality trait manifesting itself in situations in general. Porter, however, offers a double explanation: "... persistence is not a generalized trait, and at least some of the tests are not valid tests of persistence" (loc. cit.). This way of explaining the results is highly confusing, since these same results cannot be used to test both the validity of the hypothesis that persistence is a generalized trait and at the same time the validity of the tests chosen to measure this trait.

In his review of persistence studies, Feather (1962) presents the classical comprehensive work by Hartshorne, May, and Maller (1929) as the only illustration of the nonfactorial trait approach to the problem, but it should be noted that the investigators themselves do not consider persistence as a general trait of the individual. Rather, persistence is conceived as a function of previous experience in the activity in question, or, from another point of view, as a function of interests, and it may therefore vary from one situation to another (Hartshorne et al., 1929, pp. 279 f.). Nevertheless, the study may serve to elucidate the trait question, since it includes a series of persistence tests.

The persistence problem was examined in a group of nearly 900 school-children of both sexes in grades five to eight, representing a wide variety of social backgrounds, intelligence, and emotional stability (ibid., pp. 7, 169 ff., 328 ff.). A rich diversity of tasks were used, including on the one extreme apparently meaningless physical persistence tasks such as standing on one foot (ibid., pp. 342 f.), and on the other hand clearly ideational tasks, such as solving various kinds of puzzles (ibid., pp. 295 ff.). The reported correlations between the various persistence measures in terms of time spent at the tasks varied from -.11 to +.42, most of them being in the range between +.10 and +.20 (ibid., pp. 332, 348).[1]

Thus, neither the results obtained by Porter nor those from the study by Hartshorne, May, and Maller lent much support to the apprehension of persistence as a personality trait manifesting itself rather independently of the characteristics of the tasks in question. On the other hand, higher correlations between persistence measures are obtained in other correlational studies. Thus Howells, administering 11 different persistence tests to a sample of university students, reports intercorrelations among the measures (in terms of time spent in the persistence situations) ranging from +.18 to +.72 (1933, p. 23). Another example, mentioned in the review by Ryans (1939b, p. 726), is provided by the results from Cushing's study (1929) with young children as subjects, where the intercorrelations among several persistence test results were relatively high, with an average of +.42, thus suggesting a common factor. It should, however, be noted in this connection that the test set applied by Howells, at least, is a fairly homogeneous one, measuring persistence in terms of resistance to physical pain caused in various ways (op. cit., p. 15), so that of course the results say little about the generality of a possible trait of persistence.

The studies considered above suffice to demonstrate the lack of clarity as to the results obtained by the nonfactorial approach to the persistence problem. The pic-

---

1. Some of these correlations refer to a small subsample of that described above (ibid., pp. 347 f.)

ture revealed does not, however, seem very surprising, taking into consideration the diversity of tasks used in several of the studies as well as the differences in tasks from one study to another. Compared with these studies, the factorial trait investigations represent a methodological advance which makes possible a differentiation between various kinds of persistence. Thus, the factorial studies represent at least a certain drifting away from the conception of persistence as an entirely general personality trait, manifesting itself independently of the situation characteristics.

The Factorial Trait Investigations. One of the early factorial trait studies is that by Crutcher (1934), where 40 boys and 43 girls from about seven to sixteen years of age were given six different tasks to perform: card-house building, two mechanical puzzles, addition tasks, picture copying, and cancellation of A's. The intercorrelations between the time spent on each of the persistence tasks varied from +.23 to +.71. A subsequent Spearman-type analysis of tetrad differences led Crutcher to the very cautious conclusion that "... the results begin to look as if there might be present a general factor and specific factors as well" (ibid., p. 414). It is, however, to be observed that the tasks used here are relatively homogeneous, compared with for example those used by Hartshorne and his associates (cf. pp. 24 f. a circumstance which makes finding a "general" factor more likely. This also means that the statement about the "generality" of the factor becomes rather uninteresting.

The generality problem is further illustrated in a later study by Ryans (1938a) conducted on a group of 40 college students. A variety of measures were obtained, including time spent at ideational and physical persistence tasks as well as ratings of persistence by instructors and by the subjects themselves. Factor analysis revealed three factors, the first one being interpreted as a persistence factor (ibid., p. 349). According to Ryans there is "... more than sufficient evidence in favor of the view that a common or general factor of persistence does exist when situations such as were employed in this study are compared and analyzed" (ibid., pp. 349 f.). This conclusion seems, however, somewhat problematic in light of the fact that some of the a priori selected persistence tests had low or even negative loadings on the persistence factor. As to this point, Ryans himself in his later review article (1939b, p. 730) argues, in a way similar to that of Porter (cf. p. 24), that some of the original measures were not valid indicators of the trait. This way of reasoning seems to make it impossible to refute the hypothesis that persistence is a general factor, as tests not supporting the hypothesis are considered as invalid! Obviously, the results could be interpreted in another way. A study by Thornton exemplifies this.

26

In the Thornton study (1939), which was based on a larger sample than that of Ryans, consisting of 135 male and 54 female psychology students, a large number of varying types of persistence tests were administered, including such tasks as for example holding the breath, maintaining handgrip, word building, reading difficult material, etc. The data are mostly time scores, and the results are somewhat similar to those obtained by Ryans. On the basis of these results it is concluded that "... whether factorized or not, the intercorrelations between these supposed tests of persistence do not reveal evidence of any universal factor" (ibid., p. 28). The analyses revealed five group factors, two of which were said to bear a resemblance to certain aspects of persistence (ibid., p. 29).

More recent studies are those by Rethlingshafer (1942) and by MacArthur (1955). The results from the former (Rethlingshafer, 1942, p. 75), referring to a sample of 38 college students, are in accordance with Thornton's finding that persistence tests do not all measure the same thing. MacArthur's study is characterized in the review by Eysenck (1970, pp. 77 f.) as the most satisfying one methodologically of those considered, probably because the influence of mental abilities on persistence was removed. The study is based on a relatively large sample, 120 secondary school boys. Twenty-one persistence tests were used, representing a wide variety of tasks. In addition, twenty-one measures of ability were available, and these measures were intercorrelated and factor-analysed. Next, the influence of the five ability factors revealed by the factor analysis was removed from the correlations between the persistence tests. Of those 210 partialled intercorrelations between the persistence measures, 57 were significantly positive ($p < .05$), 100 were non-significantly positive, and 53 were non-significantly negative (MacArthur, 1955, p. 48). The factor analysis of the partialled correlation matrix of persistence measures resulted in five significant factors. One of them runs positively through all twenty-one persistence measures, and is interpreted as a general persistence factor (ibid., p. 46). It should, however, also be noted that this persistence factor had low loadings in several of the persistence tests (ibid., p. 49). It does not seem that these data warrant the conclusion made by MacArthur, that a strong general persistence factor emerged (ibid., p. 53).

An Evaluation. Even though we have dealt with a restricted number of the studies where persistence is conceived as an underlying personality trait, those reviewed suffice to demonstrate the unclarity as to the implications of such studies. The introduction of factor analytic techniques admittedly represented a methodological advancement compared with the earlier simple correlational methods, by creating the possibility of differentiating between various kinds of persistence. However, our restricted review has shown that the results as well as the interpretations of them vary in the same way as those deriving from the correlational studies. Hence, it is difficult to see the justification of the statement in Eysenck's review that the evidence for persistence as a trait of relatively unitary nature is fairly conclusive (1970, p. 79). If "unitary nature" means something in the way of "independent of other characteristics", the conclusion seeems too strong. Obviously, Eysenck relies heavily on the previously cited work of MacArthur (1955), but the method chosen in that study, that of removing the effect of, for example, mental abilities on the persistence test results, seems at least indirectly to allow for the interpretation that the manifestation of persistence depends on other characteristics too. In other words, we are here not far from an interactional-psychological viewpoint on persistence, but such interactional viewpoints are not explicitly set forth in MacArthur's report.

Then, the results considered hitherto are far from clear-cut. They are interpreted by the investigators both in favour of and against persistence as a general trait of personality. A consideration of all studies together does not, however, make it improbable that much of this unclarity is due to the diversity of the persistence tests used as well as to the somewhat different ways of analysing the data. But even if more comparable sets of tests had been used, and more consistency had appeared in the results, the trait approach considered here is from a theoretical point of view encumbered with another weakness which reduces its significance, and which therefore merits a closer scrutiny.

In the foregoing we have mainly been concerned with studies of persistence in behaviour carried out by investigators who have designated the trait itself persistence. This clearly underlines the circularity in the work, which reduces the value of their persistence concept. Thus, the term persistence suffers from a misuse similar to that pointed out by Mowrer (1960, p. 174) in connection with the curiosity concept, when it is used both as an explanation and as a description of behaviour. Persistence should be considered either as a behaviour phenomenon to be explained or it should be considered as a personality trait producing certain effects. Persistence cannot be both cause and effect simultaneously. Needless to say, explanation is not furthered by inferring both cause and effect from the same measures. To serve this purpose, cause and effect should be identified independently, which means that there should be at least one logical step between the explanatory construct and the behaviour criterion.

From this point of view most of the studies considered belong on the classification or description level, and as such they might be valuable. Individuals can be grouped as more or less persistent according to the scores on various persistence tests, but this does not explain persistence in behaviour. Explanation means accounting for what lies behind behaviour, and this demands theories on a level at least slightly higher than that of description. A suggestion in this direction is found in the work by Hartshorne and his associates referred to previously (pp. 24 f.). They regard persistence as a function of learning experiences or of interests. However, with little further account of what this implies, it can scarcely represent much more than a renaming of the phenomenon. Indeed, the investigators themselves are aware of this weakness, admitting that it is hardly an adequate explanation of an activity to refer to some interest as its cause (Harsthorne et al. , 1929, p. 280). In this connection they also hint that individual differences in capacities of one sort or another may be involved, some minds being for example more capable of great enthusiasm for standards of honour than others (ibid. , p. 281). A related viewpoint is also stated by Ryans, who recognizes that one and the same incentive may appeal to one individual and not to another, wherefore the resulting behaviour may differ (1938c, p. 90). These ideas are not spelled out in any further detail either by Hartshorne and his associates nor by Ryans, but they are held to some extent to foreshadow the conceptualization within the achievement motivation theory, where motives are seen as capacities for the experience of positive or negative affects in certain kinds of situations.

Then, to sum up, although circularity in the reasoning is a dominating feature in the studies presented, there are nevertheless some weak traces of a more explanation-oriented way of considering the problem of persistence. In addition to those hints of explanation that we have called attention to above, some of the studies in which persistence is regarded as an underlying personality trait also relate persistence in behaviour to other personality characteristics, thus offering something more than merely a circular description. In the following some examples will be given of results concerning relationships between persistence and a few individual characteristics.

Persistence in relation to other individual characteristics

Persistence as Related to Sex.   The reason for focusing upon this aspect at present is more empirical than theoretical. Thus, as pointed out by Carlson and Carlson (1960, p. 482), there is a sizable accumulation of evidence that males and females react differently to many situations. This may also be the case in persistence situations. Yet, to take the studies with which we have been concerned hitherto, this problem is not mentioned at all by Porter (1933) or in the article by Ryans (1938a), although both sexes are included in their samples, and Rethlingshafer (1942) does not even report the sex of her subjects. Further, in the study by MacArthur sex is said to be held constant in the analyses (1955, p. 46), but it can be seen from the report that this just means that the study was restricted to boys only, a circumstance representing a clear limitation as to the generality of the results.

There are, however, some studies in which the question of sex differences is explicitly dealt with. For instance, Crutcher, using six persistence tests of such a kind that physical strength should be of little importance for performance (as to the tests used, cf. p. 26), found the persistence scores, in terms of time spent in working at the task, to be higher for boys than for girls in every case (1934, p. 412). He draws, however, the somewhat unexpected conclusion that the results as a whole do not indicate that boys are more persistent than girls, arguing that the differences in all cases but one are small.

A result similar to that obtained by Crutcher is reported by Ryans (1939a, pp. 259 f.) from a sample of 230 males and 230 females, aged 14 to 25. The persistence score was based on three subtests measuring continued learning effort, self-estimation of persistence, and endurance of the cumulative effects of muscular fatigue. While the mean persistence score was found to be higher for boys than for girls, Ryans concludes in a way similar to Crutcher that the difference is so small that there is no likelihood that a true difference exists (ibid., p. 260). In this connection it also seems pertinent to ask whether the difference found is due to a sex difference in strength, since the result on one of the subtests is probably influenced by physical strength. This aspect has been given attention by Howells (1933), and by Thornton (1939).

While Howells found that men achieved significantly higher persistence scores than women, it should here be recalled that his data refer to a particular kind of situation, i.e. where some sort of physical pain is inflicted upon the subjects (cf. p. 25). In this connection Howells also suggests that the sex difference in persistence might partly be explained in terms of differences in physical characteristics such as weight, a suggestion also supported by his data (Howells, 1933, p. 26). Yet he concludes that apparently men are more persistent than women, even aside from any weight advantage they may have (loc. cit.). It does not, however, seem that control for weight only is an adequate check upon the possibility of physical sex differences influencing the persistence scores.

This matter is recognized by Thornton (1939), who included some of Howell's tests in his persistence test battery, and who found the scores on these tests to be clearly related to what he labels a sex-strength factor, involving such aspects as for example handgrip strength, height, and weight (ibid., pp. 24, 31, 35 f.).

In this connection it should also be noted that in Thornton's study sex alone is not systematically related to persistence at the ideational persistence tests (ibid., p. 22).

The same lack of consistency is found in the results presented by Hartshorne, May, and Maller (1929). They found differences from one persistence test to another, boys being more persistent on some of them, girls on others, but on the whole the results seem here to be in favour of girls (ibid., pp. 380 ff., 513 f.).

Thus, the question of sex differences in persistence is far from settled. Males have been found to be more persistent than females at tasks requiring physical strength, a relatively uninteresting result in view of the clear sex difference in physical characteristics. As to persistence at tasks where physical strength is of little importance, Crutcher has been seen to report a slight tendency in favour of boys, while Hartshorne, May, and Maller found a slight tendency in favour of girls. Therefore, the results from the studies considered do not provide any basis for expectations of sex differences in persistence, except in cases where physical strength plays an important role. This does not, however, necessarily mean that sex is an uninteresting variable in this connection. The problem will therefore be given more attention at a later stage.

Persistence and Intelligence. It may seem more or less self-evident that if an individual is to display persistence when confronted with a task, he must have a minimum of capacity or ability to work at the task. This aspect was indirectly commented upon in the previous section, where physical strength represented one such capacity in connection with certain kinds of persistence tasks. Similarly, it seems reasonable to look for a relationship between measures of intelligence and persistence at least at ideational tasks. The problem has already been touched upon in connection with the reference to the study by MacArthur (cf. pp. 27 f.), in which the influence of mental abilities on the persistence measures was removed. His report does not, however, state anything about what kind of relationship was observed between persistence scores and the ability measures obtained by him.

The significance of mental abilities for persistence seems, however, to be indicated by the results from studies such as that by Hartshorne, May, and Maller (1929, p. 371), Crutcher (1934, p. 412), and Brintnall (1940, p. 585), as well as that from a recent motivation study by Battle (1965, pp. 215 f.). These studies revealed positive correlations between intelligence (ability) measures and persistence measures, most of them in the range between +.20 and +.30. On the other hand, the study by Howells (1933) reports only a very low correlation ($r = +.10$) between intelligence scores and persistence scores (ibid., p. 27), while Ryans (1938b, pp. 356 f.), Thornton (1939, pp. 22 ff.), and Rethlingshafer (1942, pp. 75, 80) did not find any systematic relation at all between ability measures and persistence scores.

Finally, to underscore the complexity of the question, the result obtained in a recent motivation study by C. P. Smith (1964, p. 526), with 146 college students as subjects, should also be noted in this connection. In this study a significant negative relationship was obtained between intelligence score and persistence in terms of time spent at two different examinations ($r = -.21$, and $r = -.19$). It might, however, be pertinent to ask whether these negative correlations only reflect the simple fact that highly intelligent students need a shorter time to solve the tasks than the less intelligent ones. This possibility is not mentioned by Smith.

On the whole, then, there is no clear pattern in the results concerning the relationship between intelligence and persistence. This may in part be due to the diversity of persistence tasks used, but the pattern does not become much clearer even if we focus upon ideational persistence tasks only (cf. for example Ryans, 1938b, p. 357). Nevertheless it seems reasonable to regard ability level as an important variable in connection with the problem of persistence, primarily because an individual's ability level is assumed to be an important determinator of his expectancy of success or failure at the tasks to be performed. This expectancy, as already noted (cf. p. 21), plays an important role within the achievement motivation theory. According to this theory, which will be examined in detail in the next chapter, a certain expectancy of success or failure may have positive or negative effects, depending upon whether the individual is dominated by a motive to achieve success or by a motive to avoid failure. So far as the individual's expectancy is determined by his intelligence, this also implies that the relationship between intelligence and persistence may very well vary from positive to negative, as it has been seen to do in the studies with which we have been concerned.

Finally in this account of individual-oriented approaches to the persistence problem we shall deal with another personality characteristic which has been focused upon by Kounin (1941). Since his study clearly aims at explaining persistence-related problems and is also frequently cited in psychological literature, it should be considered in some detail.

Persistence and Rigidity: Kounin's Study. The study by Kounin rests upon Lewin's assumption (1935, pp. 206 ff.) that the person region of life space is differentiated into parts or cells by boundaries of different rigidity. The term "rigidity" refers to that property of the boundaries which prevents an occurrence in one cell from having an effect upon neighbouring cells, as for example in terms of spread of tension. Thus, occurrences in one cell may have different effects on neighbouring cells, dependent on the rigidity of the boundaries. As regards persistence this means that what happens in one cell in the person region may or may not influence the persistence of behaviour related to another cell.

The theory further postulates that rigidity is a positive monotonous function of chronological age, and that mental age corresponds to the degree of differentiation, i.e. the number of cells, in the person region. The latter means that rigidity is also a positive monotonous function of the degree of feeble-mindedness, since this is defined as the ratio between mental age and chronological age. From this it follows that, other things being equal, the older and/or more feeble-minded the individual, the less effect will an occurrence in one cell have upon the state of the neightbouring cells.

To test this derivation an experiment was planned so as to create experimentally a differentiation of an equal number of cells for all subjects, to produce a change in one of the cells, and to ascertain the effect of this change upon the neighbouring cells (Kounin, 1941, p. 256). To obtain the same degree of differentiation three groups of subjects with equal Binet mental age were chosen: An old feeble-minded group, a young feeble-minded group, and a young normal group, 63 subjects altogether. The first group should, according to what has been said above, be characterized by most rigidity, the last one with least rigidity.

Each subject was initially made conversant with four simple drawing activities: drawing cats, bugs, turtles, and rabbits. Then, in a situation as free as possible he was allowed to draw cats until he became satiated and wanted to draw no more. After that he was asked if he wanted to draw bugs, and so on with turtles and rabbits.

It was expected that the satiation of the cell of "drawing cats" should result in different degrees of co-satiation of the neighbouring cells (those of "drawing bugs", etc.) for the three groups characterized by different rigidity. A small amount of co-satiation should result in drawing bugs for almost as long a time as drawing cats. The expectation was clearly confirmed by the results, revealing least co-satiation in the old feeble-minded group and most in the young normal group (ibid., p. 258).

The prediction focused upon the relationship between time spent at each of the drawing activities, thus disregarding the absolute satiation time or persistence. However, the results in terms of group differences in absolute satiation time are at least equally conspicuous. Thus, there was a dramatic increase in persistence from the young normal group via the young feeble-minded group to the old feeble-minded group at all drawing activities (ibid., p. 259; see also Fig. 3-14 in Baldwin, 1967, p. 117). These results may in a way be said to provide additional support for the rigidity hypothesis set forth by Kounin, as they imply that the smaller amount of co-satiation found in the old feeble-minded group occurred in spite of their larger absolute satiation time or persistence, while generally one would expect that the more time a person spends at one activity, the less time he should spend at a subsequent related activity. On the other hand, however, the results do also represent a problem, in that the group differences in absolute time spent on the drawing activities cannot be accounted for by the rigidity hypothesis.

Then, while Kounin's work aimed not only at describing, but also at explaining differences in behaviour, his own results can only be partially explained by the rigidity theory. In this connection it should also be noted that Kounin's work has been repeatedly criticized (see for example the review by Spitz, 1963, pp. 17 ff., and by Zigler, 1962, pp. 145 ff.), the most extensive criticism being that by Zigler, who focuses upon possible motivation differences between the groups (1961, p. 413; 1962, pp. 150 ff.). Thus, Zigler argues that institutionalized feeble-minded children are often relatively deprived of adult contact and approval, and accordingly they have a higher motivation to secure such contact and approval than normal children. This contact and approval may be maintained by being persistent in the experimental situation. This makes Zigler argue that the differences reported by Kounin were related to motivational differences between the groups, rather than to differences in rigidity. From this point of view the group differences in persistence at all tasks in Kounin's experiment are far from surprising.

In summary, then, Zigler's explanation seems to represent a reasonable alternative to that offered by Kounin, and is also seen to cover a greater part of the results obtained. This does not, however, preclude that motivational effects other than those primarily focused upon by Zigler might have been present in Kounin's experiment. One such possible effect will be discussed in Chapter 4.

Concluding remarks

In this section the problem of persistence has been focused upon from an individual-oriented point of departure. It seems, however, that we are at least as far away from an explanation of the persistence questions now as when we started. Other primarily individual-oriented studies of the persistence problem not referred to in the foregoing, such as for example that by Thornton (1940; 1941), Schofield (1943), J.W. French (1948), and Edmiston and Jackson (1949), do not alter this impression. According to the investigators' conclusions there is evidence both for and against persistence as a general trait of personality. In addition, many of these studies are characterized by a circularity in the reasoning which makes the conclusions drawn rather uninteresting. There is no clear trend as to the influence of sex upon persistence. While several investigators have failed to find any relationship between intelligence and persistence, there are also results indicating a relation between these variables. The relationships observed have, however, varied from significantly positive to significantly negative. Finally, the results which are assumed by Kounin to provide support for his rigidity hypothesis, seem to be better explained in terms of motivation differences.

On the whole, then, there are conflicts and contradictions both in the data and in the theoretical viewpoints presented which means that there is very little clarity left. Maybe this despondent state of affairs is the reason why very few persistence studies have been reported in the last two decades (cf. Psychological Abstracts for the last twenty years). The lack of clearness is, however, supposed to be at least partially due to the extensive variation in the tasks included, both within and between studies. In other words, there has been too little systematic control or variation of situation variables in the primarily individual-oriented studies.

In the next section we shall consider some studies with the opposite basis, i. e. studies where the situation characteristics are in focus.

PERSISTENCE CONSIDERED FROM A SITUATION-ORIENTED POINT OF DEPARTURE

Within achievement motivation research related to persistence, attention has been called to one group of situation-oriented investigations, those concerned with the problem of resistance to extinction (Feather, 1962, pp. 99 ff.). These studies are relevant because the extinction situation is similar to that type of persistence situation in which a subject is confronted with a very difficult or insoluble task. Here we shall in addition later pay some attention to the other end of the difficulty continuum, i. e. to situations where the task in question is a very easy one.

But first let us pay some attention to the extinction studies. The point of departure for the following examination is found in the review of extinction studies by Jenkins and Stanley (1950) and by Lewis (1960) as well as Feather's discussion (1962) of some of these studies. Only aspects of the studies which are particularly relevant to the problem of persistence as outlined in the introductory section will be dealt with. For more comprehensive coverage of the literature on extinction the reader is referred to the reviews mentioned.

Persistence considered as resistance to extinction

In the introductory section three key variables were pointed out in connection with the achievement motivation concept: motive, incentive value, and expectancy. The last one, expectancy, covering the strength of the individual's anticipation that engaging in an activity will lead to a particular result, has been offered some attention within extinction studies too. These studies may therefore be of some interest here, and in this connection the reinforcement pattern is a very central variable.

Reinforcement Pattern and Expectancy. According to Jenkins and Stanley the general findings of the extinction studies can be summarized in this way: "All other things equal, resistance to extinction after partial reinforcement is greater than that after continuous reinforcement when behavior strength is measured in terms of single responses" (1950, p. 222). These results seem, as pointed out by Humphreys (1939b, pp. 150 f.), quite reasonable from an expectancy theoretical viewpoint. The line of reasoning runs as follows (Humphreys, 1939a, p. 298; 1939b, pp. 150 f.): Irregular reinforcement results in an expectancy of irregular reinforcement, uniform reinforcement in an expectancy of uniform reinforcement. It is easier to change from an expectancy of one kind of regularity to one of another kind of regularity than it is to change from an expectancy of irregularity to one of regularity. More specifically, it is easier to change from an expectancy that each trial is followed by reinforcement to the expectancy that reinforcement does not occur at any trial than it is to change from an expectancy that only some trials are followed by reinforcement to the expectancy that no reinforcement will occur. Subjects given irregular reinforcement in a training session should probably increase their expectation of reinforcement during the first unreinforced trials in the extinction session.

The expectation viewpoint presented here received empirical support in an experiment by Humphreys (1939a), carried out on a group of 78 male and female college students. The subjects were trained under two reinforcement conditions, uniform reinforcement (one light following another one each time) and irregular reinforcement (the light following the first one only 50 per cent of the time in un-predictable order). The subjects' guesses as to whether or not they would get re-inforcement (i. e. whether or not the second light would appear) served as the conditioned response, and extinction referred to the change in the verbalized expectations of reinforcement. The results from the extinction stages revealed that the subjects developed an expectancy of uniform nonreinforcement more quickly after having been uniformly reinforced in the acquisition stage than after having been irregularly reinforced in the acquisition stage. In the latter case they even displayed an initial increase in expectation of reinforcement, followed by a gradual decrease (ibid. , pp. 297 f.).

A closely related way of explaining results like those referred to above is found in the discrimination hypothesis, advanced by Mowrer and Jones (1945, pp. 303 ff.). Briefly, it states that resistance to extinction is a function of the similarity of the acquisition situation to the extinction situation. When the subject is only intermittently reinforced in the training stage, the acquisition and extinction situa-tions are relatively similar. In this case it should be relatively difficult to dis-cover that the extinction situation is a different one. Hence, extinction should take longer. Where the subject gets continuous reinforcement in the training stage, the extinction situation is obviously quite different. Discrimination is easier, and therefore there should be less resistance to extinction.

This type of analysis also made apparent the importance of distinguishing be-tween the continuity-discontinuity factor and the regularity-irregularity factor, especially in studies with human subjects (ibid. , p. 305). Human subjects are able to count and may therefore discover the pattern in partial but regular rein-forcement conditions. In such a case the change from the acquisition to the extinc-tion stage should be easily observed. Therefore, to ensure the usual partial re-inforcement effect in terms of greater resistance to extinction, the reinforce-ments should be not only intermittent, but also irregular. Results such as those by Longenecker, Krauskopf, and Bitterman (1952, pp. 585 ff.), obtained in a group of thirty male undergraduate students, illustrate this point. In their ex-periment a simple alternating pattern of reinforcement and nonreinforcement, i. e. regular partial reinforcement, resulted in quicker extinction of a con-ditioned galvanic skin response than reinforcement administered in a random fashion. In the former case the regularity is supposed to be easily observable, and therefore the extinction situation should be quickly classified as different from the acquisition situation.

Further results explicitly related to and lending support to the discrimination hypothesis are presented for example by Bitterman, Fedderson, and Tyler

(1953, pp. 459 ff.), Elam, Tyler, and Bitterman (1954, pp. 382 f.), and Fehrer (1956, pp. 168 ff.), all based on animal subjects.

Thus far we have noted what seems to be a well-established effect of partial reinforcement in terms of greater resistance to extinction, and we have considered two related ways of explaining this effect. However, although the effect of partial reinforcement was first investigated in a group of human subjects (Humphreys, 1939a), most subsequent research on this matter has been conducted on animals (cf. the studies reviewed by Jenkins and Stanley, 1950, and by Lewis, 1960). In this connection it should be noted that while there are a few deviations in the many results reported from animal studies as to the effect of partial reinforcement, such as that reported by M. R. Denny (1946, pp. 384 f.) and by Finger (1942, p. 126), the deviations seem to be much more frequent in the relatively few studies reported where human subjects were employed. Thus, for example, Diciaula (1970), Grant, Riopelle, and Hake (1950, pp. 55 ff.), and Lester (1966a; 1966b) failed to replicate the typical partial reinforcement effect obtained in most animal studies, and in the above-mentioned study by Grant et al. (eyelid conditioning) the randomly reinforced group even showed a clearly more rapid decrement in reponse magnitude in the extinction stage than the other participating groups. Further, in a review and discussion article by Battig (1968) it is also argued that the S-R behaviour theory is inadequate as an explanation of paired-associate learning and extinction (ibid., pp. 150, 166), although such learning tasks represent the simplest and closest counterpart to the simpler conditioning and animal learning situation in which the S-R behaviour theory was originally formulated. This, Battig further argues, is an indication of even greater inadequacy for the multitude of situations that are more complex than the paired-associate learning situation, or, in other words, that the theory suffers from a considerable lack of generality (ibid., p. 166). Among other things this lack of generality may be due to the neglect of a possible relationship between the subject's skill and attainment of reinforcement.

Internal versus External Control of Reinforcement. In connection with the assertion of lack of generality it should be of some interest to take the work by James and Rotter (1958) on partial reinforcement into account. In the same way as Battig (1968) they call attention to the fact that most extinction studies have dealt with very simple responses, where the possibilities for symbolic behaviour have been minimized. Further, they emphasize that in studies with human subjects the learning situations have been so arranged that the subjects have probably regarded reinforcement as being beyond their control and primarily contingent upon external conditions. It is not a matter of course that the effect of continuous versus partial reinforcement is just the same whether the subjects regard reinforcement as being a result of their own skill - that is, where the achievement aspect is the primary one - or whether it is regarded as having been manipulated by the experimenter. In the study by James and Rotter this skill dimension was a central one. Since their work deals with problems closely related to that of the subjects' possibility to succeed and thereby also partly concerns achievement motivation questions, it merits somewhat more detailed consideration.

In general, James and Rotter can be said to rely on the previously mentioned discrimination hypothesis (cf. p. 37). Thus, in a training situation with continuous reinforcement the subject gets no cues of nonreinforcement, and therefore, when the extinction series begins, the first nonreinforcements function as cues that the situation has changed. Then, if reinforcement is regarded as being outside his control, a sudden decrease in expectancy of reinforcement is presumed to follow, and, as a consequence of this, rapid extinction. Where the training situation involves partial reinforcement, the cues of nonreinforcement are present from the start, and therefore they cannot serve as cues in the extinction stage that the situation has changed. As a result, extinction should here take longer.

However, as pointed out by James and Rotter (op. cit. , pp. 397 f.) and by Feather (1962, p. 101), there is an important difference between the situation where reinforcement is outside the subjects' control, being manipulated by other people, and that where it is perceived to depend on the subjects' own skill. Under skill conditions it is less likely that the subject will recategorize the situation when reinforcement disappears, and ascribe the disappearance to a situation change. Rather, it will probably be attributed to the lack of skill. Then, since the continuously reinforced group should have more confidence in their skill than the partially reinforced group, the first one should be more resistant to extinction. In other words, we have arrived at a prediction quite opposite to that stated in earlier extinction studies. True enough, James and Rotter did not go that far. Their hypothesis is the more restricted one that a partially reinforced group would show less superior resistance to extinction under skill conditions than under chance conditions (1958, p. 399). However, their empirical results, obtained in a sample of 80 college students, males and females, revealed a much clearer interaction than hypothesized.

The study contrasted 100 per cent and 50 per cent irregular reinforcement under conditions where half of the subjects were instructed that success in a card-guessing game was a matter of luck and half that it was a matter of their own skill. Before each trial the subjects were asked to state their expectancy of success on an 11-point scale. In the test session following the training session the subjects were considered extinguished when their verbalized expectancy fell to either 0 or 1 on three consecutive trials. In accordance with most earlier results the 100 per cent reinforced chance group was less resistant to extinction than the 50 per cent reinforced chance group. Under skill conditions the reverse was the case (ibid. , p. 401).

In the James and Rotter study the chance-skill variable was a manipulatory one, i. e. the difference between the chance and skill conditions was established, not by using different kinds of tasks, but by differential instructions. Then an adjacent question is whether their findings are replicable in situations where the nature of the tasks themselves rather than the instructions differ.

To examine this problem, Rotter, Liverant and Crowne (1961) compared the effect of different reinforcement schedules in two different tasks, a card-guessing task similar to that used by James and Rotter (1958), and a motorial skill task involving steadiness. The latter consisted of lifting a platform with a ball on it to a specified height. The ball was held on the platform by an electro-magnet, which could be switched on and off by the experimenter. While Rotter et al. recognized that some subjects may have felt that skill was involved in the card-guessing task, their over-all assumption was that success at this task for the group as a whole would be considered to be much more determined by chance, luck, or random factors than success at that used as a skill task (op. cit. , p. 164).

For each task a group of 20 female students were given 25 per cent, 75 per cent, and 100 per cent reinforcement over eight training trials. Following this all groups underwent experimental extinction through continuous failure. Expectancies for success were reported prior to each trial, and the subjects were here too considered extinguished when their stated expectancies were 1 or 0 on an 11-point scale.

The findings corresponded very well to those in the James and Rotter study. Thus, neither the skill-chance variable itself nor the reinforcement schedule variable produced significant effects alone, but the interaction between reinforcement schedule and the skill-chance variable was highly significant (ibid. , pp. 171 ff.). At the skill task the continually reinforced group was more resistant to extinction than the partially reinforced group, while the reverse was the case at the chance task.

Admittedly, the findings of Rotter and his colleagues concerning greatest persistence under skill conditions among those most frequently reinforced were not replicated in a later anagram experiment by Diciaula, Martin, and Lotsof (1968,

p. 741), carried out on a group of female students. Nevertheless the results
weaken the broad generalization that resistance to extinction after partial reinforcement is greater than after continuous reinforcement. In other words,
these results seem to support the notion articulated by Battig (1968, p. 166)
that S-R behaviour theory in its present form suffers from a considerable lack
of generality, especially as far as human behaviour is concerned.

An Evaluation. In the foregoing only a restricted number of extinction studies
have been considered, but nevertheless enough to get an impression of some of
the problems stirred up by this research tradition. We have seen that the investigators within this area have been concerned not only with the description
but also with the explanation of resistance to extinction, or in other words, with
the explanation of persistence in behaviour. Yet the development in recent years
does not seem to have resulted in a much clearer picture of this problem area,
rather the contrary. This is clearly illustrated in the reviews of extinction studies
by Jenkins and Stanley (1950) and by Lewis (1960). The former ends thus: "Sti-
mulus-response learning theory concepts and those stemming from an expectancy
point of view are discussed as explanations of partial reinforcement data. It
appears that S-R principles provide a framework accounting for the phenomena
in this area" (Jenkins and Stanley, 1950, p. 231). In contrast to this relatively
clear conclusion the review published 10 years later ends as follows: "The writer
feels no desire at present to carry cudgels for any of the 'theories' now available,
nor does he have a theory of his own to contribute that he has any confidence in,
nor does he think it sporting to take further 'pot shots' at the existing theories"
(Lewis, 1960, p. 24).
On the other hand it may be argued that attaining a better understanding of resistance to extinction or persistence in behaviour does not necessarily imply revealing only simple relationships. Thus, to cite Battig again "... the simpler
the empirical underpinnings of a theory of behavior, the less likely that theory
is to apply generally to more complex behavioral situations" (1968, p. 166).
To exemplify: Jenkins and Stanley arrive at the following practical implications
of the extinction studies: "If one desires behavior to be maintained for long periods of time in the absence of externally presented reward, partial reinforcement should be used in training" (1950, p. 230). Taking the later results by
James and Rotter (1958) and by Rotter et al. (1961) into consideration, contrasting skill and chance conditions, the implications are seen to be less simple,
in that continuous reinforcement under certain conditions may even result in
greater resistance to extinction than partial reinforcement. The latter findings

41

might be said to complicate the picture, but may nevertheless be said to have contributed to a better understanding of the matter. Thus, these findings emphasize the importance of taking both the expectation aspect and the chance-skill dimension into consideration. The last aspect has been neglected in early extinction studies, which have been concerned with situation characteristics only.

The work by Rotter and his colleagues implies that in extinction studies attention ought also to be directed towards personality characteristics. Certainly, in their studies the chance-skill variable was in fact a manipulatory one, but the skill term itself serves as a cue to what should be the next step: Since individuals differ in skills as well as in other personality characteristics, such significant characteristics should be introduced in a systematic way in extinction studies. In this connection Rotter himself calls attention to one particular variable, i.e. to the individual differences in the tendency to perceive reinforcement as being contingent on one's own skill or independent of it, and he has also participated in the preparation of a scale for measuring such differences (Rotter, 1966, pp. 9 ff.). While the inclusion of this personality variable in extinction investigations may possibly represent a fruitful course of action, hitherto no results along these lines seem to have been published which throw new light on the problem of resistance to extinction. However, since we shall consider in a later chapter the problem of persistence within an achievement motivation context, it is of some interest to note that Rotter also assumes the strength of the above-mentioned tendency for an individual to regard what happens to him as being dependent upon his own skill, to be related to the strength of his achievement motive (ibid., pp. 21 f.).

Other extinction studies are reported where personality variables have been included. Thus, in the investigation by Taylor (1951) and that by Spence and Farber (1953) the extinction rate was related to manifest anxiety scores. However, since in these cases there was no variation in reinforcement pattern, this represents only a simple individual-oriented approach to the extinction problem. A study where both reinforcement pattern and personality characteristics were taken into account is that by Lester (1966a) referred to previously (p. 38). In that study chronological and mental age were included (without revealing any interaction effects). Nevertheless, on the whole the neglect of individual characteristics represents, as pointed out by Feather (1962, p. 102), a main objection towards extinction studies. Stated otherwise, the possibility of an interaction between individual and situation characteristics has most often not been considered in these studies. Such more interaction-oriented considerations will be given attention later, but first we shall focus upon another situation-oriented line of research which seems significant in this connection.

In the foregoing the expectation concept has been emphasized as an explanatory one in connection with resistance to extinction: Subjects engage in activities expected to have rewarding or pleasant effects and avoid activities expected to have noxious or unpleasant effects. Accordingly, if an individual is asked to participate in an activity, he should be more persistent if the activity is expected to have pleasant effects than if it is expected to have unpleasant effects. Then, the general question of what determines whether a situation will be experienced as pleasant or unpleasant becomes an important one. In this connection the concept of an optimal level of stimulation, used by psychologists like Fiske and Maddi (1961), Hebb (1955), and Leuba (1955; 1961) among others, seems to be a central one. In the following the persistence problem will therefore be considered in light of optimal stimulation viewpoints.

Persistence and the concept of optimal stimulation

Understimulation - Overstimulation.   Within theories concerned with motivation and learning problems the tension reduction principle has been given a prominent position. This principle implies that motives are conceptualized as deficit tensional states which energize the individual's actions until the tension is reduced, a viewpoint that occurs, although in somewhat differing language, in such influential theories as those of Freud (1946), Hull (1943), and Miller and Dollard (1941). On the other hand results from studies in restricted stimulation, such as those by Bexton, Heron, and Scott (1954), Karsten (1928), and Lilly (1956) among others, seem to indicate that under certain conditions individuals behave so as to increase stimulation rather than reduce it. Relying on other similar results, Leuba (1955) argues that the concept of optimal stimulation is a central one in connection with behaviour. This concept implies that those reactions are strengthened which are accompanied or followed by stimulation within an optimal range of intensities. This means that Leuba does not reject the tension reduction principle of learning, but regards this principle as only one aspect of the more general principle that subjects tend to learn those reactions which produce an optimal level of stimulation. In light of this principle the most obvious interpretation of the results from studies where subjects have learned to do the things which were drive-reducing, should be that these subjects were overstimulated and therefore learned to do what returned the stimulation to a moderate level (ibid. p. 28). The corresponding interpretation of results from the studies where subjects have learned reactions followed by an increase in stimulation then should be that these subjects were understimulated and, in the same way as the overstimulated ones, learned to do what resulted in a moderate level of stimulation. Such situations offering too little stimulation are held not to be unusual in daily life:

> ... at both home and school he [the child] is frequently living under circumstances which are lacking in adequate stimulation and are at least mildly boring. Actions which increase stimulation and produce excitement are strongly reinforced, sometimes to the dismay of parents and teachers, as compared with the reactions performed during more humdrum stimulation. Another way of saying this is that reactions which bring the environment to bear upon the sense organs and increase the stimulating capacities of the environment are reinforced over other reactions (ibid., pp. 28 f.).

Finally it has to be noted that according to Leuba the concept of optimal stimulation is closely related to that of pleasantness and unpleasantness. Thus, pleasantness is held to be an accompaniment of optimal stimulation, and unpleasantness an accompaniment of excessive stimulation:

> A specific stimulus will ordinarily be sensed as pleasant if, together with the background of stimulation at the moment, it forms a pattern of over-all stimulation which falls within a range of moderate or optimal intensities, or is part of a change in that direction from either inadequate or excessive stimulation. And contrariwise, a specific stimulus will ordinarily be sensed as unpleasant if, together with the background of stimulation present at the moment, it forms a pattern of over-all stimulation which falls within a range of very intense stimulation, or is part of a change in that direction and away from optimal stimulation (Leuba, 1961, p. 322).

The position taken by Leuba has a close parallel in that taken by Hebb (1955) and that by Fiske and Maddi (1961). Thus, according to Hebb (op. cit., p. 250) the drive or level of arousal increases with the amount of sensory bombardment, and the individual will be attracted to conditions that maintain arousal at an optimal level. Fiske and Maddi suppose that the individual's momentary level of activation or arousal is directly related to the combined impact of all stimuli impinging upon the individual at a given moment (op. cit., pp. 19 f.), and that the individual will experience negative affects when the level of activation or arousal differs markedly from the optimal level, and positive affects when arousal approaches the optimal level (ibid., p. 46).

According to the stand taken by these psychologists the relationship between stimulation level, activation or arousal level, and attractiveness can, as pointed out by Berlyne (1963, p. 318), be summarized as in Fig. 1, showing arousal level to be an increasing monotonic function of stimulation, and attractiveness to have an inverted U-shaped relation to the degree of arousal. The curve illustrates the individual's taste for excitement, which implies that "... up to a certain point, threat and puzzle have positive motivating value, beyond that point negative value" (Hebb, 1955, p. 250).

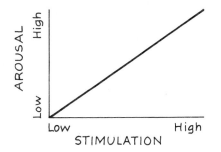
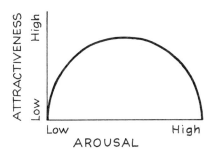

Fig. 1. The relationship between stimulation, arousal, and attractiveness as
hypothesized by Fiske and Maddi (1961), Hebb (1955), Leuba (1955),
among others. (Adapted from Berlyne, 1963, p. 318. Copyright 1963
by the McGraw-Hill Book Company, Inc. Used with permission of
McGraw-Hill Book Company, Inc.)

However, there is at least one problem connected with the assumptions illustrated in Fig. 1. The problem is implied in the assumed linear relationship between degree of stimulation and arousal level, and is clearly illustrated in the
results from the studies in restricted stimulation referred to previously (cf. p.
43). We shall therefore pay somewhat closer attention to these studies, turning
first to that by Bexton, Heron, and Scott (1954). In their experiment on restricted
stimulation, subjects with their primary needs met were paid handsomely to do
nothing, see nothing, hear or touch little for 24 hours a day. However, the results showed that after a few hours the subjects became increasingly restless
and unhappy, seeking increased stimulation of one kind or another, for example
by talking or whistling to themselves, or by exploring the cubicle in which they
were placed (ibid., p. 71.). The deprivation situation seemed to be experienced
as extremely unpleasant, an impression strengthened by the circumstance that
the subjects could stand only a few days despite the lack of exertion and the fact
that the pay was more than double what they could normally earn. As an example,
one of the subjects in real need of money gave up the reward of $ 20 a day for
participating in the experiment to take up a job involving hard labour paying $7
or $8 a day (reported by Hebb, 1955, p. 247).

A similar result is reported from the experiment by Lilly (1956), where the
subjects were placed in a tank containing slowly flowing water of a temperature
such that they felt neither hot nor cold. The subjects wore masks, much of the
pressure on the body caused by gravity was lacking, and the sound level was very
low. On the whole, the environment was described as one of the most even and
monotonous the investigator had experienced (ibid., p. 5). After an initial period
of relaxation, the same characteristic restlessness as that observed in the study

by Bexton et al. appeared: ".. the tension may ultimately develop to the point of forcing the subject to leave the tank." (ibid., p. 6).

In the experiment reported by Karsten (1928) the subjects were instructed to perform monotonous repetitive tasks, such as drawing horizontal or vertical lines, reading a short poem over and over again, drawing simple figures such as moon faces repeatedly, etc. Here too the subjects were observed to be increasingly uncomfortable, trying to decrease the restlessness by introducing variation into the tasks to be repeated, and at last refusing to continue (ibid., pp. 175 ff.).

The results from these and similar studies (e.g. S. Smith & Myers, 1966, p. 1160; S. Smith, Myers, & Johnson, 1967, p. 266) are observed to be at variance with the assumption of a linear relationship between degree of stimulation and arousal level, illustrated in Fig. 1, in that they seem to reveal a high degree of arousal under conditions providing very scarce stimulation. Thus, Lilly points out that the brain not only stays active despite the lowered levels of stimulation, but accumulates surplus energy to extreme degrees (op. cit., p. 7). Working within the psycho-analytical tradition he describes this as increase of amount of libido with time of deprivation. If libido is not discharged somatically, discharge starts through fantasy, but this, he says, does not result in an adequate rate of discharge in the presence of the rapidly rising arousal level, and therefore more definite phenomena, such as hallucinations, delusions, etc., appear at some point (ibid., p. 8).

Another way of accounting for results like those referred to above is in terms of a boredom drive concept, used by such psychologists as Fenichel (1951), Berlyne (1960, 1963), and Myers and Miller (1954).

The Boredom Concept. The researchers using this concept suggest that the subject becomes satiated when exposed to enduring mild, familiar or unchanging stimulation. Then, if he is compelled to remain in the situation after he is satiated, that is, after the point at which he would voluntarily refuse to continue, boredom occurs. Thus, according to Myers and Millers, such monotonous stimulation provides the basis for a boredom drive:

> Indeed, the observation of small children who are required to sit absolutely still, the reports of prisoners subjected to solitary confinement, and the difficulty of Bexton, Heron, and Scott (1954) in retaining Ss in their experiment on the effects of decreased sensory variation would indicate that such conditions can produce strong motivation. Therefore we suggest that drives produced by homogeneous or monotonous stimulation, enforced inaction, etc., may be reduced by sensory variety, freedom of action, etc., ...
> (1954, p. 435).

The same position is taken by Berlyne (1960, 1963), arguing that both intense stimulation and lack of stimulation is unpleasant (1963, p. 310). The lack of stimu-

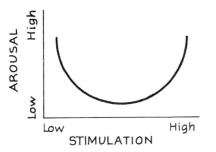
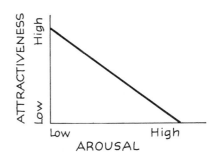

Fig. 2. The relationship between stimulation, arousal, and attractiveness as
hypothesized by Berlyne. (Adapted from Berlyne, 1963, p. 319. Copyright 1963 by the Mc Graw-Hill Book Company, Inc. Used with permission of Mc Graw-Hill Book Company, Inc.)

lation is unpleasant because it produces a rise rather than a fall in arousal, that
is, it produces a boredom drive. According to this viewpoint drive is regarded
simply as a U-shaped function of stimulation, as illustrated in Fig. 2, and attractiveness as a decreasing monotonic function of arousal. Then, the drive strength
is high both under threatening stimulation and under conditions where stimulation is extremely scanty.

Berlyne indicates several reasons behind the suggestion that boredom works
through a rise in arousal (1960, pp. 189 ff.). First, he points out that the human
being when experiencing boredom does not look like a creature with low arousal,
but rather shows the restlessness, agitation, and emotional upset that usually
coincide with high arousal. This is also in accordance with the EEG findings in
the Bexton, Heron, and Scott study (1954) indicating heightened arousal (Heron
in personal communication referred to by Berlyne, 1960, p. 190), as well as
with the results from J. A. Vernon's sensory-deprivation experiments, showing
skin conductance (GSR), having been taken as an index of arousal, to be greater
after a period of confinement than before (Vernon in personal communication referred to by Berlyne, 1960, p. 190).

On the other hand Berlyne points out that a state of low arousal is a state of
drowsiness or sleepiness, and, says he, "It is common knowledge that a lack of
stimulation also has the tendency to put people to sleep" (1960, p. 189). Being
lulled to sleep or lying motionless in a quiet room is not generally reckoned as
unpleasant or distressing, but as agreeable and comforting when one is tired or
ill. But as the study by Bexton, Heron, and Scott (1954) revealed, it is extremely
trying to have such conditions forced upon one when one is healthy and rested.
Scanty stimulation is held to be highly distressing when one is urgently motivated

to do something. In other words, while there are times when monotonous stimulation is agreeable, such as when one is tired, there are other times when it is highly distressing.

A Comparison of Viewpoints. At this point it is worth noting that even though the theories of Fiske and Maddi, Hebb, and Leuba on the one hand, and that of Berlyne on the other rest on different assumptions, they nevertheless yield the same relationship between stimulation level and attractiveness, i.e. both positions imply an inverted U-shaped relation between stimulation level and attractiveness. Berlyne's theory seems, however, to fare considerably better when confronted with the results from the studies in restricted stimulation referred to above, than that of Fiske and Maddi, Hebb, and Leuba, and therefore plays a considerable part in the following theorizing. Nevertheless the theories should in a certain sense be regarded as complementary rather than as mutually exclusive. Thus, Berlyne primarily emphasizes the negative aspect of the motivation problem. Arousal is something negative, something to be reduced or avoided, and it is connected with either too low or too high stimulation. This unpleasant, negative state of affairs can be reduced or avoided by turning to situations offering a moderate degree of stimulation. Actually, nothing is said about possible positive affects connected with such stimulation, but one comes very close to this problem by referring to phenomena like attractiveness and rewarding conditions (Berlyne, 1960, p. 167; 1963, p. 318). On the other hand, Fiske and Maddi, Hebb, and Leuba, emphasize just this positive aspect. They assume pleasantness to be connected with a moderate degree of stimulation. This particular part of their position does not seem to be at variance with the assumptions made by Berlyne, but seems to represent an important supplement to his theory. The importance of emphasizing both the positive and negative aspects is clearly underlined in the achievement motivation theory, which is the main theme of the next chapter.

Summing up and Evaluation. According to what has been said in the foregoing, positive affects should be connected with situations which provide a moderate degree of stimulation and negative affects with situations that provide either very low or very high stimulation. This assumption is obviously significant in connection with the persistence problem. If the situation provides either very scanty or very intense stimulation, the individual should display little persistence in it, while he should be highly persistent in situations providing a moderate degree of stimulation. The significance of the optimal stimulation principle becomes even clearer when it is related to the learning process and the expectancy theory line of reasoning considered in a previous section (cf. pp. 36 ff.). Thus, as a result of the learning process, stimuli associated with for example very high or very low stimulation, and thereby with negative affects, may in later situations release an expectancy or anticipation of negative affects which is assumed to serve at least as a partial determinant of the individual's action. The individual is thought to resist engaging in situations expected to be accompanied or followed by such negative affects. On the other hand, cues associated with a moderate degree of stimulation, and thereby with positive affects, may later release an expectancy or anticipation of positive affects which in turn results in engagement and persistence. Following this line of reasoning it can be seen that both anticipated decrease and increase in stimulation may motivate the individual to engage as well as to resist engaging in an activity, depending upon the level of stimulation at the time.

While the viewpoints presented in the foregoing are judged to contribute to the understanding of the persistence problem, the circumstance that they are primarily situation-oriented implies that they suffer from much the same objections as the works on extinction problems (cf. p. 42). Characterizing the optimal stimulation approach as primarily situation-oriented means, however, that the personality aspect has not been completely neglected. Thus, it has been touched lightly on by for example Leuba, who points out that for some people all intensities of certain sensations may, as a result of learning, be unpleasant (1961, p. 319), and that in general pleasant stimulation intensities seem to include higher levels for children than for adults (ibid. , p. 320), thus implying that the amount of stimulation which is unpleasant to adults is not necessarily so to children. A somewhat similar way of accounting for the role of the personality is employed by Berlyne (1950, p. 72), who argues that for the human infant very little is familiar, and that the reaction which a stimulus originally evoked may disappear as the stimulus becomes familiar to the individual.

These indications of the role of the personality do not, however, change the main impression that on the whole very little has been done within optimal stimulation research to take personality differences systematically into account. In other words, variation in reactions to a given stimulus due to personality differences has usually been treated as a part of error variation. Here it should, however, be stressed that while the optimal stimulation principle implies that individuals will be persistent in situations providing a moderate degree of stimulation, and display resistance towards engaging in situations providing either very low or very high stimulation, this does not necessarily mean that they will

4

all seek the same kind of environment. Thus, we are here arguing for a relativistic stimulation concept.. The key point in this connection, more or less
neglected by the advocates of the optimal stimulation viewpoint, is that the degree to which a given situation will be experienced as distressing or exciting, or
to what degree it will release positive or negative affects, varies from one individual to another, depending upon the individual's personality characteristics.
It is anticipated that if the optimal stimulation principle is supplied with such
personality-oriented viewpoints, we shall arrive at a better understanding of
the persistence problem. Further, it is maintained that the achievement motive
is a personality characteristic of high relevance in this connection, indicating
the degree to which an individual will experience positive or negative affects
and accordingly act more or less persistently in a given situation. We shall
therefore in the last section of this chapter focus upon some viewpoints which
are clearly related to those set forth by achievement motivation theorists.

TOWARDS AN INTERACTION-ORIENTED CONSIDERATION OF PER-
SISTENCE: SOME VIEWPOINTS RELATED TO THE ACHIEVEMENT
MOTIVATION CONCEPT

The increasing interest in what may be called the individual's tendency to try to
master his environment in an effective way is probably one of the clearest trends
within motivational psychology of today. This tendency, as shown in a review
article by White (1959), has been dealt with in different ways, some of which,
having at least implicitly to do with the problem of persistence, will be considered here. One of the psychologists concerned with this area of human behaviour is Ives Hendrick, who works within the psychoanalytic theory field.

An instinct to master

According to Freud an instinct is a force of biological origin, producing tensions
the release of which is experienced as pleasure. With this as a starting point,
Hendrick (1942, p. 40) refers to what he calls "an inborn drive to do and to learn
how to do" as an "instinct to master", the aim of which is the pleasure in exe-
cuting a function successfully (ibid. , p. 41). This instinct manifests itself in the
development of motor abilities, such as grasping, reaching, handling, turning

over, etc. These abilities appear at very definite times in an infant's life, but their effective use is not immediately established:

> In achieving locomotion, for example, the child repeats a step supported by both hands, by one hand, then uses neither, but steps towards a place of safety; then it relies on a single support, and eventually tries walking unassisted. During these weeks a considerable amount of its behavior will be concentrated in practicing these stages of learning to master space with his legs. But, when the child has learned to walk, this compulsion to repeat over and over a certain locomotor movement, to practice it for its own sake, disappears, and the function is then at the disposal of the ego for use in a multitude of situations (Hendrick, 1942, p. 42).

What Hendrick says here is clearly related to the problem of persistence: As long as an activity is not fully mastered, the child is motivated to perform it once more, i.e. he will be persistent in the activity, but as soon as the child masters the task, the motivation or tendency to perform is weakened, i.e. the child will no longer display persistence at the task. This, Hendrick thinks, is a fundamental principle of human behaviour, so fundamental that he prefers to regard mastering behaviour as instinctive.

The theoretical position taken by Hendrick has much in common with that of those arguing for a built-in tendency of the individual to actualize his capacities by dealing with the environment, represented in this connection by outstanding psychologists like Woodworth (1958), Piaget (1966), and White (1959).

The tendency to deal with the environment

Woodworth holds drive to be the main motivational variable, but while most drive theorists emphasize the role of internal needs such as hunger or thirst as the primary basis for drives, Woodworth also holds environmental incentives to be important drive causes. Instead of saying that behaviour directed towards mastering the environment is secondarily motivated by organic needs, he holds ". . . the tendency to deal with the environment as a primary drive, and indeed as the primary drive in behavior" (1958, p. 133). The capacities for dealing with the environment offer outlets for this primary drive. This tendency to actualize one's capacity finds a close parallel in Piaget's developmental theory.

The work of Piaget focuses on problems of cognitive development, and motivational terms have not occupied a prominent place in his production, but nevertheless his theory has much to say about problems of motivation. Piaget's interest is in the development of cognitive structures or schemas, and one of the main characteristics of a schema is its built-in need to function, i.e. to

assimilate anything assimilable in the environment (Piaget, 1966, pp. 32 ff.).
As an example, let us consider the grasping schema, a cognitive structure with
reference to grasping activity. An eight-month-old child may be able to pick
up a ball from the floor. He grasps it over and over again, but the same child
does not try to pick up a little button lying in front of him. The object must appear graspable before the schema is activated, or, in Piaget's terms, the schema
must assimilate the object to a certain degree. In other words, the situation must
represent a challenge, and this challenge is present when the object or task in
question is assimilable, but not completely assimilated. When the child can grasp
the ball in an effective way, the ball no longer represents a challenge to the grasping schema. The task is completely assimilated, and therefore the child is no
longer motivated for this activity, that is, he will no longer be persistent at it.

This intrinsic tendency to assimilate more and more of the environment is
the force behind the cognitive development, according to Piaget. Thus, what
Hendrick refers to as an instinct to master, and Woodworth refers to as actual-
izing one's capacities, is an important aspect within the system of Piaget too.
This line of thought seems to reach something of a climax in the article by White
(1959) on motivational problems. Because his position is that which is most explicitly related to the achievement motivation theory, which will be the main theme
in the next chapter, we shall give it a more thorough examination.

White does not deny the role of bodily needs such as hunger, sex, etc. in human
behaviour, but after having reviewed several motivational theories he tries to
take care of some of the important phenomena left out by drive theory by introducing the concept competence motivation or effectance motivation as a primary
kind of motivation, held to be of high adaptive value:

> The behavior that leads to the building up of effective grasping, handling,
> and letting go of objects, to take one example, is not random behavior
> produced by a general overflow of energy. It is directed, selective, and
> persistent, and it is continued not because it serves primary drives, which
> indeed it cannot serve until it is almost perfected, but because it satisfies
> an intrinsic need to deal with the environment (1959, p. 318).

This effectance motive is not a deficit motive; it is assumed to be neurogenic,
"... its 'energies' being simply those of the living cells that make up the nervous
system" (ibid. , p. 321). Therefore we find no consummatory acts, and the satisfaction lies in the arousal and maintaining of activity, rather than in its decline
to passivity. This subjective side of effectance motivation is described by White
as a "feeling of efficacy" (ibid. , p. 322).

This kind of motivation is aroused only under certain stimulus conditions. It
is not aroused when the stimulus field is of such a character that it releases

only reflex behaviour or other well-learned behaviour patterns. A prerequisite for the arousal of effectance motivation is that the stimulus field releases a certain degree of uncertainty, a viewpoint close to that of Piaget. When a situation has been explored to the point where it no longer presents some uncertainty or new possibilities, no effectance motivation will be aroused. Activity will no longer involve a "feeling of efficacy". In such situations the individual is not expected to be persistent.

It can thus be seen that effectance motivation may have reference to a wide spectre of behaviour, such as visual exploration, grasping, walking, thinking, exploring novel objects, etc. All these kinds of behaviour may, but do not necessarily, produce a "feeling of efficacy". Here, the interaction aspect appears clearly: A situation may, or may not, release effectance motivation, depending upon the degree to which the individual expects to master the situation. This expectation is a result of individual characteristics as well as of situation characteristics.

The effectance motivation concept has its close parallel in the achievement motivation concept. In fact, White himself holds achievement motivation to be an aspect of effectance motivation:

> In infants and young children it seems to me sensible to conceive of effectance motivation as undifferentiated. Later in life it becomes profitable to distinguish various motives such as cognizance, construction, mastery, and achievement. It is my view that all such motives have a root in effectance motivation. They are differentiated from it through life experiences which emphasize one or another aspect of the cycle of transaction with the environment (1959, p. 323).

An Evaluation. Although the positions considered in the foregoing all to a certain degree reflect an interactional-psychological way of considering such problems as persistence, they are not developed to the extent that they are very serviceable for explanation purposes. Thus, as Bolles (1958, p. 4) points out, one way to make a theoretical construct such as drive succeed as an explanatory device is to determine its functional relationships to both antecedent conditions and to certain features of behaviour. However, one of the main arguments set forth against the concept the tendency to deal with the environment, presented under somewhat different labels, is that it is too loosely defined, often on the basis of observed variations in activity. Thereby one gets a concept which assumes all that it was intended to predict. To cite Bolles again: "Inferring drives from behavior without reference to antecedent conditions may do no more than restate the facts that the drive was called out to explain" (1958, p. 4). In the same way Estes, also emphasizing the antecedent and the consequent relationships, says that the usefulness of the drive concept breaks down "... when enthusiastic proponents extend usage of the term to situations in which only one of the defining relations can be identified, thereby generating such ill-endowed mutants as 'exploratory drive' and even 'activity drive' (1958, p. 34). From this point of view the advocates of the tendency to deal with the environment concept are, although highly concerned with explanation of behaviour, subject to much the same criticism as those arguing for persistence as an underlying personality trait (cf. pp. 27 ff.).

GENERAL SUMMARY

In this chapter examples of three possible ways of considering the persistence problem have been presented: examples of the individual-oriented approach, the situation-oriented approach, and to a certain extent interaction-oriented approach. The individual-oriented approach implies accounting for differences in persistence by referring to differences in an underlying personality characteristic. Very often this characteristic itself has been designated persistence, and has been inferred from the time spent on a wide variety of tasks. The circularity implied in such reasoning leaves these works little, if any, explanatory value. In addition, the empirical results are found to be rather divergent.

A few examples of efforts to relate persistence to other characteristics, such as the subject's sex and intelligence, have also been considered, but here too there seems to be a considerable lack of consistency in the results. On the whole, little light is shed on the persistence problem by the individual-oriented approach.

The situation-oriented viewpoint explains persistence differences by referring to differences in situation characteristics. Two such approaches were considered: Studies of extinction problems, and works concerned with the problem of optimal stimulation. A central concept in connection with both is expectation: The individual displays persistence in activities expected to result in reward or in stimulation within a moderate range.

However, neither the individual- nor the situation-oriented approach in their pure form take account of the possibility of an interaction between individual and situation characteristics. This interaction aspect is to a certain degree taken into consideration in positions focusing on what may be called the tendency to deal with the environment. According to these positions persistence should be displayed as long as the situation represents a challenge to the individual. This is supposed to be the case when the task in question is neither too difficult nor too easy. However, the positions considered have not been developed so far as to suggest an independent identification of the strength of the tendency to deal with the environment. The theorists rather restrict themselves to inferring the tendency from the behaviour which is to be explained. Avoidance of such a tautological explanation is attempted in the achievement motivation theory, with which we shall be concerned in the next chapter.

CHAPTER 2

THE ACHIEVEMENT MOTIVATION THEORY

In connection with the expectation and optimal stimulation aspect dealt with in the
previous chapter some attention was paid to the significance of affects for persistence in behaviour. The viewpoints considered implied that subjects should persist
in behaviour expected to have pleasant effects and resist engaging in activities expected to have unpleasant effects. A somewhat similar line of reasoning is developed in the affective arousal model, presented by McClelland, Atkinson, Clark,
and Lowell in Chapter II in The Achievement Motive (1953).

THE AFFECTIVE AROUSAL MODEL

Psychologists seem to agree that certain types of stimulation are innately painful,
but it is more unusual to see the other logical possibility being taken into consideration, namely, that other types of stimulation are innately pleasurable.
McClelland and his collaborators hold that there is convincing evidence for certain innate pleasures, and ". . . any theory of motivation should take account of
the active comforts and pleasures of life as well as the discomforts, tensions
and their relief" (McClelland, Atkinson, Clark & Lowell, 1953, p. 12). There
are for example, according to the same investigators, undoubtedly intrinsic
pleasures connected with such universal experiences as learning to walk, talk,
write, and so forth (ibid. ; p. 78). This is a viewpoint very close to some of those
briefly presented in the last part of the previous chapter (pp. 50 ff.), one of which
being that advocated by Piaget. Piaget also holds that affects such as pleasure or
pain are linked to the modalities of the activity itself (1968, pp. 15 f.), and has
published a long series of observations of children which seem to lend support
to this view (cf. e.g. Piaget, 1966).

These unlearned affective states are the prerequisites for the development of
motives, but they are not themselves motives. McClelland and his associates'
viewpoints on the development of motives rest on an initial premise of a con-

stantly active individual. The newborn child displays activities of various sorts, and intrinsic pleasures or pains are assumed to be connected with these activities, thus providing a basis for affective conditioning. Such conditioned affects are held to be motivating. Thus a motive is said to be "... the redintegration by a cue of a change in an affective situation" (McClelland et al., 1953, p. 28). This definition sums up what is expressed in a more easily understandable way in an earlier work by McClelland (1951, p. 466). " ... a motive becomes a strong affective association, characterized by an anticipatory goal reaction and based on past association of certain cues with pleasure or pain." In other words, stimuli, internal or external, which are present when an individual experiences positive or negative affects may later redintegrate parts of the same experiences. The individual learns to anticipate positive or negative affects which motivate him to approach or to avoid the situation respectively.

Following this line of reasoning all motives are regarded as learned. What is meant by this can probably best be illustrated by a quotation from Atkinson (1954, p. 60), where hunger is used as an example:

> This view would not deny that on the first occasion of food deprivation some important changes take place within an organism which produce diffuse reactions of various sorts including, presumably, a negative affective state. But it would not speak of the organism as motivated until the cues of the hunger state had been followed a number of times by the sensory pleasure of eating and subsequent affective changes when food is digested. After a number of such occasions, the cues produced by the state of food deprivation would arouse anticipatory representations of the events that had previously followed. We could then speak of a food motive or motive to eat and mean by this an anticipatory goal state, a state of anticipation of the affective consequences of eating, or, said another way, an anticipation of the affective change contingent upon eating.

What is said above clearly emphasizes the directional aspect of motivation within the affective arousal model. There is no food motive until the child has eaten food and the internal need-produced stimuli have obtained the capacity to redintegrate an affective change such as that connected with eating. But, as Brown (1961, p. 181) points out, McClelland and his collaborators say nothing about whether the unlearned affects have motivating effects, i.e. are energizing, even though they are not motives. What Brown here clearly has in mind is the common drive-theoretical viewpoint that it is deficit tensional states which cause the apparently random activity of the child. It may seem as if the McClelland group's assertion that the newborn child does not have a food motive means much the same as Brown's statement that the child, although hungry, cannot be said to have a drive for food (1953, p. 8). The drive qua drive is not assumed to have this directional function. Thus, as Brown (1961, p. 181) also mentions, the motive in the affective arousal model seems to be roughly the same as Hull's reaction (excitatory) potential $(_SE_R)$ (Hull, 1943, pp. 239 ff.). In the same way as the reaction potential, being equivalent (strongly simplified) to Habit $(_SH_R)$ x Drive (D), would be zero if $_SH_R$ were zero, so the motive would be non-existent until a habit had been formed, even though some primary affect were present. The reaction potential guides behaviour in the same way as the motive does. However, in spite of the parallel indicated by Brown there remains an important difference between the position taken by the McClelland group and that of the Hull inspired psychologists, in that the McClelland group does not presuppose a deficit tensional state as the first cause of activity. The drive problem has no place in their theory, since they assume a constantly active individual. Then the central problem is seen to be that of change from one activity to another. Obviously, this may also be considered as a persistence problem. The achievement motive is assumed to be an important determinator of persistence in a broad spectre of situations, and we shall therefore now turn to what distinguishes this motive from others.

THE ACHIEVEMENT MOTIVE: A PERSONALITY CHARACTERISTIC

Since a motive within the affective arousal model is said to be a general capacity to anticipate satisfaction or pain in connection with certain kinds of incentives, one may distinguish between different motives by referring to classes of incentives which produce essentially the same kind of expectancies of satisfaction or pain. As to the achievement motive, the expectations are, according to McClelland and his collaborators,

> ... built out of universal experiences with problemsolving - with learning to walk, talk, hunt or read, write, sew, perform chores, and so forth. ... The tasks can be done quickly and efficiently or clumsily and slowly. They can also be done better or faster than someone else. ... The child must begin to perceive performance in terms of standards of excellence so that discrepancies of various sorts from this perceptual frame of reference (AL) can produce positive or negative affect (McClelland et al., 1953, pp. 78 f.).

In other words, as a consequence of experiences in connection with behaviours like those mentioned above the child develops an achievement motive, which is a general capacity to anticipate positive affects in terms of pleasure or pride or negative affects in terms of shame or embarrassment in achievement situations, i.e. in situations where the behaviour is to be evaluated in terms of some standard of excellence. According to McClelland and his associates the evaluation in relation to the standard may be done either by others or by the subject himself, and the consequence of the subject's action must be either a favourable or an unfavourable evaluation (success or failure).

Then, since there are two possible outcomes of the evaluation, it becomes appropriate to distinguish between two aspects of the achievement motive, according to whether the affects involved are positive or negative: a motive to achieve success in achievement situations, here designated M_s and implying anticipation of positive evaluations (positive affects), and a motive to avoid failure in such situations, here designated M_f and implying anticipation of negative evaluations (negative affects). Since the development of the motives is held to be a result of experiences in achievement situations, especially in early childhood, it follows that their strength should vary from one individual to another, the variation reflecting individual differences in childhood experiences. Then, depending upon the relative strength of the two motives M_s and M_f, there is a "characteristic center of gravity" (Heckhausen, 1967, p. 22) for each individual. Thus, individuals dominated by the motive to achieve success " ... consider the probability of success rather than that of failure; they judge their levels of achievement against a general background colored with success expectation" (ibid. , p. 22). The reverse should be true for individuals dominated by the motive to avoid failure, i.e. they should consider the possibility of failure rather than that of success, and judge their achievements against a general background of failure expectations.

While the strength of the motive is assumed to vary from one individual to another, the emphasis placed on childhood experiences makes it clear that its strength is considered to be relatively stable for the same individual over time. We shall consider some of the arguments presented in favour of this viewpoint (McClelland, 1951, pp. 441 ff.), arguments which are based on well-known learning principles.

The importance of early learning

While there is scarcely any clear-cut dichotomy between the learning conditions in early childhood and those later in life, there are differences in degree which may account for the greater persistence and strength of what is learned early in life.

First, however, it has to be pointed out that, as distinct from the laboratory situation, the real life learning situation is characterized by so much irregularity, change, and inconsistency that one may wonder how anything is ever learned. But, says McClelland,

> ... things are learned under such conditions and when they are, they should be very hard to unlearn because the learning is so general in the first place, so compounded of different cues, responses, rewards, and punishments, that it will be hard for the person ever to discover that conditions have changed, that some general expectation he has formed is no longer being confirmed (ibid., p. 442).

This obscurity in the learning situation is held to be most pronounced in early childhood, before the child has developed symbolic capacities to any great extent, which could help him create regularity in external irregularities. Consequently, what is learned in early childhood should be more difficult to extinguish than what is learned later on. This point is further underlined by the circumstance that because of the development of the discriminatory ability, much of what is learned earlier is learned under cue conditions which it is impossible to reinstate, and when the cue conditions cannot be reinstated, it will be difficult to unlearn the associations involving them.

The characteristics considered so far must be seen together with what McClelland calls "the greater over-all responsiveness of the infant to stimulation" (ibid., p. 443), implying that more of the child's associations than of those formed later in life will involve an affective component, being accompanied by some kind of discharge in the autonomic nervous system. Such associations, involving autonomic discharge, are held to be stronger and harder to extinguish than associations involving more differentiated cortical control. As the child grows older, the affective component decreases and becomes more attached to specific cues or responses.

According to these arguments early childhood should offer the best possibilities for the learning of strong, general, and persistent associations. This means that early childhood should also be of special importance for the development of motives. Since more of the conditions promoting the learning of strong, general associations are apt to occur in childhood, motives become harder to form with age. Later in life the possibility is greater for developing what McClelland calls achievement habits. An achievement habit is tied to rather particular situations and rewards, in contrast to an achievement motive, which is based on a generalized association between various responses and possible achievement rewards (ibid., p. 451).

Then, to sum up, the achievement motive is assumed to be a relatively stable and general personality characteristic, developed in early childhood as a result of experiences in performance situations. This underlining of the importance of learning experiences calls for a somewhat further examination of two important problems. For one thing, what is said so far does not seem to have resulted in any clear distinction between the achievement motive and other achievement-related motives. In the second place, very little is said about the relationship between the positive and the negative aspect of the motive, i.e. between M_s and M_f. Both these questions must be of great significance in achievement motivation studies.

Two problems related to the achievement motive concept

The Achievement Motive as Distinct from Other Achievement-Related Motives.

According to the arguments presented in favour of the significance of early learning for the formation of motives, the reinforcement following performance must be regarded as a decisive factor. Then it seems natural to regard, as McClelland seems to do (1951, p. 450), the achievement motive as being mainly a product of reinforcement obtained from parents or other persons in the child's environment. In other words, the achievement motive then is regarded as a result of social learning. This line of thought is clearly expressed by V. J. Crandall, Preston, and Rabson (1960, pp. 243 f.):

> Presumably, the achievement need, like other need systems, is a product of social learning situations and reinforcements which children experience in their daily life. Achievement behavior of children, like other social behaviors, should increase as children experience satisfactions and rewards for their efforts and decrease when such reinforcements are not forthcoming. It might be expected, then, that children who display strong achievement propensities by nursery school age or grade school age are those who, in earlier learning situations, have frequently received approval from others for their accomplishments. Children who are rewarded for achievement striving and for proficient performance should, in time, come to value achievement activities as potential sources of satisfaction and security. In addition, these children should develop expectations that their achievement efforts will be successful. Thus, because they have come to value achievement as a potential source of satisfaction and have expectations that their efforts will lead to successful attainments and approval, these children should develop strong achievement motivation and should seek out and participate in achievement activities when these activities are available.

Undoubtedly, the reinforcement administered by persons in the environment must be regarded as important for the formation of motives, but nevertheless it seems that Crandall and his associates, by regarding the development of the achievement motive in this way, overlook another kind of reinforcement which is equally, or probably more important for the formation of the achievement motive than the social reinforcements referred to, i.e. the kind of self-reinforcement which has been demonstrated in children's behaviour such as that observed by Piaget (1966) in his studies of cognitive development. In these studies the children have been found to display a characteristic tendency to repeat actions producing environmental effects. Further, these actions are observed to be accompanied by positively toned emotions. Similar observations have been called attention to by Atkinson (1969, pp. 200 f.) in an attempt to deemphasize the importance of social reinforcement for the development of the achievement motive. Another leading investigator within achievement motivation research, Heinz Heckhausen, has considered this aspect more thoroughly. Starting with experiences from daily life, he says:

> Every mother has to realize that even her more dramatic negative social sanctions so often cannot extinguish her child's activity in dealing with certain objects which the mother thinks are inappropriate or even dangerous for the child's transactional curiosity. Can there be any doubt that the experience of produced effects has in itself a reinforcing value for the infant, and that a feeling of efficacy, as Robert White (1959) has put it, is sufficiently and intrinsically rewarding? (1969, p. 130.)

There is also another important characteristic referred to by Piaget in his studies of this kind of behaviour, which seems to be directly related to the achievement motive concept, i.e. the significance of the difficulty of the task in question. The tendency to repeat the actions and the emotions accompanying them decrease as the child approaches an effective level of performance, i.e. as the task becomes easy. In the case of the small child the grasping of for example a small marble, may represent a challenging task at a certain stage of development, and at this stage the child enjoys grasping it over and over again, but he does not spend the rest of his life grasping small marbles. In other words, the affective arousal is experienced only insofar as the task to be performed is of a certain difficulty. Mastering such a task means reaching a certain standard of excellence. Then we are, according to what is said on the preceding pages, talking about an achievement motivation problem.

Heckhausen discusses the same point, and since his reasoning results in an important distinction between the achievement motive and other achievement-related motives, it should be considered in some detail. Referring to the importance of the standard of excellence in connection with performance, he says:

> Thus, the very origin of achievement motivation is identical with the first appearance of a self-reinforcement contingent on an activity requiring a certain mastery. That is to say, the result of one's

own activity is evaluated within a reference system of standards of excellence and tells the actor how good, how competent he himself has been at a given task. What previously has been mere pleasure from activity effects in the environment becomes now pride in own success; and prior displeasure from nonappearance of looked-for effects becomes now a feeling of shame because of failure (1969, p. 131).

Thus, it is assumed that social reinforcement is not a necessary condition for the development of the achievement motive. Indeed, Heckhausen puts it even more strongly, arguing that if it is social approval or disapproval that is aspired to or avoided, then it is not appropriate to speak of achievement motivation. One ought instead to speak of achievement-related behaviour in the service of the approval motive (ibid., p. 132).

So much for the de-emphasizing of the significance of social approval in connection with the achievement motive. Nevertheless, social approval or disapproval is not irrelevant in this connection, since it must be regarded as one of the sources of information which lead to the building up of a reference system, a standard of excellence, against which performance is evaluated. The point is, however, that behaviour activated by the achievement motive is not primarily intended to attract social approval, but is undertaken because of the pleasure in mastering the activity itself. And even though it is found that behaviour pursued for its own sake and behaviour intended to yield social approval are closely correlated (Kagan & Moss, 1962, pp. 120 f., and Appendix 32C ff.), the distinction pointed out above is seen to be of importance when designing studies of achievement motivation questions. If this viewpoint is valid, one would for example expect a clearer relationship between achievement motive strength and behaviour when the person is working at an achievement task alone in a room where no one is aware of his behaviour than when he is working with an audience. In the first case, we expect achievement motivation, which is directed towards the task itself, to be at least the main, if not the only, motivation. In the second case we expect in addition a motive for social approval to be aroused, which will also be of significance for behaviour. The more such irrelevant (from an achievement motivation viewpoint) motivation enters the picture, the more unclear the relationship between achievement motive strength and behaviour should be.

The above discussion is most strongly related to the positive aspect of the achievement motive (M_s). However, a similar line of reasoning may also be applied to the negative aspect of the achievement motive (M_f), since the experiences of negative affects in achievement situations are not dependent on social reinforcements alone.

Another problem which has been given little attention so far in this work is that of the relationship between the positive and negative aspects of the achievement motive.

The Relationship between the Positive and the Negative Aspects of the Achievement Motive. In the studies of achievement motivation one of the problems which comes up is that of the relationship between M_s, the motive to achieve success, and M_f, the motive to avoid failure. McClelland and his co-workers have regarded the relationship between these two aspects in two different ways: partly as two mutually exclusive personality characteristics, partly as two relatively independent characteristics. The first appears from the McClelland group's early anchoring of both characteristics in the same measuring instrument. They then assumed a low or a moderate score to reflect a relatively strong motive to avoid failure and a high score to reflect a relatively strong motive to achieve success (McClelland & Liberman, 1949, p. 242).

On the other hand, the motivation model developed by Atkinson (1964, pp. 240 ff.) presupposes independency between M_s and M_f to be meaningful. In later years Atkinson and his colleagues have taken the consequence of this by anchoring the two motive aspects in the scores on two different instruments (see for example Atkinson & Feather, 1966, pp. 75 ff.).

In this connection Rand (1965, pp. 23 ff.) points to several circumstances which make it reasonable to assume that the two motive aspects are relatively independent of each other. First, the child's experiences in achievement situations will usually be very varied, and the outcome of efforts to solve a task need not necessarily be an absolute success or an absolute failure. Rather, the success may be greater or smaller and so may the failure, and the solution of a task may be composed of a series of actions, each of which is more or less successful. According to this line of reasoning it may be assumed that the strength of M_s will be dependent upon the number and intensity of success experiences, and the strength of M_f dependent upon the number and intensity of failure experiences. This makes Rand conclude: "The relative strengths of these tendencies would be independent of each other in so far as the experiences of praise and blame are independent of each other" (ibid., p. 24). On this basis Rand takes an intermediate position, assuming the two tendencies to be mutually rather independent, but nevertheless probably correlated.

Of course this basic question is very hard to study experimentally, not least because the measuring problem is a very difficult one, so that the relationship obtained will to a certain extent be dependent upon the kind of instruments used. The measuring problem will be considered later, but it is stressed even now that since we know so little about the relationship between the two aspects of the achievement motive, it is all the more important to employ measuring instruments which are as far as possible unbiased in relation to this problem.

So far we have considered the achievement motive, which can be divided into a motive to achieve success and a motive to avoid failure, and which is further characterized as a general and relatively stable personality characteristic. But this emphasis on its stability and generality does not mean that it is assumed to manifest itself to the same degree in all kinds of performance situations. In this connection the question of what conditions arouse the motive, i.e. lead to the anticipation of pleasure or embarrassment, becomes a very important one, and here we turn our attention to situational factors.

The key role of situational factors

In Chapter 1 we met advocates of the view that the tendency to deal with the environment manifests itself only as long as an activity is not fully mastered (cf. pp. 50 ff.), a view in accordance with that expressed within achievement motivation theory. The anticipation of affects is assumed to depend on some uncertainty as to whether one will succeed or fail at the task in question (McClelland et al., 1953, p. 78). The point is illustrated by Atkinson:

> There can be little question that expectancies and incentives vary greatly from situation to situation. The individual's motivation to achieve, for example, is not aroused to the same extent as he lies sunning himself on a beach as when he enters his office on the day of an important business transaction. It is presumed, however, that the strength of his motive to achieve - that is, his tendency to strive for achievement when the situation offers an opportunity for achievement - does not change. His basic personality is the same whether on the beach or at the office, though his momentary interest and behavior will differ in these two situations (1958, p. 435).

In other words, the motivation or action tendency is a result of an interaction between the motive and particular learned cognitive expectancies elicited by the situation. These cognitive expectancies are assumed to be learned later in life than the motive, and are therefore also more situation-bound and more easily modified than the motive (loc. cit.).

This interaction viewpoint is further elaborated in Atkinson's achievement motivation theory, in which the question of what conditions arouse the motive plays a prominent role (1964, pp. 240 ff.).

ATKINSON'S ACHIEVEMENT MOTIVATION THEORY

In correspondence with the previously presented distinction between a positive and a negative aspect of the achievement motive, Atkinson considers the achievement motivation for a particular activity to be composed of a motivation or tendency to achieve success and a motivation or tendency to avoid failure. Let us first turn to the tendency to achieve success.

The tendency to achieve success (T_s)

Atkinson assumes that as a consequence of past experiences an individual's expectancy that an action will lead to success may be strong, as well as moderate or weak, and in his theory this expectancy is related to the subjective probability of success (P_s). Thus, expectancies can be graded from .00 to 1.00, where for example a P_s of .90 means that the individual is almost certain of success, a P_s of .10 that he has a very weak expectancy of succeeding, and a P_s near .50 that he is maximally uncertain as to the outcome. Further, Atkinson suggests that not all instances of success are equally satisfying, and more specifically that the probability of success, in addition to being the determinant of expectancy, also determines the incentive value of succeeding. Relying on the work of Escalona (1940, pp. 258 f.), Festinger (1942, pp. 237 ff.), and Lewin, Dembo, Festinger, and Sears (1944, pp. 356 ff.) on level of aspiration problems, showing that accomplishment of difficult tasks is more attractive than accomplishment of easy tasks, Atkinson holds that the incentive value (I_s) is inversely related to the ease of attainment, that is $I_s = 1 - P_s$.

The two above-mentioned situational variables, P_s and I_s, are assumed to combine multiplicatively with the motive to achieve success (M_s) which the individual carries with him from situation to situation into an actual tendency to achieve success: $T_s = M_s \times P_s \times I_s$. This simple principle of motivation has the clear implication, as can be seen from Table 1, that the tendency to achieve success will be strongest when a task is neither too easy nor too difficult, i.e. when the task appears to be of intermediate difficulty. Or stated in another way, the anticipation of pleasure implied in the motive concept is modified by situationally aroused cognitive expectancies in such a way that anticipated pleasure is at a maximum in tasks of intermediate difficulty. Further, it can be seen that the tendency to achieve success is stronger when M_s is strong than when M_s is weak, but that the difference in the strength of the tendency to achieve success is substantial only when the task is of intermediate difficulty.

66

Table 1. Tendency to achieve success (T_s) as a joint function of motive to achieve success (M_s), expectancy of success (P_s), and incentive value of success (I_s) for individuals in whom $M_s = 1$ and $M_s = 10$.

Task	P_s	I_s	$T_s = M_s \times P_s \times I_s$ When $M_s = 1$	When $M_s = 10$
A	.90	.10	.09	.90
B	.70	.30	.21	2.10
C	.50	.50	.25	2.50
D	.30	.70	.21	2.10
E	.10	.90	.09	.90

(Adapted from Atkinson, 1964, p. 242. Copyright 1964 by Litton Educational Publishing, Inc. Published by D. Van Nostrand Reinhold Company.)

So far we have considered only the positive aspect of achievement motivation in Atkinson's theory, i.e. the tendency to achieve success. However, the negative aspect, i.e. the tendency to avoid failure, plays an equally important role.

The tendency to avoid failure (T_f)

Parallel to the expectancy of success there may also, as a result of past experiences in situations similar to the one confronting the individual at the moment, be an expectancy that the action will lead to failure, defined in terms of the subjective probability of failure (P_f). And if success and failure are alternative outcomes, then P_f must be weak when P_s is strong, and vice versa. In other words, P_s and P_f are assumed to add up to 1.00. Further, still relying on Escalona (1940), Festinger (1942), and Lewin et al. (1944), it is assumed that the embarrassment of failure is normally greater when the task is easy than when it is difficult, and consequently the incentive value of failure (I_f) is equal to the probability of success with a negative sign: $I_f = -P_s$. The minus sign means that the incentive represents something noxious, and therefore something to be avoided.

P_f and I_f combine multiplicatively with the motive to avoid failure, M_f, into a tendency to avoid failure: $T_f = M_f \times P_f \times I_f$, and, in the same way as the tendency to achieve success, this tendency will be strongest when a task is regarded as of intermediate difficulty. Table 2 spells out the implications of this part of the theory.

Table 2. Tendency to avoid failure (T_f) as a joint function of motive to avoid failure (M_f), expectancy of failure (P_f), and negative incentive value of failure (I_f) for individuals in whom $M_f = 1$ and $M_f = 10$.

Task	P_f	I_f	$T_f = M_f \times P_f \times I_f$	
			When $M_f = 1$	When $M_f = 10$
A	.10	-.90	-.09	-.90
B	.30	-.70	-.21	-2.10
C	.50	-.50	-.25	-2.50
D	.70	-.30	-.21	-2.10
E	.90	-.10	-.09	-.90

(Adapted from Atkinson, 1964, p. 244. Copyright 1964 by Litton Educational Publishing, Inc. Published by D. Van Nostrand Reinhold Company.)

T_s and T_f: A summing up

As is evident from what is said above, the expectancies become central facts in Atkinson's theory of achievement motivation. We have noted that Atkinson, in the same way as McClelland, regards motives as general tendencies to anticipate positive or negative affects as results of actions (cf. p. 57). But these affective expectations, which are developed in early childhood, are modified by a cognitive or perceptual kind of expectancy, which is the result of later experiences of the environment, and the manifest motivation or tendency to achieve success or to avoid failure depends on both kinds of expectancies. The cognitive expectancy $(P_s$ or $P_f)$ seen in isolation is not motivating. An individual may know that he will succeed in a task, but if this knowledge is not combined with what Brown calls a motive-type expectancy (1961, p. 247), i.e. an affectively toned expectancy, nothing will happen. In the same way, the subject may know that he will fail, but unless this knowledge combines with an affective expectancy it has no effect on behaviour. And if an individual has developed a capacity to anticiapte affects in achievement situations, this capacity is, as we have seen, aroused to the highest degree in situa-

68

tions where the uncertainty as to the outcome is greatest, i.e. where P_s or P_f is near .50. If the situation involves no uncertainty, then according to the achievement motivation theory the capacity to anticipate affects will not be aroused at all, meaning that the individual is not motivated. On the other hand, since the theory assumes that all individuals may have both a motive to achieve success (M_s) and a motive to avoid failure (M_f) (Atkinson, 1964, p. 246), both motives will be aroused as soon as there is some uncertainty as to the outcome. Then, the question of the relationship between the two aroused tendencies, T_s and T_f, becomes an important one.

The relationship between T_s and T_f

The key to Atkinson's view of the relationship between the two tendencies lies in the incentive value, which we have seen can be positive or negative. A positive incentive value combines with the motive into a positive tendency, while a negative incentive value is a determinant of the strength of the tendency not to engage in an action. If actions are expected to lead to failure and the individual is disposed towards affectivity in connection with failure, i.e. has a motive to avoid failure, then such actions will be avoided whenever possible. The person is negatively motivated, or motivated not to perform. On the behavioural level the motivation or tendency to achieve success manifests itself in positive interest and active pursuit of success, while the motivation or tendency to avoid failure functions by steering an individual away from achievement-related activities. In this connection Atkinson says:

> Viewed this way, a disposition to be anxious provides no motor for performance of an activity but is conceived as the source of inhibition of activity. With no positive "inducement" to choose between one and another activity which differ in apparent difficulty, a hypothetical person who has only a strong disposition to avoid failure should, according to what is stated in the theory, not act at all (1964, p. 245).

Hence, the tendency to avoid failure does not, according to Atkinson, excite any action at all, neither task-solving nor avoidant actions. The tendency to avoid failure is not motivating at all in the traditional sense of the word, but functions by dampening the positive tendency to achieve success, thereby representing a resistance to achievement-oriented behaviour.

Then, taking into consideration the assumptions presented earlier (pp. 66 ff.), that the positive incentive value is inversely related to the probability of success, i.e. $I_s = 1 - P_s$, and that the negative incentive value of failure is greater the easier the task, i.e. $I_f = -P_s$, the achievement motivation theory can be summarized symbolically in the following way:

$$T_{ach} = T_s + T_f = (M_s \times P_s \times I_s) + (M_f \times P_f \times I_f)$$

$$= \left[M_s \times P_s \times (1 - P_s) \right] + \left[M_f \times (1 - P_s) \times - P_s \right]$$

$$= \underline{(M_s - M_f) \times P_s \times (1 - P_s)}$$

As the formula indicates, a main task within achievement motivation research becomes that of assessing the strength of the two personality characteristics M_s and M_f. We shall therefore, before turning to research concerning achievement motivation and persistence, briefly consider the most usual ways of measuring the motives M_s and M_f.

USUAL WAYS OF MEASURING THE MOTIVES

The motive to achieve success (M_s)

Relying on the traditional psychoanalytic assumption that motivation has effect on fantasy, McClelland and his associates have developed a Thematic Apperception Test to measure the motive to achieve success (TAT nAchievement) (1953, pp. 97 ff.), which has been extensively used in achievement motivation research. In this test the subjects are presented with a set of relatively uninformative pictures, usually four to six, resembling those in the Thematic Apperception Test developed by Murray (1938), and are requested to create a story around each of the pictures. A modified version of the test for use with children has been described by Winterbottom (1958, pp. 459 f.), where, instead of creating stories around pictures, the subjects are asked to finish a set of incomplete stories. Another variant, the Test of Insight, has been developed by E. G. French (1958). In this test the subjects are presented with a set of items each of which describes behaviour which is characteristic of a person, and are asked to write a story as to why the person behaves as he does (ibid., pp. 244 f.). In all three cases it is assumed that the strength of the motive to achieve success can be estimated from the frequency with which certain types of imagery, i.e. imagery with some reference to achievement, appear in the stories. The stories are then scored by counting, according to a set of rules, the number of relevant reactions to the pictures presented.

A combination of projective technique and multiple-choice is found in the Iowa Picture Interpretation Test (IPIT), described by Hurley (1955). In this test a series of TAT pictures is presented, each picture accompanied by a set of four alternative interpretations. One of the interpretations reflects achievement-orientation, the others blandness, insecurity, and hostility. The subject has to rank these interpretations, and M_s strength is inferred from the sum of ranks for the achievement-oriented interpretations throughout the whole series of pictures (ibid. , p. 373).

Looking for a moment at the validity of the M_s tests under consideration, this has been questioned, primarily because of the apparent inconsistencies in the empirical results (Klinger, 1966). As Klinger's review shows, the relationship between scores on various M_s tests and performance level has varied from significantly positive to significantly negative. It should, however, be clear that the question of the validity of the test is closely related to the validity of the theory on which it is based. As pointed out by Krause (1967, p. 281), the failure of an instrument to produce results consistent with the derivations from the theory discredits the instrument only if the theoretical propositions are treated as if they were true. Since the validity of the test and that of the theory are tangled in this way, we shall not be further concerned with these problems at the present stage. Instead, the reader is directed to subsequent chapters where results concerning the relationship between motive strength and behaviour criteria like persistence and performance are dealt with in detail. These results provide a basis for a broader validity evaluation.

Turning now to the reliability problem, the coding reliability or interscorer agreement should not represent any difficulty in connection with the IPIT, where the scoring procedure has been seen to be a very simple, objective one. Satisfactory interscorer agreement has also been reported from studies where the TAT nAch method has been used. For instance, Feld and Smith report scores from novice coders and expert coders to correlate mostly in the range from +.80 to +.90 (1958, p. 238).

The test-retest reliability is more problematical. As to the TAT.nAch scores a coefficient as low as +.22 is reported by McClelland et al. (1953, p. 192) for two sets of three pictures each, given a week apart. Similarly, Krumboltz and Farquhar report a coefficient of only +.26 over a nine-week interval (1957, p. 227). It has, however, been suggested that the test-retest method is inadequate for this kind of instrument, since taking one test may "spoil" the subject for a retest (McClelland, 1958, p. 19). Nevertheless, Haber and Alpert report a more satisfactory test-retest reliability, r = +.54, over a three-week interval with two parallel sets of six pictures each (1958, pp. 660 f.). A similar result for the IPIT is presented by Hurley, who obtained a test-retest coefficient over a six-week interval of +.52 (1955, p. 374), while Himelstein and Kimbrough report a test-retest coefficient for the Test of Insight over a seven-week interval of +.36 (1960, p. 739).

Another indicator of the stability of M_s over time is provided by the findings from longitudinal studies such as that by Moss and Kagan, where there was a correlation of +.31 between TAT nAch scores from adolescence and scores obtained 6 to 15 years later (1961, p. 507).

In summary, the results seem to justify the methods' being used for group comparisons in experimental research. This is all the more justified since, as pointed out by Heckhausen (1967, p. 20), the reliability is probably underestimated, owing to the circumstance that the subjects might have been "spoiled" during the first test.

In most of the studies to be considered later on, the motive to achieve success has been measured by one of the tests referred to above.

The motive to avoid failure (M_f)

Since M_s and M_f, the two aspects of the achievement motive, were initially regarded as two poles on a continuum (cf. pp. 64 f.), the TAT nAch scores were held to reflect both tendencies, a low score reflecting a relatively strong motive to avoid failure, and a high score a relatively strong motive to achieve success. However, the anchoring of M_f in a low score on this projective test soon appeared questionable, among other things because behaviour results seemed to indicate a higher motive to avoid failure in subjects with moderate scores on the test than in those with low scores (McClelland et al. , 1953, pp. 226, 269 ff.). As a consequence of this, an attempt to arrive at separate measures for each of the two achievement motive aspects was made by counting separately the approach and avoidance reactions. This method did not, however, prove successful (ibid. , p. 273).

A new approach has been introduced by Atkinson and Litwin (1960), based on the research carried out by the Mandler-Sarason group on test anxiety (Mandler & Sarason, 1952; S. B. Sarason & Mandler, 1952; S. B. Sarason, Mandler, & Craighill, 1952). Mandler and Sarason have developed a test anxiety questionnaire (TAQ) for measuring anxiety reactions occurring in test situations. This scale consists of 42 questions concerning subjects' feelings before and during test situations like a course examination or an intelligence test, such as uneasiness, heartbeat, sweating, and worry (Mandler & Sarason, 1952, p. 167; S. B. Sarason & Mandler, 1952, p. 810). The questions are answered on a Likert-type scale, and the test anxiety score is obtained by summing the scores on the individual items. This questionnaire aims at measuring test anxiety in adults. A corresponding scale of test anxiety in children (TASC) has since been developed (S. B. Sarason, Davidson, Lighthall, & Waite, 1958), containing 30 questions about reactions in test situations which have to be answered by "yes" or "no". The score is made up of the number of "yes" answers given.

Satisfactory internal consistency as well as test-retest reliability has been reported for both TAQ and TASC. For instance, S. B. Sarason and Mandler report a split-half coefficient of +.91, and a test-retest reliability coefficient over six weeks of +.82 (1952, p. 811). For TASC, S. B. Sarason and his associates report split-half coefficients ranging from +.82 to +.90, and a test-retest reliability of +.71 over a two-month interval (1958, p. 108).

After having compared the test anxiety concept and the motive to avoid failure concept, Atkinson and Litwin hypothesized that the test anxiety scores indicate the strength of the motive to avoid failure (1960, p. 52). Results from a group of 49 college men regarding distance at which shots were taken in a ring toss game, time spent on an examination, etc., provided support for the hypothesis (ibid., pp. 54 ff.). In later achievement motivation studies it has therefore been usual to employ a test anxiety questionnaire to measure the strength of M_f (Atkinson, 1964, pp. 248 ff.; Atkinson & Feather, 1966; Gjesme, 1968; 1971b; 1971c; Nygård, 1967; 1968; 1969; Rand, 1965).

It has also been both implicitly and explicitly suggested by Atkinson that even the score on the Manifest Anxiety Scale (MAS; Taylor, 1953) can be taken as an indicator of the strength of the motive to avoid failure (Atkinson, 1960, p. 266; 1964, pp. 250, 254). This scale consists of 50 items agreed upon by four out of five clinicians to indicate manifest symptoms of anxiety. The subject is asked to indicate whether the statements are true or false as regards him, and the score is made up of the number of items marked in such a way as to reflect the presence of anxiety as a personality trait. Split-half reliability reported by Hilgard, Jones, and Kaplan (1951, p. 96) indicates high internal consistency ($r = +.92$). As to the test-retest reliability, Taylor has reported coefficients varying from +.89 over three weeks to +.81 over an interval of 9 to 17 months (1953, pp. 286, 289). Since the MAS scores have been taken as an indicator of M_f strength, it is also of interest to note that the TAQ scores and the MAS scores are normally correlated about +.50 (I. G. Sarason, 1959, pp. 273 f.; 1961, p. 196).

In subsequent chapters we shall be concerned both with studies where the TAQ or TASC and the MAS have been used to assess individual differences.

Final comments regarding the motive measurement

Before leaving the measurement question there is another matter to which attention should be paid, since it is of particular significance in connection with the interpretation of results from studies where only one of the motives M_s and M_f has been measured. Thus, most studies have shown no significant relationship between the M_s and M_f measures (e.g. Atkinson & Litwin, 1960, p. 59; Litwin, 1966, p. 104; Mahone, 1960, p. 255; C. P. Smith, 1964, p. 526; Vislie, 1972, pp. 248 ff.). This implies that the average M_f strength should be about the same among high and low M_s subjects, or, from the opposite point of departure, that the average M_s strength should be about the same among high and low M_f subjects. Then, as pointed out by Atkinson and Litwin (1960, p. 61), given only M_s scores one can assume that in a group of subjects with high scores M_s is relatively strong in relation to the unmeasured M_f ($M_s > M_f$), while in the group with low M_s scores the reverse should be the case ($M_s < M_f$). When only M_f is measured, one can similarly assume that individuals with a high score as a group have an M_f which is relatively strong in relation to the unmeasured M_s ($M_s < M_f$), while the reverse should hold for the group with low M_f scores ($M_s > M_f$). Needless to say, one can have more confidence in the inference of the relative strength of the motives where both a test assumed to measure M_s and a test assumed to measure M_f have been used.

Lastly, since most achievement motivation studies have used college students as subjects, a reservation has to be made in connection with the inference of the strength of M_s and M_f. As pointed out by Atkinson and Litwin (1960, p. 61), it seems likely that most people in whom M_f is stronger than M_s are eliminated long before the college level. Thus, in a group of college students the average M_s is probably stronger than the average M_f. This implies that in such selected groups one should not too quickly assume the <u>absolute</u> M_f strength to be greater than the <u>absolute</u> M_s strength even among those who score high on the M_f test and low on the M_s test.

GENERAL SUMMARY

In this chapter the achievement motivation theory has been considered in some detail. According to this theory motives are regarded as learned, relatively stable personality characteristics. The motive to achieve success (M_s), considered as a capacity to anticipate positive affects in achievement situations, combines with the situationally aroused expectancy of success (P_s) and the incentive value of success (I_s) into a motivation or tendency to achieve success (T_s). In the same way, the motive to avoid failure (M_f), considered as a capacity to anticipate negative affects in achievement situations, combines with the situationally aroused expectancy of failure (P_f) and the negative incentive value of failure (I_f) into a negative tendency, a tendency to avoid failure (T_f). The resultant motivation or tendency to engage in a particular task equals the tendency to achieve success minus the tendency to avoid failure.

The strength of M_s has usually been assessed by the Thematic Apperception Test for need Achievement or some variant of it (Test of Insight, Iowa Picture Interpretation Test). The strength of M_f has usually been inferred from the scores on test anxiety scales (TAQ or TASC), but also from the scores on the Manifest Anxiety Scale (MAS).

Obviously the achievement motivation theory has clear relevance to the problem of persistence in behaviour. This problem has, however, been given relatively little explicit consideration in the present chapter. In the next chapter we shall be directly concerned with research on persistence based on the achievement motivation theory.

CHAPTER 3

A CHIE VE ME NT MOTIVATION AND PERSISTENCE:
PREVIOUS RESEARCH

Within achievement motivation research the persistence problem has been investigated
in different ways. The simplest kind of study has compared subjects with different
scores on the tests assumed to reflect the M_s or M_f strength with respect to persistenc
in achievement situations. The comparison has been based on the assumption that the
scores at least to a certain degree reflect differences in motivation for the task at
hand. As pointed out in the previous chapter, this motivation is held not only to be a
function of the strength of the individual's motives, but also to depend on certain
situation characteristics. Therefore, more sophisticated investigations have included such situation variables in one way or another. We shall first consider the
simpler way of investigating the problem, starting with the motive to achieve success.

SIMPLE COMPARISONS OF MOTIVE STRENGTH AND PERSISTENCE

Although the style of presentation in the following implies a certain amount of
repetition, nevertheless, for the sake of simplification, the relationship between M_s
measures and persistence will be dealt with first, then that between M_f measures and
persistence, and finally the relationship between combined motive measures and persistence. The fact that in most of the recent achievement motivation studies both
motives have been taken into account also means that much the same studies will be
referred to under all three headings.

Motive to achieve success (M_s) and persistence

The achievement motive is assumed to be elicited under achievement-oriented conditions, and therefore one has expected to find a simple positive relationship between
M_s strength and persistence in such situations. Such a relationship has been observed
both under experimental conditions and in more natural situational settings.

One of the first experiments which focused upon this question was conducted by
Winterbottom (1958) as part of an investigation of the relation of the achievement motive

to early learning experiences. In this experiment 29 eight-year-old boys were observed in a situation where they were given a puzzle test said to tell how clever they were compared with others in the class, and where they were invited to stop work and rest at certain intervals. The results showed that boys scoring above the median on the TAT nAch (adapted for use with children, cf. p. 70), which is assumed to measure the motive to achieve success, refused the invitation to stop work and rest more often than those scoring below the median (ibid. , p. 475). In other words, using refusals of the invitation to stop work as an indicator of persistence, the group assumed to be high in M_s was more persistent in this situation than that assumed to be low in M_s.

Thomas (1956) also found the scores on the achievement motive test to be positively related to persistence in a problem-solving situation, but since no details are reported, the importance of his result cannot be evaluated. This experiment was, however, followed up by one conducted by E. G. French and Thomas (1958), in which 92 male subjects of approximately equal intellectual ability, but with varying M_s strength according to the scores on the motive test (French Test of Insight), were asked to solve a complicated mechanical problem presented to them as a measure of competence. All the facts necessary for solution were learned beforehand, and the subjects were told that they had 35 minutes to solve the problem and that they could use as much of this time as they wished. The results pertaining to persistence were quite clear, in that the mean working time for the group scoring above the median on the achievement motive test was more than twice that of those scoring below the median (ibid. , p. 46). Even more, this result represents a clear under-estimation of the difference between the groups, since 22 of the 47 high M_s subjects worked until the time limit, as compared with only one of the 45 low M_s subjects (loc. cit.).

A positive relationship between M_s strength and persistence is also reported by Evans (1967). His study was mainly directed towards the motive effect upon learning under two different incentive conditions, i.e. an achievement-oriented condition, and an extrinsic incentive (monetary reward) condition. The results obtained in a sample of 195 students, sex not reported, showed that subjects scoring high on the motive test (Iowa Picture Interpretation Test) spent more time on the learning task than those scoring low under both conditions (ibid. , p. 198). This led Evans to suggest that persistence is the primary mediating factor in the observed positive relationship between motive strength and learning. His suggestion was also supported by the fact that when time spent on the learning task was used as a control variable, no relationship was observed between motive strength and learning (ibid. , p. 199).

The relation between M_s strength and persistence in an examination situation has been studied by Atkinson and Litwin (1960), and by C. P. Smith (1964).

Atkinson and Litwin examined the relationship between M_s strength and persistence in a sample consisting of 49 male college students enrolled in a psychology course, using the time spent working on the final examination as a measure of persistence. In the same way as in the studies referred to in the foregoing the subjects with scores above the median on the motive test (French Test of Insight) were more persistent than those with scores below the median on the test (op. cit., p. 56).

A similar study is reported by C. P. Smith (1964), where the relationship between M_s strength and persistence was examined in a sample of 146 college psychology students. Information as to sex is not reported. Smith did not, however, obtain the same clear relationship as that observed in the study by Atkinson and Litwin. Thus, Smith's correlations between motive scores (French Test of Insight) and time spent on a midterm and a final examination were only +.05 and +.09 respectively (ibid., p. 526).

A similar lack of influence of M_s (TAT nAch) is reported by Barker (1968) from a study of persistence in college, where persisting students were defined as those still enrolled in college three years after entry.

However, one question immediately presents itself, at least in connection with the "unexpected" results obtained by C. P. Smith (1964), and it is not discussed by the investigator himself. Thus, at least in the final examination, to which Smith pays most attention, the students could use as much time as they wanted, since there was no upper time limit (ibid., p. 526). Whether the upper limit of 65 minutes for the midterm examination was sufficient for all the students to complete their work, does not appear from the data reported. Anyhow, it might be asked whether the lack of a clear positive relationship between M_s measures and persistence in the examination situation simply reflects that high M_s subjects work harder and therefore complete their work faster than low M_s subjects. From such a point of view it even seems more reasonable to expect a negative relationship between M_s strenght and persistence than a positive one, and this in turn means that the results of the study by Atkinson and Litwin (1960) already referred to, in terms of a positive relationship between M_s strenght and persistence in the examination situation should become the problematical ones. However, for some reason, the data presented by Smith do not indicate that high M_s subjects worked more efficiently than low M_s subjects, the correlation between the M_s measures and final examination results being .00, compared with a correlation of +.09 between the M_s measures and persistence in terms of time spent in the examination (op. cit., p. 526). A greater effi ciency should have manifested itself in a higher positive correlation between M_s score and grade than between M_s score and persistence. Further analyses carried out by Smith, and dealt with in some detail in the section concerning complex relationships between motive strength and persistence, also indicate that the negligible relationship between M_s measures and persistence obtained here cannot be explained simply in terms of greater efficiency among high M_s subjects.

Then, to sum up, although there is considerable evidence in favour of the hypothesis of a positive relationship between M_s strength and persistence, studies are also reported in which one has failed to find any clear relationship. Thus, the results considered so far do not seem to warrant any strong conclusion regarding this matter.

There is less research concerning the relationship between M_f strength and persistence. However, two of the studies already cited, that by Atkinson and Litwin (1960) and that by C. P. Smith (1964) also deal with this question.

Motive to avoid failure (M_f) and persistence

Since the motive to avoid failure is considered as a capacity to anticipate negative affects in achievement situations, one should expect to find a simple negative relationship between M_f measures and persistence. This expectation was supported by the results from the Atkinson and Litwin study previously referred to, which had as one of its main aims the investigation of the construct validity of the Test Anxiety Questionnaire (TAQ) as a measure of M_f (cf. pp. 72 f., where the motive measurement question was dealt with). The results revealed, as expected, that subjects with test anxiety scores above the median, i. e. subjects held to have a strong M_f, left the final examination sooner than those with scores below the median, i. e. subjects held to have a weak M_f (Atkinson & Litwin, 1960, p. 57).

Turning to C. P. Smith's study again, we find an even clearer disagreement with Atkinson and Litwin's results than that in connection with the M_s variable. Thus, Smith found a significant positive relationship between persistence at both the midterm and final examinations and TAQ score, taken as an indicator of M_f strength. The correlations were +.31 and +.27 respectively (C. P. Smith, 1964, p. 526). The possibility of a greater efficiency among high M_s subjects than among low M_s subjects was discussed in the preceding section. Here it is reasonable to ask whether these positive correlations only reflect that the higher the M_f strength, the less efficient the work. From this point of view high M_f subjects should take longer to complete their examination than low M_f subjects, a possibility also touched upon by Smith (ibid., p. 524). According to the achievement motivation theory, however, the high M_f subjects should wish to leave the examination early because of the potentially painful consequences of it. The more thorough-going analyses reported by Smith, which we present in the section on complex relations between motive strength and persistence, also indicate that the explanation of the positive relationship between M_f measures and persistence is not simply that high M_f subjects are less efficient than low M_f subject.

The study by Atkinson and Litwin (1960) and that by C. P. Smith (1964) seem to be the only ones where simple comparisons between M_f measures and persistence are made. Since the results from these two studies are quite contradictory, there is so far no basis for any conclusion regarding the relationship between M_f strength and persistence.

Finally in this section some attention should be paid to the relationship between combined motive measures and persistence.

Combined motive measures and persistence

Since the achievement motivation theory emphasizes the _relative_ strength of the two motives M_s and M_f, (cf. pp. 69 f.), the expectation of a positive relation between M_s strength and persistence together with that of a negative relation between M_f strength and persistence also implies that subjects high in M_s and low in M_f (here designated the $M_s > M_f$ group) should be more persistent than those low in M_s and high in M_f (here designated the $M_s < M_f$ group). Data related to this matter are also reported by Atkinson and Litwin (1960), who in addition to treating each of the motive variables separately, also classified their subjects into four motive groups according to whether their scores on the two tests used were above or below the median. Subjects scoring above the median on the French Test of Insight and below the median on the TAQ were classified as having $M_s > M_f$, while those below the median on the former test and above the median on the latter were classified as having $M_s < M_f$. Individuals with high or low scores on both tests were thought to fall between these groups, that is, to have $M_s \approx M_f$. As one would expect from the cited results related to each of the motive measures separately, a clear difference was found between the $M_s > M_f$ group and the $M_s < M_f$ group, the first one being more persistent in the examination situation (ibid. , p. 57). While the high M_s/high M_f group fell between the two extreme motive groups in persistence, the low M_s/low M_f group was the least persistent one.

It has been pointed out previously that C. P. Smith (1964) obtained results opposite to those in the Atkinson and Litwin study when focusing upon each of the motive variables separately. Accordingly, it is no surprise that this was also the case when the joint influence of M_s and M_f on persistence was examined. In the same way as Atkinson and Litwin, Smith classified his subjects into four motive groups on the basis of median splits on the motive score distributions, and then compared these groups with respect to time spent on the final examination. While there was no significant difference between these groups, Smith nevertheless points out that " . . . there was a tendency for subjects with _relatively_ strong Motive for Success $[M_s > M_f]$ to leave the final exam sooner than subjects with _relatively_ strong Motive to Avoid Failure $[M_s < M_f]$" (ibid. , p. 527).

In addition to classifying the subjects into motive groups, Smith also used another indicator of the relative strength of M_s and M_f, based on the subjects' standard scores (Z scores) on the motive tests. The difference between these standard scores was calculated, and a high score was assumed to indicate a relatively strong M_s, a low score a relatively strong M_f (ibid. , p. 525). This difference score correlated slightly negatively with persistence at both the midterm and final examinations, the coefficients being -.18 and -.12 respectively. That is, when inferring motive strength by this difference method, subjects held to have a strong M_s were also found to be, if anything, less persistent in the examination situation than those held to have strong M_f.

Finally, results related to the question of the joint effect of M_s and M_f on persistence are reported by Heckhausen, who focused upon such a "free" activity as that of doing homework. In a group of 47 psychology students he found the $M_s < M_f$ students (according to the scores on Heckhausen's version of the TAT nAch) to hesitate longer before turning to homework and to interrupt their work more often than did $M_s > M_f$ students (1963, pp. 236 f. ; 1967, p. 114). On the basis of results presented in an unpublished work by Vukovich, Heckhausen, and von Hatzfeld (1964) it is also concluded that in the face of failure and difficulties success-motivated subjects tend to pursue a goal more persistently than failure-motivated subjects (Heckhausen, 1967, p. 114).

On the whole, then, the results reported by Heckhausen seem to correspond well with the impression left by the Atkinson and Litwin study that the $M_s > M_f$ group is more persistent than the $M_s < M_f$ group. Then, we are once more left with the question of why C. P. Smith obtained results quite contrary to those reported by Atkinson and Litwin. Some attention has earlier been paid to the possibility of differences between the motive groups in efficiency at work, but it was concluded that this does not seem to represent a satisfactory explanation. Another more interesting possibility, indicated by C. P. Smith himself (op. cit. , p. 527), is that there may be a difference in perceived difficulty of the task between his sample and that of Atkinson and Litwin. This difficulty variable has been seen to be a very central one in the achievement motivation theory. It will therefore be a main theme on the following pages, where Smith's results will also be further discussed.

Summing up and evaluation

Although we have seen on the preceding pages that M_s measures, M_f measures and combined motive measures have been found to be positively as well as negatively related to persistence, most results from the simple comparisons of motive strength and persistence have been in the expected direction. Nevertheless, studies of this kind are of rather limited interest, since the interactional theoretical viewpoint found in the underlying achievement motivation theory has been given a very restricted, if any, place in the empirical work. The studies are mainly individual-oriented, comparing subjects with different motive strength with respect to persistence, without varying the situational factors in any systematic way. Such a systematic investigation of persistence as the result of an interaction between motive and situation variables was conducted for the first time by Norman T. Feather. His work will be considered in the following section.

COMPLEX RELATIONS BETWEEN MOTIVE STRENGTH AND PERSISTENCE

The motivation model

As pointed out several times on the preceding pages, the achievement motivation theory assumes that the achievement motivation for a particular task is the result

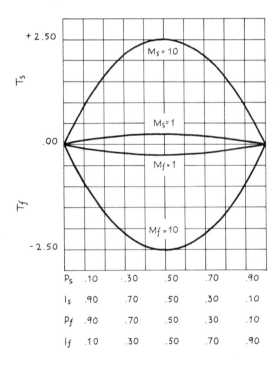

Fig. 3. Tendency to achieve success (T_s) and tendency to avoid failure (T_f) as a function of motive strength (M), expectancy (P), and incentive value (I). ($I_s = 1 - P_s$, $P_f = 1 - P_s$, $I_f = -P_s$, $T_s = M_s \times P_s \times I_s$, $T_f = M_f \times P_f \times I_f$).

of an interaction between motives and situational factors. This is the basic assumption behind Feather's work on persistence (1961; 1962; 1963). However, since his reasoning may appear somewhat complicated, it may facilitate understanding to start by summing up the implications of the achievement motivation theory by means of illustrations. This is done in Fig. 3 and Fig. 4.

Fig. 3 is an illustration of the content of Table 1 and Table 2. It shows the motivation or tendency to achieve success, or to avoid failure, for individuals with different motive strength when the probability of success varies, that is, when the tasks are perceived to vary in difficulty.

The theory assumes that all individuals have both motives. We can, therefore, as pointed out in the previous section, differentiate between three hypothetical groups of individuals according to the strength of each of these motives: a group with $M_s > M_f$, a group with $M_s \approx M_f$, and finally a group with $M_s < M_f$. It should be recalled that the resultant achievement motivation or tendency is thought of as the algebraic sum of the motivation or tendency to achieve success and that to avoid failure (cf. pp. 69 f.).

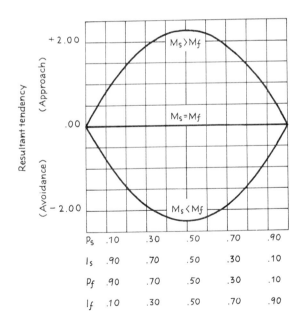

Fig. 4. Resultant tendency as a function of expectancy (P) and incentive value (I) when $M_s > M_f$ ($M_s = 10$, $M_f = 1$), $M_s = M_f$, and $M_s < M_f$ ($M_s = 1$, $M_f = 10$).

Then, using the motive strengths from Fig. 4 as examples, the motivational implications of the differentiation in groups when tasks vary in perceived difficulty are illustrated in Fig. 4.

The activity in an achievement situation is also assumed to be influenced by extrinsic motivation, i.e. by motivation attributable to motives other than M_s and M_f. The total motivation to perform an act therefore equals achievement motivation $(T_s + T_f)$ plus extrinsic motivation (Atkinson, 1964, p. 247). It should in this connection be noted that, according to the achievement motivation theory, if the $M_s < M_f$ group is to perform at all, enough extrinsic motivation must exist to oppose and overcome its avoidance motivation.

Let us then turn to persistence investigations related to the model outlined in Fig. 4.

Investigations related to the motivation model

Feather's Investigations. In the first experiment to be considered (Feather, 1961) 34 male college students assumed to belong either to the $M_s > M_f$ group (high TAT nAch/low TAQ) or to the $M_s < M_f$ group (low TAT nAch/high TAQ) were asked to perform four tasks presented to them as items in an important test. Each item was a diagram where all lines should be traced without lifting the pencil from the figure or retracing any line. The experimenter made it clear that the subjects were free to quit the initial item and turn to the next (alternative) one whenever they wished. Since Feather's reasoning is a very instructive application of achievement motivation theory, it will be followed in some detail. At certain points alternative arguments to those of Feather will also be presented.

Feather's primary interest was in persistence at the first task.. Half of each motive group was told that this task was an easy one: "... at your age level ... approximate 70 per cent of college students are able to get the solution" (ibid. , p. 556). The other half was told that the initial task was a very difficult one: " . . . approximately 5 per cent of college students are able to get the solution" (loc. cit.). However, all subject experienced repeated failure at the initial task, since it was in fact insoluble.

It should further be noted that the subjects were instructed that some items were harder than others. However, the difficulty of the alternative task was not reported the subjects until they gave up the initial task. Nevertheless, although not explicitly dealt with by Feather, it seems reasonable to assume that since the initial task was presented as either very difficult or very easy, and the tasks were said to vary in difficulty, the alternative task to which the subjects could turn was initially anticipat to be of about moderate difficulty. His hypothesis 4, which will be considered later also presupposes that this was the case.

Ostensibly to permit derivation of hypotheses about persistence at the initial task, Feather introduced the following assumptions: (1) Both extrinsic motivation to perform the initial task and extrinsic motivation to perform the alternative task were equal for the two experimental conditions. (2) Extrinsic motivation to perform the initial task was stronger than extrinsic motivation to perform the alternative task, owing to the fact that the subjects were requested by the experimenter to begin the initial task first. (3) The subjective probability of success for the alternative task was constant across experimental conditions (ibid., p. 553).

The presentation of the initial task as an easy one for half of the subjects although it was in fact insoluble, forces us, before proceeding, to question the third of the assumptions cited above. Thus, Feather held failure at the initial "easy" task to result in a decrease in P_s for this task during work. But it seems very unlikely that the discrepancy between the experimenter's statement (that the initial task was easy) and the subject's own experience (that it was difficult) had no effect at all upon how he regarded his chances of succeeding at the alternative task. Rather, it appears reasonable to argue that the decrease in P_s for the initial task also generalizes to the alternative task. That is, while the alternative task was probably initially anticipated to be of some moderate difficulty ($P_s \approx .50$), the experience that the initial "easy" task was much more difficult than stated probably soon resulted in an anticipation that the alternative task was a very difficult one. On the other hand, for the other group, instructed that the initial task was a difficult one, there should be no such discrepancy between stated difficulty and own experiences. Accordingly, there should not be any reason to expect a corresponding change in P_s for the alternative task in that group. While these assumptions are in disagreement with Feather's third one, we shall see that rather than weakening the basis for the hypothesis set forth by Feather, they seem to strengthen it.

Focusing now upon the development of these hypotheses, it was assumed that the subjects would persist at the initial task as long as total motivation (achievement motivation plus extrinsic motivation) to perform it was stronger than total motivation to perform the alternative available to them.

Let us then consider the group with $M_s > M_f$. From Fig. 4 it can be seen that when this group starts with a task presented to it as easy (i.e. $P_s > .50$) and undergoes repeated failure, the motivation or tendency to achieve increases as the probability of success falls towards .50, and then decreases. When this group starts with a task presented as difficult (i.e. $P_s < .50$), the motivation is seen to decrease from the start because of the repeated failure resulting in a decrease in P_s away from .50. When the motivation to perform the initial task becomes weaker than the motivation to perform the alternative one, the subject should quit the initial task and turn to the alternative. This should happen first for the group told that the initial task was a difficult one. Therefore, Feather hypothesized (1) that for the $M_s > M_f$ group persistence at the initial task should be greater when initial P_s was high (i.e. $P_s > .50$) than when it was low (i.e. $P_s < .50$).

It should be pointed out here that the indication of a probable change in P_s for the alternative task in the experimental group which had been told that the initial task was an easy one and no corresponding change in the group told that the initial task was difficult, strengthens confidence in this hypothesis. Thus, while motivation for the alternative task should remain relatively high for those told that the initial task was difficult, it should decrease for the other group, because of the decrease in P_s away from .50. That is, contrary to what is assumed by Feather, it is suggested that the two $M_s > M_f$ groups with which we are concerned here soon became <u>differently</u> motivated for the alternative task as well in a way that made a shift to the alternative task less likely among those with high P_s at the initial task.

Applying a corresponding analysis to the $M_s < M_f$ group, it should first be recapitulated that for this group the total motivation or tendency is positive only on the assumption that the extrinsic motivation is strong enough to outweigh and overcome the avoidance tendency due to M_f. Turning next to the dynamics of changing motivation during work at the initial task, it appears that when the initial task is presented as easy (i.e. $P_s > .50$ or $P_f < .50$), repeated failure first results in a decrement in P_s in the direction of .50, implying an increase in avoidance motivation, and thus a decrease in total motivation for the initial task. From Fig. 4 it can also be seen that when P_s decreases below .50, avoidance motivation decreases, and thus total motivation increases again. When the initial task is perceived as difficult (i.e. $P_s < .50$ or $P_f > .50$), failure, followed by a decrease in P_s, is seen to result in a decrease in avoidance motivation and thus an increase in total motivation from the very outset. Hence, Feather argues that $M_s < M_f$ subjects should continue to perform the initial task indefinitely (<u>ibid.</u>, p. 555). Feather therefore hypothesized (2) that for the $M_s < M_f$ group persistence at the initial task should be greater when initial P_s was low (i.e. $P_s < .50$) than when it was high (i.e. $P_s > .50$).

Before we leave this hypothesis, some more attention should be paid to its basis. Firstly, Feather's argument that the low P_s group should work indefinitely at the initial task deserves some comment, since a similar argument plays an important and apparently debatable role in a later study by Feather (1963), with which we shall be concerned later on. While the argument of indefinite work has an apparently clear theoretical basis, it deviates too far from what we know about the reality. Thus, no matter what the theory says, we may be quite sure in advance that subjects in whom $M_s < M_f$ also stop working at a difficult task sooner or later if they are allowed to work long enough. Then, rather than arguing in absolutes like Feather, it seems more easonable to think in terms of probabilities: After all, the probability of a shift to he alternative task during the experimental session should be lower among those told hat the initial task was a difficult one than among those told that it was easy. This is lso in accordance with hypothesis 2.

Another comment concerns the consequence of a possible change in P_s for the lternative task as indicated previously. Here too, such a change is seen to strengthen he basis for the hypothesis. Thus, for the experimental group instructed that the nitial task was easy there should, on the assumption that the decrease in P_s for the nitial task also generalizes to the alternative ($P_s \approx .50$), be a decrease in avoidance notivation and thus an increase in total motivation for the alternative task. This hange in motivation for the alternative should increase the likelihood of a shift. here is no reason to expect a corresponding change in motivation for the alternative n the experimental group instructed that the initial task was a difficult one.

Two additional hypotheses were also set forth: (3) When initial P_s was high (i.e. $P_s > .50$), the $M_s > M_f$ group should persist longer at the initial task than the $M_s < M_f$ roup, and (4) when initial P_s was low (i.e. $P_s < .50$), the $M_s < M_f$ group should per- ist longer than the $M_s > M_f$ group at the initial task.

The derivation of these two hypotheses is not presented by Feather, but the former ollows more or less directly from the analysis presented above, and the latter from eather's assumption that the $M_s < M_f$ group should work indefinitely at the initial task. lowever, as we shall see, the achievement motivation theory does not imply that the $M_s < M_f$ group should be more strongly motivated for the initial difficult task than the $M_s > M_f$ group. An attempt will nevertheless be made to show that hypothesis 4 is a easonable one.

Turning to Fig. 4 again, it can be seen that according to the model, motivation should be stronger in the $M_s > M_f$ group than in the $M_s < M_f$ group in all cases except where P_s is exactly 1.00 or .00, and in neither of the two extreme cases should motivation be higher in the $M_s < M_f$ group. In other words, as long as P_s at the nitial task is above .00, the $M_s > M_f$ group should be more strongly motivated for he initial task than the $M_s < M_f$ group, and not even in the extreme case where $P_s = .00$ is there any basis for predicting higher persistence in the $M_s < M_f$ group vhen focusing upon the initial task only. This prediction can be set forth only when aking the motivation for the alternative task into consideration. We have assumed hat this task was initially anticipated to be of moderate difficulty, and further that or the particular experimental group under discussion here (the one told that the first ask was difficult) P_s for the alternative remained relatively constant. Then, while he $M_s > M_f$ group should be somewhat more motivated for the initial task than the $M_s < M_f$ group, it should be much more strongly motivated for the alternative

($P_s \approx$ 50) task than the $M_s < M_f$ group. Taking into consideration both the relatively small difference between the groups in motivation for the initial task in favour of the $M_s > M_f$ group and the relatively large difference in motivation for the alternative task (this task being attractive to the $M_s > M_f$ group and unattractive to the $M_s < M_f$ group) the hypothesis of greater persistence at the initial task among $M_s < M_f$ subjects than among $M_s > M_f$ subjects seems to rest on a sound basis. Feather himself does not present any arguments along these lines. However, his underscoring at the outset of the report of the importance of the motivation for the alternative task indicates that he has nevertheless reasoned in the same way.

Since the main points may have been forgotten during this rather lengthy account of and comments on the theoretical basis for Feather's persistence experiment, they are briefly summarized below by repeating his four hypotheses:

(1) When $M_s > M_f$, persistence at the initial achievement task should be greater when initial P_s is high (i. e. $P_s > .50$) than when initial P_s is low (i. e. $P_s < .50$).

(2) When $M_s < M_f$, persistence at the initial achievement task should be greater when initial P_s is low (i. e. $P_s < .50$) than when it is high (i. e. $P_s > .50$).

(3) When initial P_s is high (i. e. $P_s > .50$), subjects in whom $M_s > M_f$ should persist longer at the initial achievement task than subjects in whom $M_s < M_f$.

(4) When initial P_s is low (i. e. $P_s < .50$), subjects in whom $M_s < M_f$ should persist longer at the initial achievement task than those in whom $M_s > M_f$.

Turning now to the data, time and trials scores were reported to be perfectly correlated, which is why only the analysis of persistence in terms of the number of trials at the first task is presented by Feather. The major results are presented in Table 3. It can be seen that there was no difference in persistence at the initial task between the $M_s > M_f$ group and the $M_s < M_f$ group when the stated difficulty of the task was disregarded. Neither was there any difference in persistence between the subjects told that the initial task was easy and those told that it was difficult when motive differences were overlooked. In other words, there were no main effects of personality differences or situation differences. However, when the results were cross-tabulated, a very clear interaction between personality and situation characteristics appeared, lending convincing support to all four hypotheses. These results therefore serve as an eminent illustration of the basic contention behind the present study that persistence can only be understood as an interactional function of individual and situation characteristics.

Additional data bearing upon the theoretical analysis presented in the foregoing are reported by Feather (1963). This study is essentially a replication of parts of the persistence study considered above. In this study 60 male students were tested for persistence at the same task as that used in Feather's first study (1961). The task was presented to the subjects as very difficult: "In fact, only about 5%

Table 3. Number of subjects high and low in persistence in relation to motive constellation and task difficulty.

TAT nAch (M_s)	Test Anxiety (M_f)	Difficulty level	Persistence High (above mdn.)	Low (below mdn.)
High	Low		8	9
Low	High		9	8
		Easy	9	8
		Difficult	8	9
Cross-tabulated:				
High	Low	Easy	6	2
		Difficult	2	7
Low	High	Easy	3	6
		Difficult	6	2
			17	17

(Results from Feather, 1961, p. 558. Copyright 1961 by the American Psychological Association. Reprinted by permission.)

of University students are able to pass it, so the chances of success are very low indeed" (op. cit. , p. 606). Since the task was in fact insoluble, it produced an experience of repeated failure. The subjects were here, too, free to turn to an alternative, similar task whenever they wished, but in contrast to the conditions of the previous study they were here clearly informed about the difficulty level of this alternative before they started to work at the initial task: "The second item is of average difficulty. About 50% of University students are able to pass it, so the chances of success are 50/50" (ibid. , p. 606).

Feather's hypothesis of a longer persistence at the initial task among $M_s < M_f$ subjects than among $M_s > M_f$ subjects is identical with his hypothesis 4 in the previous investigation (cf. pp. 87 f.), but in contrast to in his first report the investigator here refers explicitly to differences between the groups in motivation for the alternative, moderately difficult task as a basis for the hypothesis.

The persistence results, in terms of number of trials at the first task, were in the expected direction, but the difference was rather small (p < . 10, one-tailed test; ibid. , p. 606). This may be due to facts recognized in additional hypotheses.

In addition to the prediction of a difference between the motive groups in persistence, Feather also hypothesized differences within the $M_s > M_f$ group, based on the fact that although the initial task was described as very difficult, the initial expectations of success differed, some having higher expectations than others. Hence he predicted, what can be seen to follow from the model in Fig. 4, that persistence should relate positively to initial expectation of success for the $M_s > M_f$ group. This is so because the higher the initial expectation of success, the more unsuccessful attempts at the task are necessary to reduce expectancy, and thus total motivation, to the low level at which total motivation to perform the initial task becomes lower than the motivation to perform the alternative. As can be seen, this hypothesis is in fact the same as hypothesis 1 in Feather's first experiment (cf. pp. 85 f.). The difference is only that in his first experiment the P_s variable was manipulated by instructing half of the group that the task was an easy one and the other half that it was difficult, while in the present study P_s was inferred from the subjects' reported initial expectation of success at a task stated to be very difficult.

As to the $M_s < M_f$ group, Feather argues that when P_s at the initial task is below .50, which he assumed to be the case for all subjects in the present study, and the alternative task is one of intermediate difficulty, the subjects should according to the theory persist at the initial task indefinitely. A similar argument was also presented in connection with Feather's first study (cf. pp. 86 f.). For the $M_s < M_f$ group he therefore predicted no difference between those with initially relatively high and low expectancy of success.

The analyses lent clear support to these hypotheses, persistence being positively related to initial expectation of success among subjects in whom $M_s > M_f$, and unrelated to initial expectation of success among subjects in whom $M_s < M_f$. Since we shall later discuss these results in more detail, they are presented in full in Table 4.

Even though the results were stated to favour both hypotheses, there is nevertheless something strange about Feather's prediction of no relationship between expectation of success and persistence among subjects with $M_s < M_f$. Thus, following the same general line of reasoning as that behind hypothesis 2 in his first experiment (cf. p. 86), the avoidance motivation due to M_f should be lower for those with a relatively low P_s (e.g. $P_s < .05$) than for those with a relatively high P_s (e.g. $.50 > P_s > .05$), i.e. the total motivation for the initial task should be lowest for the subjects with a relatively high initial expectation of success. Then, while all $M_s < M_f$ subjects should have a strong motivation to avoid the

Table 4. Number of subjects high and low in persistence at a difficult task with an alternative task of intermediate difficulty in relation to estimates of initial probability of success and motive constellation.

TAT nAch (M_s)	Test Anxiety (M_f)	Estimated P_s	Persistence trials	
			High (above mdn.)	Low (below mdn.)
High	Low	High	6	3
		Low	0	9
Low	High	High	5	4
		Low	5	4
Total			16	20

(Results from Feather, 1963, p. 606. Copyright 1963 by the American Psychological Association. Reprinted by permission.)

alternative, moderately difficult ($P_s \approx .50$) task, the difference between the motivation to avoid the initial task and that to avoid the alternative task should be least for those with a relatively high expectation of success at the initial task. Furthermore, if subjects with a relatively high expectation of success at the initial task (i.e. $P_s > .05$) also overestimate their chances of success at the alternative task (i.e. $P_s > .50$), this should make the difference between the motivation to avoid the initial task and that to avoid the alternative task even less (cf. Fig. 4). In any case, the probability of a shift should increase with the probability of success at the initial task. Therefore the prediction here, in contrast to Feather's, would be that if any shifts to the alternative task occurred in the $M_s < M_f$ group, the frequency of shifts should be higher among subjects with a relatively high initial P_s than among those with a relatively low initial P_s

We have, however, seen that the results rather lent support to Feather's somewhat "unexpected" prediction of no relationship between initial expectation of success and persistence among $M_s < M_f$ subjects. If this support had been in terms of no shifts in the $M_s < M_f$ group, there would be no reason to pursue this matter any further, but in fact, as appears from Table 4, nearly half of the $M_s < M_f$ subjects quit the initial task. Thus, there must be something wrong or unrecognized somewhere.

In this connection some closer attention should be paid to the P_s variable, which is possibly something of a joker here. Focusing only upon the left half of the motivation model ($P_s \leq .50$) presented in Fig. 4, which is of primary interest here, it can be seen that the resultant achievement motivation or tendency is positively related to P_s for the $M_s > M_f$ group, and negatively related to P_s for the $M_s < M_f$ group. In other words, the achievement motivation theory does not assume any main effect of P_s, but rather a P_s by M_s and a P_s by M_f interaction effect. Nevertheless, Feather in fact observed a main effect of P_s (cf. Table 4), the group reporting a relatively high expectation of success at the initial task being more persistent than that reporting a relatively low expectation of success. This need not represent any challenge to the theory, since it might be argued that clearly M_f-dominated students will not go to college, and therefore the average M_s strength among college students, from which this sample was taken, is probably stronger than the average M_f strength (cf. Atkinson and Feather, 1966, pp. 22, 342). It appears from the motivation model in Fig. 4 that the lack of a main P_s effect should be observed only in a group where the average strength of M_s and M_f is the same. Anyhow, a main P_s effect was observed in Feather's data, and on closer scrutiny it looks as if it is this main effect which makes the results from the $M_s < M_f$ group appear to turn out in an "expected" or "unexpected" direction, depending upon the way one looks at it. The pattern of the results in Table 4 indicates that the main effect obscures a clear P_s effect in the $M_s < M_f$ group as well.

To show that this is the case, the frequency results obtained by Feather and presented in Table 4 are converted to persistence scores, by giving those high in persistence the score 1 and those low in persistence the score 0. True enough, the following analyses should preferably have been based on continuous data, but such data are not available here. However, we can see no reason why the use of the dichotomous data should imply any systematic error, assuming that the underlying variable is continuous.

Table 5a, being in substance identical with Table 4, shows the mean values of these persistence scores for each of the estimated motive/probability of success groups. Following the simple procedure described by Guilford (1965, pp. 294 f.), the main effect of P_s is removed by adjusting each cell mean in such a way that the mean for the high P_s group as well as that for the low P_s group equals the total mean. The deviations of the row means from the total mean represent the P_s effect. The high P_s group mean is .62, i.e. .17 above the total mean, and the low P_s group mean is .28, i.e. .17 below the total mean. The P_s effect is then removed by adding a constant of -.17 to the two means within the high P_s group, and a constant of +.17 to those of the low P_s group. The result of this correction is presented in Table 5b. Since the main effect of P_s is now stripped away, the cell means of this table have to be interpreted as the main effect of motive constellation plus

Table 5. Mean persistence scores at a difficult task with an alternative task of intermediate difficulty

a) without correction for effects of motive constellation and P_s

	$M_s < M_f$	$M_s > M_f$	Both motive groups
High P_s	.56	.67	.62
Low P_s	.56	.00	.28
Both P_s groups	.56	.34	.45

b) corrected for main effects of P_s

	$M_s < M_f$	$M_s > M_f$	Both motive groups
High P_s	.39	.50	.45
Low P_s	.73	.17	.45
Both P_s groups	.56	.34	.45

c) corrected for main effects of P_s and motive constellation

	$M_s < M_f$	$M_s > M_f$	Both motive groups
High P_s	.28	.61	.45
Low P_s	.62	.28	.45
Both P_s groups	.45	.45	.45

N within cells = 9

Basic data in Table 4.

the interaction effect of motive constellation and P_s. To make the interaction effect quite clear the main effect of motive constellation is also removed by the same procedure, by adding a constant of $+.11$ (i.e. $.45 - .34$) to the cell means of the $M_s > M_f$ group, and a constant of $-.11$ (i.e. $.45 - .56$) to the cell means of the $M_s < M_f$ group. The result of this last correction is shown in Table 5c. The difference between mean values in the cells of this table represent the interaction effect of motive constellation and probability of success.

The above analysis illustrates clearly that the interaction effect is obscured in Feather's presentation of his results, in that it shows that, in contrast to what was hypothesized by Feather, the P_s variable also has a clear effect within the $M_s < M_f$ group, along the lines of reasoning presented earlier in this section. Thus, the mean values of persistence corrected for main motive and P_s effects are seen to be equal and highest for the $M_s > M_f$ group with a high P_s and the $M_s < M_f$ group with a low P_s, and lowest for the $M_s > M_f$ group with a low P_s and the $M_s < M_f$ group with a high P_s. The result revealed by this additional analysis is also in accordance with hypothesis 2 in Feather's first study (cf. pp. 86 f.), while it appears to be highly problematical when related to the reasoning behind his hypothesis of no effect of P_s on persistence within the $M_s < M_f$ group. This analysis indicates that Feather misinterprets the significant interaction effect of motive constellation and P_s on persistence (reported in Feather, 1963, Table 2) when he holds that it provides support for this hypothesis, i.e. when he regards the interaction effects obtained as an effect of P_s within the $M_s > M_f$ group only (ibid., p. 607). Table 5c makes it clear that the total interaction effect is as much a result of a P_s effect within the $M_s < M_f$ group.

On the whole, then, we have once more been concerned with a study providing very strong support for the notion of persistence as the result of an interaction between personality and situation characteristics. It should also be emphasized that in spite of the criticisms set forth in the foregoing in connection with Feather's persistence studies, his work on this problem is definitely among the most sophisticated within achievement motivation research. His studies have also inspired other investigators to think along the same lines, as for example Atkinson and O'Connor (1966) do in a study of persistence at a difficult task.

Other Results Lending Support to Feather's Theorizing. Atkinson and O'Connor's investigation (1966) was carried out on a group of 35 male college students and had a wider scope than Feather's persistence studies. However, as far as the relationship between achievement motives and persistence is concerned, the study is a replication of that part of Feather's first study where the initial task was presented as a very difficult one (cf. p. 84). Therefore it will not be considered in detail here. Let it suffice to note that the direction of the results was the same as in Feather's study. Thus, there was a decrease in the percentage of low per-sisters from the upper via the middle to the lower quartile on the TATnAch-TAQ (Z score) distribution (ibid., p. 311). The decrease was rather modest, but in their comments the investigators point out that the results are undoubtedly affected by some variations in the subjective probability of success. As will be recalled from the account of Feather's second study (cf. pp. 90 f.), clearer relations were observed when such variations in P_s were controlled.

Higher persistence among M_f-dominated subjects at a difficult task is also in-dicated by results reported by Mandler and Watson (1966), whose subjects were selected from the top and bottom 15 per cent of the TAQ score distribution. A group of 14 college students, males and females, who were working at a task pre-sented to them as a valid test of intelligence, experienced continuous failure at it. The subjects were free to turn to another task whenever they wished. As to this alternative they had been instructed that one did not know whether it was easy or difficult. The results showed that the high TAQ subjects were more persistent than the low TAQ subjects (ibid., p. 279). In their comments on this result, Mand-ler and Watson argue, in accordance with what would also have been done on the basis of the achievement motivation theory: "High anxiety subjects will choose any situation which is 'certain', i.e., a situation which does not produce interruption. Thus, the certainty of failing would be chosen over an uncertain situation" (ibid., p. 279).

Next in this consideration of persistence experiments we shall pay attention to a study carried out by Weiner (1965). This study was mainly directed towards the so-called inertial tendency (Atkinson and Cartwright, 1964, p. 586), or the effect of earlier aroused but unsatisfied motivation, a problem area which lies outside the scope of the present study (cf. p. 18 above). Nevertheless some of the results obtained by Weiner are of interest here, since they bear upon the problems under discussion and also seem to indicate that some assumptions made in the achieve-ment motivation theory should possibly be re-examined. They will therefore be considered briefly without going into detail about the theoretical background pre-sented by the investigator.

Results Indicating Higher Motivation among $M_s < M_f$ Subjects than among $M_s > M_f$
Subjects. In Weiner's experiment subjects classified as having $M_s > M_f$ or $\overline{M}_s < \overline{M}_f$
on the basis of the difference between the score on the TAT nAch and on the TAQ
(Z scores) were given an achievement task to perform (a digit-symbol substitution
test). The subjects knew that they could move on to an activity unrelated to achievement (answering various questions about advertisements) whenever they wished.
Two experimental conditions were created, one with continuous success at the initial
task when the reported probability of success was .70, and another with continuous
failure when the reported probability of success was .30. Experiences of success
or failure were created by allowing the subjects to complete each card in the test,
or by interrupting them before completing the cards (Weiner, 1965, p. 435).

The procedure implies that there should be a relatively clear difference between
the $M_s > M_f$ group and the $M_s < M_f$ group in motivation for the initial task at the outset (cf. the motivation model in Fig. 4, for $P_s = .70$ and $P_s = .30$). However, according to the procedure one would also expect P_s to reach a very high ($P_s \rightarrow 1.00$),
or a very low level ($P_s \rightarrow .00$) after some time. Under such extreme P_s conditions
there should, according to the motivation model, be only a very small difference
in motivation between the $M_s > M_f$ group and the $M_s < M_f$ group. In other words,
there should be a gradual decrease in the motivation difference between the $M_s > M_f$
group and the $M_s < M_f$ group during work.

This decrease in the difference between the groups in motivation for the initial
task, along with the fact that the alternative activity is not an achievement-related
one, and therefore does not differ in its attractiveness to the two motive groups, implies that one would expect only a modest difference between the groups in persistence, in favour of the $M_s > M_f$ group. This should be the case in both experimental
conditions, and thus also across conditions.

Unfortunately, the results, stemming from a group of 59 male college students,
are not reported for each of the experimental conditions, but for both conditions
together there was only a slight difference between the two motive groups in persistence in terms of number of trials at the initial task. Thirty-two per cent of the
$M_s > M_f$ subjects and 46 per cent of the $M_s < M_f$ subjects persisted to the maximum
number of trials which the time allowed, and had to be interrupted by the experimenter (ibid., pp. 437 f.). The trouble is, however, that the difference lies in the
opposite direction to what one would expect. That is, if anything, the $M_s < M_f$ group
was the most persistent one. From the reported within-groups results it can be
inferred that the results from the easy condition must have contributed more to this
difference in favour of the $M_s < M_f$ group than those from the difficult condition.

On the other hand, the fact that the only difference observed within the motive groups was an insignificant one in terms of lower persistence following success than following failure among $M_s > M_f$ subjects,[1] indicates that the persistence results for both conditions together do not cover up any clear underlying interactions.

Since the result was in the opposite direction of what would be predicted from the achievement motivation theory, it should not be dismissed only by referring to the small size of the difference. In this connection some attention should first be paid to the possible influence of extrinsic motivation. Thus, as recognized by Feather (1961, p. 553), the fact that the subjects find themselves in a social situation where they are asked by the experimenter to work at a task, probably implies a considerable amount of extrinsic motivation for this initial task. It therefore seems reasonable to expect that all subjects, including those with $M_s < M_f$, work at the initial task for some time. From a persistence point of view the motives M_s and M_f may therefore be considered as being of little significance in this first phase of work. However, as a result of continuous success or failure, depending on the experimental conditions, P_s should increase or decrease during this first phase. It may therefore be that when the extrinsic motivation alone is no longer sufficient to get the subjects to continue at the initial task, P_s has reached a markedly high or low level. It does not appear from Weiner's report whether all subjects really worked at the initial task for some time. But if they did, which seems a reasonable assumption, his results indicate, if anything, a tendency towards higher persistence among $M_s < M_f$ subjects than among $M_s > M_f$ subjects in relatively extreme P_s conditions. As will be recalled, Feather (1961; 1963), Atkinson and O'Connor (1966), and Mandler and Watson (1966) all found subjects assumed to be relatively strongly M_f-dominated to be the most persistent ones at a very difficult

---

1. Weiner's interest is mainly in the between-conditions difference in persistence for each of the motive groups. Thus, according to Atkinson's motivation theory, individuals with $M_s > M_f$ should lose interest in the initial task after about the same number of trials in the two experimental conditions, on the assumption that P_s increases after success at the same rate as it decreases after failure. If there is an inertial tendency following failure, there should be greater persistence in the failure condition than in the success condition. There was an insignificant difference in this direction, but this difference may equally well be explained on the basis of the tendency among $M_s > M_f$ subjects to overestimate their P_s (Atkinson, 1957, p. 367). This overestimation should, according to the motivation model in Fig. 4, imply a higher motivation for the $M_s > M_f$ subjects in the failure condition than in the success condition.

task. However, while the latter results were explained in terms of a difference between the $M_s > M_f$ and the $M_s < M_f$ group in motivation for an alternative, moderately difficult task in favour of the $M_s > M_f$ group, the results obtained by Weiner cannot be explained in this way, since in this case the alternative was not an achievement task. Weiner's results should therefore be taken as a cue to examine whether, contrary to what is assumed in the achievement motivation theory, $M_s < M_f$ subjects are in fact more strongly motivated for extremely easy and extremely difficult tasks than $M_s > M_f$ subjects. If this should happen to be the case, Feather's, Atkinson and O'Connor's, and Mandler and Watson's results have a double explanation: The $M_s < M_f$ subjects were more persistent at the initial, very difficult task than the $M_s > M_f$ subjects not only because of the avoidance motivation for the alternative, moderately diffi- cult task, but also because they had a stronger motivation for the initial, very difficult task than the $M_s > M_f$ subjects. The results with which we shall finally be concerned serve as another indicator that the possibility of a higher motiva- tion among $M_s < M_f$ subjects than among $M_s > M_f$ subjects should be considered where P_s is very high or low.

Earlier in this chapter (pp. 78 ff.) we dealt with some of the results reported by C. P. Smith (1964) from a study of the relationship between motive strength and persistence at a midterm and a final examination. To recapitulate, TAQ scores (M_f) were positively related, nAch scores (M_s) were not related, and nAch-TAQ scores were negatively related to persistence in both examinations (ibid. , p. 526). Recognizing that these results were quite contrary to those ob- tained in a similar study by Atkinson and Litwin (1960), Smith argues that the lack of agreement might be accounted for if the perceived difficulty of the examina- tions was different in the two studies, either because the subjects in his study had a higher average ability, or because they had a somewhat easier examination, or both (op. cit. , p. 527). Some indications that there were such differences in ability level and examination difficulty are also reported.

While no measure of perceived difficulty was obtained in this study, Smith ar- gues that the intelligence measures, in terms of Otis scores, may be taken as indicators of the subjects' perceived probability of success at the examination. Thus, subjects with high Otis scores (IQ or 127 or over) should see the examina- tion as easier than subjects with low scores (IQ < 127). However, when Smith introduces this variable into the analyses, he makes a theoretical mistake. To clarify this mistake, his argumentation has to be dealt with in some detail.

Firstly, with reference to Atkinson's and Feather's theorizing, Smith points out that subjects with a relatively high M_s will persist longer at a task of inter-mediate difficulty than subjects with a relatively high M_f, while they will persist less long at a very easy task (ibid., p. 527). Taking the Otis scores as an in-dicator of perceived difficulty level, it was then predicted (1) that for the group with high Otis scores (high P_s) persistence at the examination should be positive-ly related to test anxiety (M_f) score and negatively related to nAch-TAQ ($M_s - M_f$) score. For the group with low Otis scores the examination should be of approxi-mately intermediate difficulty, and therefore the reverse relationships were pre-dicted (2). For some reason no prediction was made concerning the relationship between nAch scores alone and persistence.

Obviously, Smith's prediction of higher persistence among $M_s < M_f$ than among $M_s > M_f$ subjects at an easy task, which the examination was supposed to be for those with high Otis scores, was meant to be a parallel to Feather's prediction of higher persistence among $M_s < M_f$ subjects than among $M_s > M_f$ subjects at a very difficult task. However, Smith did not here take into account that Feather refers to a situation where the subjects could switch to an alternative achieve-ment task whenever they wished, and that his hypothesis presupposes that the two motive groups were differently motivated for this alternative (cf. pp. 87 f.). Thus, in contrast to Feather's hypothesis, Smith's prediction of higher persist-ence among $M_s < M_f$ subjects than among $M_s > M_f$ subjects has no basis in the achievement motivation theory in its present form. As can be seen from the model presented in Fig. 4, and as has been noted earlier in this chapter, the achievement motivation or tendency should be stronger for the $M_s > M_f$ group than for the $M_s < M_f$ group for all tasks except those where $P_s = .00$ and those where $P_s = 1.00$, and in neither of these two extreme cases should there be any reversal in motivation strength. The mistake made by Smith becomes even clearer from one of his additional assumptions. Thus, Smith says:

> Strictly speaking, these predictions [predictions 1 and 2 above] can
> be derived from Atkinson's theory only if three further assumptions
> are made: first, in contrast to Feather's procedure, that the per-
> ceived difficulty of the exam does not change as the subjects work on
> it; second, that motives other than the Motive for Success and the
> Motive to Avoid failure are aroused in exam performance to an equal
> degree in subjects with relatively strong Motive for Success and in
> subjects with relatively strong Motive to Avoid Failure; third, that
> alternative activities to which the subjects will turn when they leave
> the exam are of equal attractiveness to all subjects (1964, pp. 527 f.)

The first two assumptions do not require any comments, but the third one does. It should now be clear that within the achievement motivation theory in its present form Smith's prediction of higher persistence among $M_s < M_f$ than among $M_s > M_f$ subjects at an easy task presupposes quite the opposite. That is, it can only be made when assuming that there is an alternative task which is more attractive to the $M_s > M_f$ group than to the $M_s < M_f$ group.

So much for the predictions and the missing theoretical basis for the first of them. The curious thing is, however, that the results corresponded very well to what had been predicted. Thus, the calculations gave a positive correlation of +.41 between TAQ scores and time spent on the final exam for the high Otis group, while the corresponding correlation for the low Otis group was negligible ($r = +.07$). The correlation between nAch-TAQ scores and persistence was -.27 for the high, and +.10 for the low Otis group.

The results referred to above shed additional light on the question touched upon previously of whether the difference in persistence only reflects that the $M_s > M_f$ subjects completed the exam task more rapidly than the $M_s < M_f$ subjects (cf. p. 81). If this were the case, one would for example expect to find a clear negative correlation between nAch-TAQ scores and persistence among low IQ subjects, who are assumed to regard the tasks as moderately difficult, and therefore should have the motives M_s and M_f most strongly aroused. As can be seen above, this was not the case. A related question is whether the results might be thought to reflect only a higher efficiency among subjects with high IQ, resulting in an earlier completion of the tasks. This also seems unlikely, since a transformation of the correlational results to regression lines indicates that the highest persistence occurred among subjects with high Otis scores and high anxiety scores.

Then, to conclude, it seems possible that we are here concerned with a result which, in contrast to what is implied in the achievement motivation theory in its present form, means that subjects with $M_s < M_f$ are more strongly motivated for an easy task than subjects in whom $M_s > M_f$. It should be recapitulated that a similar indication was found in the results presented by Weiner (cf. p. 98).

The complex achievement motivational approach to persistence: An evaluation.
The studies dealt with in the preceding pages very nicely illustrate the importance of taking both personality and situation characteristics into consideration when investigating the problem of persistence. Thus, to exemplify, the results presented in Table 3 clearly underline how easily a purely individual or situational approach may give wrong answers to questions of this kind. Considered separately there was no relationship between motive constellation alone and persistence, or situation type alone and persistence. However, the simultaneous consideration of personality characteristics (motives) and situation characteristics (P_s) revealed that they were nevertheless both clearly important. The individual who persists under

one situation condition, does not necessarily do so under another. Or, from the opposite point of view, the same situation which makes one individual engage in a task and persist at it, releases resistance and avoidance behaviour in another individual. The analyses have shown that many of these differences can be predicted from achievement motivation theory, implying that the achievement motivational approach is a fruitful one when applied to this problem area. It should, however, be emphasized that most experiments have been restricted to male college students only, and usually to the extreme groups on the motive variables, i.e. to subjects with $M_s > M_f$ and those with $M_s < M_f$. These facts clearly limit the generalization value of the results.

Finally, while the achievement motivation theory has been seen to emphasize both individual and situation characteristics, some of the results with which we have been concerned indicate that there is one aspect of this theory to which more attention should be paid, namely the part concerning situations where the **probability of success is either very high or very low**.

GENERAL SUMMARY

This chapter has been devoted to a review of previous empirical findings concerning the relationship between achievement motives and persistence. The results of simple comparisons of motive strength and persistence were not on their own clear enough to warrant any strong conclusions. However, a more sophisticated approach to the persistence problem was introduced by Feather, who based his work on the cardinal thesis within the achievement motivation theory that the motivation for a particular task does not depend on the strength of the individual's motives only, but as much on situation or task characteristics. Even more, he realized that the degree of persistence at a task also depends on the individual's motivation for an alternative task.

The achievement motivation theory in its present form implies that $M_s > M_f$ subjects should be more strongly motivated than $M_s < M_f$ subjects for all tasks on the P_s continuum except for those where P_s is exactly 1.00 or .00. Nevertheless Feather recognized that under certain conditions the $M_s < M_f$ subjects should be not only as high but even higher persisters than $M_s > M_f$ subjects. This should be the case where the alternative task to which the subjects may switch is more attractive to the $M_s > M_f$ group than to the $M_s < M_f$ group, as a moderately difficult task should be. Several results have been presented in favour or this hypothesis.

However, we also considered a few results which indicate that $M_s < M_f$ subjects, contrary to what is assumed in the achievement motivation theory, are possibly more strongly motivated for tasks at the extremes of the P_s scale than $M_s > M_f$ subjects. These were findings from situations where no alternative achievement task was offered. Needless to say, these modest empirical indications alone do not call for a revision of the achievement motivation theory, but they serve as a cue that the possibility of higher motivation among $M_s < M_f$ subjects in particular cases should be considered. In the next chapter this possibility will be studied from a theoretical point of view.

CHAPTER 4

ACHIEVEMENT MOTIVATION: A MODIFIED THEORY[1]

In Chapter 2 the main lines in the achievement motivation theory developed by
D. C. McClelland and his co-workers and further elaborated by J.W. Atkinson
were clarified. This theory has led to vigorous research, and Atkinson's elaborated version especially has been seen to represent the foundation for a new
and apparently very promising approach to the problem of persistence. Thus,
the results obtained by Feather (1961; 1963), among others, illustrate very clearly the Lewinian nucleus in this theory, i.e. that behaviour has to be understood
as the result of a personality by situation interaction.

However, in the later part of Chapter 3 some persistence results were considered which were in disagreement with the theory. Further, the results from
studies concerned with the effect of the motives M_s and M_f on level of performance are highly divergent. Thus, while the theory assumes a stronger or weaker
positive relationship between M_s strength and performance level, the observed
relationships between M_s measures and performance level have varied from
positive (e.g. McClelland et al. , 1953, pp. 218 ff. ; Rosen, 1956, pp. 208 ff;
Wendt, 1955, p. 452) to negative (e.g. Miles, 1958, pp. 158 ff. ; C.P. Smith,
1966, p. 290; Vogel, Baker, & Lazarus, 1958, p. 110). Further, a negative relationship between M_f strength and performance level is assumed, but here too
the observed relationships between scores on anxiety questionnaires, assumed to
reflect the strength of M_f (cf. pp. 72 ff.), have varied from negative (e.g. Rand,
1960, p. 196; Resnick, 1965, pp. 223 ff. ; S.B. Sarason, Davidson, Lighthall,
Waite, & Ruebush, 1960, pp. 159 ff.) to positive (e.g. Spence, 1956, pp. 226 ff. ;
Taylor & Chapman, 1955). As regards this last group of results, it should also
be noted that the anxiety questionnaires are developed within research traditions
which do not hypothesize a simple negative relationship between anxiety strength
and performance level, but instead that the relationship may vary from negative
to positive, depending on the characteristics of the task or situation (Mandler
& Sarason, 1952 ,pp. 166 f. ; S. B. Sarason et al. , 1960, pp. 159 ff. ; Taylor 1956).

----

1. The main content of this chapter was first published in the European Journal
of Social Psychology 1975/5, published by Mouton & Co. , The Hague.

Inconsistencies between empirical results or between theory and results have often forced investigators to re-examine their notions. This has been the case within the achievement motivation tradition too. We shall initially consider two examples in this direction.

RECENT EXPLANATIONS OF UNEXPECTED RESULTS

First, faced with unexpected results like higher performance level among subjects with a low M_s than among those with a high M_s one has questioned the assumption that individuals who score high and those who score low on the motive tasks are equal in all performance relevant respects except achievement motivation (Atkinson, 1964, p. 237; Atkinson & Feather, 1966, p. 349; C.P. Smith, 1966, p. 295). Implicitly it has been suggested that superiority in "other" personality characteristics or motives has compensated for the inferiority in achievement motivation and even resulted in higher performance among low M_s subjects than among high M_s subjects. However, while it is easy to approve the questioning of the assumption of all other things being equal, the compensation viewpoint is harder to accept. On the whole, correlation rather than compensation seems to be the rule (e.g. Anastasi, 1958, pp. 378 ff.; Vernon, 1961, pp. 34 f.). Therefore, contrary to what has been suggested within achievement motivation research, we find it more likely that individuals who are inferior in achievement motivation are also inferior with respect to other performance-related characteristics, such as for example abilities. And even if the compensation viewpoint should turn out to be valid, it is not too obvious how it can explain the fact that sometimes those with a weak motive and sometimes those with a strong motive have performed at the highest level. This diversity in the results can only be explained by assuming that the effect of "other" characteristics has varied from one study to another. Of course, it is imaginable that this might have been the case. However, if one again and again post hoc has to look for differences between motive groups in other performance-related characteristics to rationalize the results, then achievement motivation research is faced with a serious dilemma.

Unexpected results have also led investigators like Atkinson and O'Connor (1966, pp. 322 f.) to put aside the simple assumption made in early achievement motivation studies that level of performance is a positive function of strength of motivation. Instead, they have returned to the old Yerkes-Dodson Law (1908), which they say states that there is an optimal level of motivation for each task, the strength of which is dependent on the complexity of the task (Atkinson & O'Connor, 1966, p. 323). If the task at hand is a simple one so that little interference from competing responses occurs, then one would expect performance efficiency to be a positive monotonic function of the strength of motivation. On the other hand, at complex tasks, calling for a cautious, deliberate approach, high motivation should cause efficiency decrement, i. e. one would expect a curvilinear relationship between motivation strength and efficiency. However, when these viewpoints are related to the achievement motivation theory as developed by Atkinson (1964), they result in a hypothesis which, if true, instead of integrating the diversity of results reported, rather appears to make them even more unexplainable. Thus, since within this theory motivation to avoid failure is assumed to dampen or weaken the motivation to undertake an activity, it follows that when the intensity of positive motivation is above optimal, the relationship between M_f strength and performance level should be positive (Atkinson & O'Connor, 1966, pp. 323 f.). Because the optimal motivation level is assumed to be lower for complex tasks than for simple tasks, a positive relationship between M_f strength and performance level should most likely appear where the task at hand is a complex one. Turning to very simple tasks, motivation can scarcely become too high. Then, since M_f functions by a dampening of the positive motivation, one should in general expect a negative relationship between M_f strength and performance level at easy tasks. In summary: Individuals with a weak M_f should perform better than those with a strong M_f at easy tasks, while at complex tasks individuals most anxious about failure should be the best performers when the strength of positive motivation is above optimal.

Even though Atkinson and O'Connor (1966, p. 320) have presented a few results in favour of this "interesting and nonobvious hypothesis" (ibid., p. 324), the overall pattern of relevant results seems, as far as we can see, to provide relatively clear evidence against the hypothesis. Thus, to exemplify, a long series of studies carried out by Spence and his colleagues have shown that anxiety enhances performance at easy tasks and impairs performance at relatively difficult tasks (see for example Spence, 1956, pp. 221 ff.).

These results aside, we should for a moment return to what is referred to by Atkinson and O'Connor as the basis for this new view, i. e. to the Yerkes-Dodson Law. Here, as regards the assertion that there is an optimal level of motivation for a given level of task difficulty, this is not exactly what Yerkes and Dodson say. Motivation in Atkinson's theory has been seen to refer to the individual's tendency to engage in an activity (or a possible tendency to display resistance towards the activity). Yerkes and Dodson do not refer to motivation in this sense, but to the intensity of stimulation, arguing that for each task there exists a most favourable level of stimulation (1908, p. 481). It seems far from reasonable to use the terms "stimulation intensity" and "motivation", in Atkinson's sense of the word, interchangeably, and one may very well imagine that the motivation or tendency to engage in an activity decreases when the intensity of stimulation passes a certain level. It should also be noted, following a line of reasoning similar to that of Spence and Spence (1966, p. 316), that, in general, to infer from a set of findings taking the form of an inverted U that there is a nonmonotonic relationship between motivation strength and performance level is only one of a number of possible assumptions. It might equally well be assumed that the relationship between the motivation and the situational variables influencing it is nonmonotonic, the relationship between motivation and performance level being a positive, monotonic one. However, in the case of Atkinson and O'Connor a double assumption of curvilinearity is in fact made. First, as previously noted (cf. p. 82, Fig. 3) a curvilinear relationship between perceived task difficulty (probability of success) and motivation or tendency to achieve success or avoid failure is assumed within the achievement motivation theory. Secondly, Atkinson and O'Connor have, as mentioned above, suggested a curvilinear relationship between motivation strength and performance level. It is far from easy to grasp the implications of this double assumption of curvilinearity, and it is also noteworthy that the first assumption mentioned, that concerning the relationship between perceived task difficulty and motivation, is passed over in silence in Atkinson and O'Connor's development of the "non-obvious hypothesis" referred to in the foregoing. Taking also the above-mentioned findings of Spence and his colleagues into consideration, the introduction of the optimal motivation viewpoint in the way done by Atkinson and O'Connor does not seem to represent a promising expansion of the achievement motivation theory.[1]

In this situation it is proposed to stick to the more simple assumption of a monotonic relationship between motivation strength and performance level until more attention has been paid to Atkinson's more central assumption of a curvilinear relationship between motivation and probability of success. The more systematic consideration of the individual's probability of success has already been judged

----

1. After the revised theory of achievement motivation was developed, a hypothesis of a curvilinear relationship between motive strength and performance level has been set forth by Rand (1973), based on the assumption that P_s is distorted upwards among $M_s > M_f$ subjects and downwards among $M_s < M_f$ subjects. However, the "unexpected" results referred to in this chapter cannot be explained in the context of Rand's way of reasoning.

to represent a promising trend in connection with the study of persistence. However, some of the results considered finally in the preceding chapter indicate that the position taken by Atkinson concerning the personality by situation interaction should be more closely scrutinized. A further indication in this direction is also found in some theory and results reviewed in Chapter 1. More specifically, attention is once more called to the optimal stimulation principle.

A RECONSIDERATION OF THE ACHIEVEMENT MOTIVATION THEORY

To facilitate understanding of the following discussion, the main points from the section in Chapter 1 on optimal stimulation are recapitulated.

Optimal stimulation: A recapitulation

Two basically different theoretical positions were considered in Chapter 1, the one represented by theorists like Fiske and Maddi (1961), Hebb (1955), and Leuba (1955; 1961), and the other by Berlyne (1960; 1963), Fenichel (1951), and Myers and Miller (1954). However, rather than paying any further attention to the difference in underlying assumptions (cf. pp. 44 ff.) attention should again be paid to the two positions' common implication in terms of an inverted U-shaped relationship between stimulation and attractiveness. This means that according to both views intense as well as very low stimulation should be unpleasant. Berlyne, Fenichel, and Myers and Miller primarily emphasize this negative aspect, while Fiske and Maddi, Hebb, and Leuba primarily emphasize the positive affects connected with a moderate degree of stimulation.

The assumption of an inverted U-shaped relationship between stimulation and attractiveness implies that the individual should display little persistence and engagement in situations providing either very scarce or intense stimulation, while he should be highly persistent in situations providing a moderate degree of stimulation. Through the learning process the individual should also become able later on to anticipate such different degrees of stimulation. Such anticipations or expectations are assumed to serve at least as partial determinants of the individual's behaviour. In motivational language, situations expected to offer very low or very high stimulation may be said to provide negative incentives, those expected to offer moderate stimulation to provide positive incentives.

In the evaluation of the optimal stimulation principle as a contributor to the understanding of persistence in behaviour it was further argued that optimal stimulation should be regarded as a relativistic concept. That is, it is assumed that the stimulation provided by a given situation varies from one individual to another, depending on the individual's personality characteristics, among which are his motives. Recent research has for example emphasized individual differences in the disposition to experience painful stimulation more or less intensely, as well as in the tolerance for sensory isolation (cf. review by Cofer & Appley, 1964, pp. 260 f. , 283 f.).

As pointed out by Birch and Veroff (1966, p. 84), a whole array of stimulation for various motivation systems constantly acts upon the person. Having hitherto been concerned with the optimal stimulation principle in a very general way, we shall in the following relate it to the specific network of motivational variables constituted by the achievement motivation system.

Basic assumptions for further work

With reference to the optimal stimulation viewpoints dealt with above, the assumption of an inverted U-shaped relationship between stimulation level and attractiveness is made the basis for a reconsideration of the achievement motivation theory. More specifically it is assumed that:

(a) There are positive affects connected with situations providing a moderate degree of stimulation.

(b) There are negative affects connected with situations providing very low or very high stimulation.

Stimulation for many different motivation systems has been said to act upon the individual. A third assumption therefore concerns what properties a situation or task must have in order to provide stimulation for the achievement motivation system. We know in a general way that situations may be attractive to a greater or lesser extent, depending on how difficult it is to manage them. This possibility for success or failure in a situation is assumed to be the crucial aspect when we talk about stimulation of the achievement motivation system. Least stimulation should be experienced in connection with tasks at which there is little or no chance of failing and tasks that are beyond the individual's capacities. Thus, the greater the individual's uncertainty as to whether he will be able to master the situation or not, the stronger the stimulation should be. In other words, it is assumed that:

(c) The strongest stimulation is provided by situations where the probability of success (or failure) is about .50, and the weakest stimulation is provided by situations where the probability of success (or failure) is about 1.00 or .00.

However, the relativistic conception of stimulation referred to previously should here be recalled. Thus, whether the stimulation provided by a situation offering a certain possibility of success is strong enough or, for that matter, too weak or too strong to be experienced as pleasant, is assumed to depend on which aspect of the achievement motive is the dominating one. To exemplify, although situations where the probability of success (or failure) is about .50 are assumed to offer the strongest stimulation to the achievement motivation system, they need not necessarily provide a stimulation too strong to be experienced as pleasant. In other words, it is assumed that the motives may be conceptualized as moderators of the stimulation provided by a given situation. First, the positive aspect of the achievement motive, i.e. the motive to achieve success, will be discussed.

The motive to achieve success (M_s) reconsidered

The behaviour of the individual is usually presumed to be determined not by a single motive, but by several different ones. However, to make the central idea clear, let us in the following imagine a group of individuals in whom the motive to achieve success is the dominant personality characteristics. This group corresponds to what Atkinson and Feather (1966, p. 368) call achievement-oriented personalities. That M_s is the dominating personality characteristic does not, of course, preclude that there are differences between the individuals in the strength of this motive.

It will be recalled from Chapter 2 that the motive to achieve success is regarded as a capacity to anticipate positive affects in achievement situations. This motive is assumed to combine multiplicatively with the subjective probability of success (P_s) and the incentive value of success (I_s) into a motivation or tendency to achieve success (T_s), i.e. $T_s = M_s \times P_s \times I_s$. The product of P_s and I_s may be conceptualized as the weighted incentive value of a task, i.e. the incentive value when the probability of success is taken into consideration. Since P_s takes values from .00 to 1.00 and I_s is inversely related to P_s, i.e. $I_s = 1 - P_s$, these weighted values vary from .00 to a maximum of .25 and to .00 again as P_s decreases from 1.00 to .00. Thus, according to Atkinson, no task can have negative incentive value as far as M_s-dominated individuals are considered. The implications of differences in the probability of success (P_s) and in the strength of the motive (M_s) for the motivation or tendency to achieve success (T_s) were spelled out in Fig. 3. This illustration makes it clear that the positive correlation between M_s strength and for example persistence should be highest when the tasks are perceived to be of intermediate difficulty, declining as higher or lower difficulty levels are approached. Then, to underline the consequence: In a situation where P_s is either very high or very low, i.e. near 1.00 or .00, M_s will, according to the theory as developed by Atkinson, have no direct influence on behaviour.[1] In such situations, individuals with a strong M_s should react identically to those characterized by a weaker M_s, other behaviour determinants being equal.

However, from an optimal stimulation viewpoint this is assumed to be too restricted a conception of the function of M_s.

Assumption (a) said that there are positive affects connected with situations providing a moderate degree of stimulation, and assumption (b) that there are negative affects connected with situations offering very low or very high stimulation. Within the achievement motivation context the most stimulating situation should, according to assumption (c) be the one where P_s is about .50. Then, since M_s is most strongly aroused where P_s is .50, and since this motive is regarded as a capacity to anticipate positive affects in such a situation, the problem of unpleasant stimulation in terms of too high stimulation should not exist for individuals in whom this motive is the dominating one. The situation where P_s is perceived as being about .50, i.e. the most stimulating situation, should be the most attractive one for these individuals. Thus far, the reasoning is clearly in accordance with Atkinson's theory.

According to assumption (c), however, the stimulation decreases as P_s increases towards 1.00 or decreases towards .00. Thus, while situations where P_s is about .50 should provide stimulation strong enough, but not too strong, to be experienced as pleasant, those where P_s is near 1.00 or .00 probably provide negligible or no stimulation to M_s-dominated individuals. In accordance with assumption (b) the latter means that M_s-dominated individuals should experience situations where P_s is about 1.00 or .00 as unpleasant, and, as a consequence, try to avoid them. This viewpoint is clearly at variance with the theory developed by Atkinson. Thus, while according to Atkinson the weighted incentive values $(I_s \times P_s)$ vary from .00 to +.25, the position taken here is that the weighted incentive value of very easy and very difficult tasks should be negative. The point is illustrated in the inverted U-shaped curve in Fig. 5, where these incentive values are designated I_{M_s} to differentiate

----

1. This does not, of course, preclude that the motive may have an indirect influence on behaviour through its contribution to the motivation to perform alternative tasks.

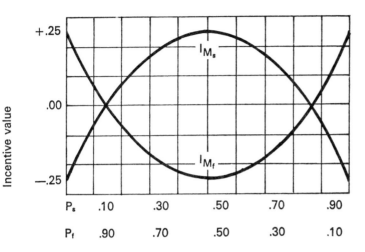

Fig. 5. Incentive values (I_{M_s} and I_{M_f}) as a function of probability of success or failure. (The I_{M_f} values are referred to later in this chapter.)

them from the I_s values in Atkinson's theory. The I_{M_s} curve takes values varying from a minimum of $-.25$ for extremely easy and hopelessly difficult tasks to a maximum of $+.25$ for tasks of intermediate difficulty. The values are rather arbitrarily chosen,[1] and it may for example be questioned whether it is reasonable to assign an equally high negative incentive value to extremely easy and extremely difficult tasks. However, the main point here is that the values chosen serve to illustrate the basic idea under consideration, and I would not, of course, quarrel with anyone arguing in favour of other values taking care of the same idea.

According to the achievement motivation theory the anticipation of positive affects, and thus the tendency or motivation to achieve when confronted with tasks of intermediate difficulty, should be stronger in individuals with a strong M_s than in those with a weak one. In a comparable way, it seems reasonable to

----

1. Actually, the incentive value for tasks with $P_s = .50$ was set equal to the product of I_s and P_s in Atkinson's theory ($+.25$). Next, negative values of the same size were assigned to the extremely easy ($P_s = 1.00$) and extremely difficult ($P_s = .00$) tasks. The other values were found by the formula $Y = -2X^2 + 2X - .25$, where $Y = $ incentive value (I_{M_s}), and $X = $ probability of success (P_s).

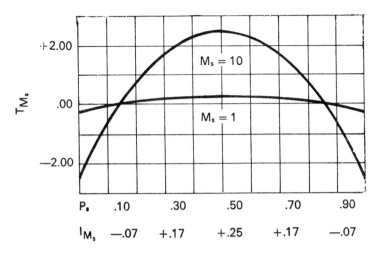

Fig. 6. Tendency to engage in an activity (T_{M_S}) in relation to P_S or I_{M_S} for individuals who differ in strength of M_S. (The I_{M_S} values are from Fig. 5.)

assume that the anticipation of negative affects when confronted with very easy or extremely difficult tasks is stronger in individuals having a strong M_s than in those having a weak one. Said in another way, individuals with a weak M_s are held to be more indifferent towards tasks of all difficulty levels. This means that the motivation or tendency to engage in an activity, here symbolized as T_{M_S}, should be a multiplicative function of the strength of the motive and the incentive value: $T_{M_S} = M_s \times I_{M_S}$. The I_{M_S} values for tasks at various perceived difficulty levels were presented in Fig. 5, and the implications of differences in motive strength and task difficulty level for the motivation or tendency to engage in a situation are shown in Fig. 6.

The figure makes clear a conception of the function of the motive to achieve success which differs at some points from that in the achievement motivation theory as developed by Atkinson: In addition to the clear difference in motivation between individuals with a strong and those with a weak M_s in connection with tasks of intermediate difficulty, there should also be important differences in the motivation for tasks at the extremes on the P_s scale, for example a pure routine task and an extremely difficult task. Individuals dominated by M_s are supposed to anticipate negative affects when confronted with such tasks, and thus to show resistance towards working on them. The strength of this tendency to resist is seen to be proportional to M_s strength.

Thus far, only the motive to achieve success has been reconsidered. In the following a comparable line of reasoning will be applied to the other aspect of the achievement motive, i.e. to the motive to avoid failure.

The motive to avoid failure (M_f) reconsidered

While we focused in the previous section upon individuals dominated by the motive to achieve success, in the following we shall turn to the other extreme, imagining a group of individuals dominated by the motive to avoid failure, corresponding to what Atkinson and Feather (1966, p. 369) name failure-threatened personalities. It is also assumed that within this group there are individual differences in the strength of this dominating motive.

As pointed out in Chapter 2, M_f is regarded as a relatively stable personality characteristic in terms of a capacity to anticipate negative affects in achievement situations. This motive combines multiplicatively with the subjective probability of failure (P_f) and the incentive value of failure (I_f) into a motivation or tendency to avoid failure (T_f), i.e. $T_f = M_f \times P_f \times I_f$. The implications of differences in P_f and in the strength of M_f were indicated in Fig. 3, which showed that M_f, like M_s, is maximally aroused in situations where the probability of success or failure is about equal. When P_f is either very high or very low, individuals with a strong M_f are assumed to behave in the same way as those with a weak M_f, other determinants being equal. However, this matter should be reconsidered in a way comparable to that in the section dealing with the M_s problem.

Since M_f is most strongly aroused where P_f is about .50 and since this motive is conceptualized as a capacity to experience negative affects in such situations, these may be said to offer an unpleasantly high stimulation to individuals dominated by this motive. In other words, taking into consideration that $P_f = .50$ also implies that $P_s = .50$, the same situation which for M_s-dominated individuals was assumed to be the most attractive one, should be the most disagreeable one for M_f-dominated individuals.

On the other hand, the problem of insufficient stimulation, which was regarded as a central one among the achievement-oriented personalities, is held to be a negligible one for the failure-threatened individuals, most situations being perceived as threatening. Instead, it does not seem unreasonable to suppose that for this group of individuals one comes closest to what may be characterized as pleasant stimulation in situations offering very little challenge, i.e. in those where P_f is near .00 or 1.00. That is, if individuals dominated by M_f do anticipate positive affects and display engagement, it seems likely that they do so only when confronted with tasks where failure is a very unlikely result (P_f near .00) or where failure is so probable that the task does not represent any realistic challenge (P_f near 1.00). While Atkinson's theory implies that no task can have positive weighted incentive value ($I_f \times P_f$) for the M_f-dominated person, the idea presented above implies that very easy and very difficult tasks may be thought of as possibly having positive value. The point is illustrated in the U-shaped curve in Fig. 5, where the incentive value is designated I_{M_f} to differentiate it from the I_f value in Atkinson's theory. Here too the values are rather arbitrarily chosen,[1] and in the same way as the I_{M_s} values they only serve to illustrate the basic idea under consideration. It may therefore well be that another set of values would represent the underlying relationship more adequately.

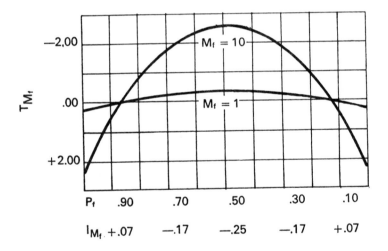

Fig. 7. Tendency to engage in an activity (T_{M_f}) in relation to P_f or I_{M_f} for individuals who differ in strength of M_f. (The I_{M_f} values are from Fig. 5.)

----

1. The incentive value for tasks with P_f = .50 was set equal to the product of I_f and P_f in Atkinson's theory (-.25). Next, positive values of the same size were assigned to the extremely easy (P_f = .00) and extremely difficult (P_f = 1.00) tasks. The other values were obtained by the formula $Y = 2X^2 - 2X + .25$, where Y = incentive value (I_{M_f}), and X = probability of failure (P_f).

Individuals with a weak M_f are held to be more indifferent towards tasks of all difficulty levels than those with a strong M_f, other behaviour determinants being equal. In other words, the motivation or tendency to engage in an activity, here designated T_{M_f}, is assumed to be a multiplicative function of M_f strength and I_{M_f}, i.e. $T_{M_f} = M_f \times I_{M_f}$. The I_{M_f} values for tasks at different difficulty levels were presented in Fig. 5, and the implications of the formula are given in Fig. 7. It can be seen that while individuals with a strong M_f should be more negatively motivated when confronted with tasks of intermediate difficulty, i.e. should reveal more resistance towards working on such tasks, than those with a weak M_f, their positions should be reversed when confronted with very easy and very difficult tasks, those with a strong M_f being most positively motivated.

Resultant achievement motivation

To make the general idea clear, we have until now concentrated upon two extreme groups of individuals, on the one hand clearly achievement-oriented personalities, i.e. those dominated by the motive to achieve success, and on the other hand failure-threatened personalities, i.e. those dominated by the motive to avoid failure. However, all individuals are assumed to have both a motive to achieve success and a motive to avoid failure, and the resultant achievement motivation may therefore be thought of as the algebraic sum of the motivation attributed to M_s and that attributed to M_f. In Fig. 8 the resultant motivation or tendency is shown for an individual with $M_s > M_f$, one with $M_s = M_f$, and one with $M_s < M_f$. While Atkinson's theory of achievement motivation (1964) implies that the resultant motivation is positive when M_s is stronger than M_f, and negative when the reverse is the case, the present reconsideration has resulted in a different conception: Whether the resultant motivation becomes positive or negative depends both upon the relative strength of M_s and M_f, and on how difficult the task is perceived to be. Individuals dominated by the motive to achieve success $(M_s > M_f)$ are presumed to engage in tasks offering an intermediate possibility of success, but are not presumed to work on very easy or very difficult tasks unless there is some extrinsic motivation present, i.e. motivation attributable to motives other than M_s and M_f, which outweighs and overcomes the tendency to resist engaging in them. In contrast, individuals in whom the motive to avoid failure is the prevalent one $(M_s < M_f)$ are presumed to show resistance towards working on tasks of intermediate difficulty, but to engage in very easy or very difficult tasks.

Thus, the revised theory of achievement motivation emphasizes the interaction principle even more strongly than Atkinson's theory, in that it implies not only

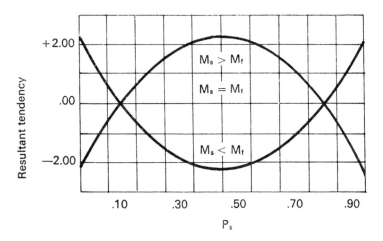

Fig. 8. Resultant tendency to engage in an activity for individuals with $M_s > M_f$ ($M_s = 10$, $M_f = 1$), $M_s = M_f$, and $M_s < M_f$ ($M_s = 1$, $M_f = 10$).

that individuals with different motive constellations should react in opposite ways to the same situation, but also that people with the same motive constellations should react in diametrically opposite ways to different situations. This understanding has been arrived at by a re-examination of the achievement motivation theory as developed by Atkinson in the light of the more general optimal stimulation principle. In the next section an attempt will be made to relate some earlier reported empirical results to this novel conception.

VALIDITY INDICATIONS

As will be recalled, we dealt in Chapter 3 with some results from persistence studies which may be taken as a first indicator that $M_s < M_f$ individuals are more motivated for extremely easy and difficult tasks than $M_s > M_f$ individuals. These results should therefore first be summed up.

Earlier considered persistence results

As we have seen, Weiner (1965) found, if anything, the $M_s < M_f$ group to be more persistent than the $M_s > M_f$ group on a digit-symbol substitution task where P_s was assumed to be either very high or very low, and C.P. Smith (1964) found higher persistence in an examination situation among $M_s < M_f$ students than among $M_s > M_f$ students where P_s was assumed to be high (i.e. among high IQ students). Further, Atkinson and O'Connor (1966), Feather (1961; 1963), and Mandler and Watson (1966) all found $M_s < M_f$ subjects to be more persistent at a low P_s task than $M_s > M_f$ subjects. It should, however, be recalled that it is possible to explain the latter results in terms of differences between the groups in motivation for an alternative, moderately difficult task, the $M_s > M_f$ group being more strongly motivated for this task than the $M_s < M_f$ group.

Before leaving the field of persistence we shall for a moment return to the study by Kounin (1941), considered in Chapter 1, since the results from that study also seem to be of some interest in connection with the revised theory. It will be recalled that the most conspicuous result in Kounin's study was a decrease in "co-satiation" and an increase in absolute "satiation-time" from the young normal group via the young feeble-minded group to the old feeble-minded group at very simple drawing tasks (cf. p. 33). Only the co-satiation results can be explained in terms of Kounin's rigidity hypothesis. In our discussion of Kounin's results we also noted the argument of Zigler (1961; 1962) that the differences might be related to group differences in the motivation for social contact and approval. It seems, however, that the differences can equally well be ascribed to differences between the groups with respect to achievement motivation. Thus, Cromwell (1963, p. 58), suggesting an approach to mental retardation problems based on social learning theory (Rotter, 1954), finds it plausible to associate the failure-avoiding tendency with the retarded individual. This idea is based on an assumption that retardates typically experience more failure than average children. Transformed to achievement motivation language, the retardates should be more M_f-dominated than normal children. If this view is related to Kounin's groups, it would imply an increase in M_f strength from the young normal group to the old feeble-minded group. Further, since all subjects were of the same mental age, the drawing task was probably perceived as about equally difficult by all groups. The task-type used, that of drawing very simple figures, along with the fact that the subjects were made conversant with the tasks beforehand, make it likely that P_s was relatively high.

Given these assumptions about relative M_f strength and P_s level, the revised theory offers an alternative explanation of the results obtained by Kounin. Thus, the increase in persistence at the initial (high P_s) task from the young normal (relatively low M_f) group via the young feeble-minded group to the old feeble-minded (relatively high M_f) group would be due to M_f-based motivation differences. However, when the old feeble-minded group eventually turned to the next drawing task, this group would also be strongly motivated for that task, i.e. a small amount of "co-satiation" among these subjects was expected and was in fact observed. In other words, if our presumptions concerning M_f differences and P_s level are correct, the revised achievement motivation theory seems capable of explaining both the differences in "co-satiation" and in absolute "satiation time".

After this initial consideration of some results referred to in previous chapters we shall next focus upon some studies dealing with the relationship between motive strength and performance level, in order to make a further evaluation of the revised theory possible.

Motive strength and performance level

In this connection no attempt will be made at an exhaustive discussion of all the research directed towards this problem. Instead, a selective review will be given, which will encompass the "unexpected" results referred to at the beginning of this chapter as well as other results which have not hitherto been reconciled by the achievement motivation theory. For a more comprehensive coverage of the literature on M_s or M_f (anxiety) strength and behaviour the reader is referred to reviews by Cofer and Appley (1964, pp. 730 ff.), V. J. Crandall (1963, pp. 435 ff.), Heckhausen (1967, pp. 127 ff.), Klinger (1966, pp. 294 ff.), and Ruebush (1963, pp. 497 ff. among others.

The revised theory has been seen to imply that the correlation between performance level and the strength of M_s as well as M_f may be positive, zero, or negative, depending on the probability of success at the task in question. As indicated at the beginning of this chapter, a great many studies have been carried out within this area, yielding relationships ranging over a wide field. However, in most of these studies the probability of success at the task has not been explicitly considered, and a post hoc arrangement of the tasks on the P_s continuum must of necessity be a somewhat risky undertaking. It also needs to be stressed again that P_s depends on the person as well as on the task and the performance situation more generally. Among the factors influencing P_s the most central ones in this connection should be mentioned.

As also pointed out by Atkinson (1960, p. 267), the complexity of the task, repeated referred to by Spence and his colleagues (e.g. Farber & Spence, 1953; Spence, 1956; Spence, Farber, & McFann, 1956), may be considered as one of the factors affecting the perceived difficulty level of the task. Secondly, P_s may be influenced by the use of norms or other kinds of instructions (e.g. of the type "Only 5 per cent of university students are able to solve the task.") as well as by reinforcements given by the experimenter (e.g. of the type "I noted you had some difficulty."). Thirdly, the perceived difficulty is in general assumed to be inversely related to the subject's ability level (Gaudry & Spielberger, 1971, p. 58; Spielberger, 1966, p. 376; Spielberger & Weitz, 1964, p. 16), a circumstance which means that one and the same task may represent a high, moderate, or low P_s task, according to whether ability level is high, moderate, or low.

With these P_s considerations in mind, let us now turn to research on performance level which can be related to the hypothesis of higher motivation among $M_s < M_f$ individuals than among $M_s > M_f$ individuals for very easy and very difficult tasks, ans let us first consider tasks at the high extreme on the P_s continuum.

Motive Strength and Performance at Easy Tasks. Such tasks have been only rarely employed within achievement motivation research. Furthermore, when easy tasks have been employed, they have often been combined with information to subjects during work that their performances were inadequate. Such information may result in only a moderate or, for that matter, a low P_s, even though the task itself is a very easy one.

An exception is found in a study by Heckhausen (1963). As part of that study a sample of 174 subjects, male and female, was required to add up a long series of pairs of one-digit figures (ibid. , pp. 228 ff.). Since the sample consisted of business school and university students, this simple arithmetical operation is assumed to represent a high P_s task. It should also be noted that Heckhausen characterizes the task as much easier than the addition task used by Lowell (1952) in a similar study, and where the high nAch subjects, i.e. those assumed to be high in M_s, were found to be superior.

Prior to the addition task Heckhausen's version of the TAT nAch test had been administered under neutral conditions. From this test a net hope (NH) score was calculated by subtracting the fear of failure score (FF) from the hope of success score (HS). The relationship between this score and addition performance was characterized as surprising, in that the group with negative NH scores ($M_s < M_f$) performed better than that with positive NH scores ($M_s > M_f$) throughout the whole test (op.cit. , p. 231). A somewhat clearer difference in the last part of the addition test was due to a deterioration of performance level on the part of the high NH scorers

$(M_s > M_f)$, while the low NH scorers $(M_s < M_f)$ were able to maintain the level of their initial performance throughout the test. Thus, while Heckhausen characterizes the results as surprising, they lend clear support to the novel hypothesis of a stronger motivation for easy tasks among $M_s < M_f$ subjects than among $M_s > M_f$ subjects, on the assumption, which seems to be a strong one, that in this case the task can be considered as a high P_s task. It is also interesting to note that in a later discussion of these results Heckhausen (1967, p. 138) in fact argues quite in accordance with the revised theory, suggesting that the superiority of the low NH group $(M_s < M_f)$ can probably be traced back to the stronger incentive value that such trivial and harmless tasks have for failure-threatened than for success-oriented individuals.

In his discussion of the results Heckhausen also refers to those obtained by Vogel, Baker, and Lazarus (1958) as being of a similar kind. These investigators found that low TAT nAch subjects attempted significantly more items than high TAT nAch subjects on a simple perceptual-motor task, that of counting as quickly and accurately as possible the number of symbols of different kinds which each of a long series of circles contained (ibid. , p. 110). In the discussion of these results we once more find arguments in accordance with the revised theory, in that it is suggested that the low nAch (low M_s) subjects have more "positive interest" in this simple perceptual-motor task than high nAch subjects. The task is said not to challenge the latter group of subjects (ibid. , p. 110).

However, the nAch test referred to above was administered after the perceptual-motor test, and the performance results did not correlate with nAch scores obtained prior to task administration. Even more, in the final third fraction of the performance session the subjects were given false norms to induce a sense of failure (decrease in P_s). These complications imply that the results cannot be said to provide the same clearcut evidence in relation to the revised theory as those reported by Heckhausen.

The results with which we have been concerned above stem from the achievement motivation research tradition in a restricted sense. But most studies comparing performance at easy and more difficult tasks have been carried out by investigators working within the anxiety research tradition. Since it has been assumed that both the scores from test anxiety questionnaires and those from the Manifest Anxiety Scale (MAS) can be regarded as indicators of the strength of M_f (cf. pp. 72 ff.), some anxiety studies which seem to provide further evidence in favour of the revised theory of achievement motivation will now be reviewed.

Turning first to the MAS studies, most of them have aimed at testing the Hull-Spence theoretical position, where behaviour is considered a function of Drive x Habit. Thus, in a simple situation, where only one habit is elicited, a high drive should produce higher performance level than a low drive. A complex situation is conceived as one where the correct response is one of a number of competing responses. In such a situation the multiplicative effect of drive should produce lower performance level when drive is high than when drive is low, because more incorrect responses are elicited when drive is high. In this connection a great number of affirmative results from anxiety studies have been reported which are too well known to be in need of detailed consideration. Thus, Spence (1956, pp. 226 ff.), Spence, Farber, and McFann (1956, pp. 300 ff.), Spence, Taylor, and Ketchel (1956, p. 308), and Taylor and Chapman (1955) all report that high anxiety students perform better than low anxiety students on simple paired-associates tasks, while the reverse was the case on complex paired-associates tasks. Similar results have been obtained among children where CMAS (Castaneda, McCandless, & Palermo, 1956), a children's version of the MAS, has been used to assess anxiety. To exemplify, Castaneda (1961), and Castaneda, Palermo, and McCandless (1956, p. 330) report performance level at a perceptual-motor task to be the result of an anxiety by task complexity interaction, the high CMAS subjects performing better than the low CMAS subjects at a simple task, and the low CMAS subjects performing better at a complex task.

Studies have also been reported where the individual's ability level has been regarded as a moderator of task difficulty. J. P. Denny (1966) investigated the effect of anxiety and ability on performance at a concept formation task. Pilot work had been done to construct a task where floor and ceiling effects were minimized, i. e. where the worst and best possible scores were rarely achieved. The measure of concept formation was the number of correct conclusions about whether or not certain attributes were included in a series of concepts. The task was administered in a sample of 64 male college students, and the results demonstrated a very clear anxiety by ability interaction: Within the high IQ group high MAS subjects were superior to low MAS subjects. The reverse was the case within the low IQ group. These results were said to be consistent with the expectations derived from Drive x Habit theory, when ability was considered as a convertor of task difficulty, high ability working through a lowering of task difficulty.

J. P. Denny's results have a parallel in the findings by Katahn (1966): higher performance level on a serial verbal maze among high MAS subjects than among low MAS subjects in a group with high aptitude scores, and lower performance level among high MAS subjects than among low MAS subjects in a sample with low aptitude scores. The same pattern of results was found when grade point average was used as criterion.

The results from the anxiety studies referred to above have all been interpreted by the investigators as being in accordance with Drive x Habit theory. However, the assumption that task complexity and/or ability level can be regarded as factors determining the subjects' probability of success means that all these results may be reinterpreted within the revised achievement motivation theory. [1] On the other hand, the superiority of the high anxiety subjects repeatedly observed where P_s is assumed to have been relatively high (simple tasks and/or high ability) cannot be accounted for by the achievement motivation theory as developed by Atkinson.

This completes our review of studies bearing upon the relationship between motive strength and behaviour criteria where the task is assumed to be perceived as an easy one. Next some results will be considered which seem to lend support to the hypothesis of a higher motivation for very difficult tasks among $M_s < M_f$ individuals than among $M_s > M_f$ individuals.

Motive Strength and Performance at Difficult Tasks. When turning to this matter there is one problem which presents itself immediately, related to the correspondence between the subjects' perceived difficulty and the objective difficulty of the task. Thus, if a task is perceived as extremely difficult and it in fact is, then there should be little or no variation in performance scores, i.e. no difference between motive groups (or any other kind of groups) would appear. Under such conditions persistence at the task should be a more appropriate criterion. Some such persistence results have been dealt with previously. It may, however, be that a very low P_s does not mean that the task is in fact almost insoluble. Where this is the case, differences in motivation strength should be reflected in variations in performance level.

A study by Miles (1958) is the only one mentioned in the extensive review of achievement motivation research by Klinger (1966) in which a significant inverse relationship between achievement motive score and performance level was obtained. It may therefore be of interest to see whether Miles's result can be reinterpreted in terms of the revised theory of achievement motivation.

Miles confronted 68 male students with a relatively complex perceptual-motor task, that of keeping a spot of light on a moving target by means of two handles on a pursuitmeter. After 12 trials at this initial task it was changed in such a way that the subjects had to make movements exactly opposite to those in the first phase to keep the light on the target. The subjects were divided into two motive groups according to the achievement imagery scores on the Iowa Picture Inter-

----

1. The soundness of the assumption that P_s rather than task complexity per se is the significant variable in connection with the anxiety by task interaction is indicated by results reported by Weiner (1966, p. 341). He found that high TAQ subjects performed better than low TAQ subjects at a complex task when they were informed that they did well (high P_s), while low TAQ subjects performed better than high TAQ subjects at a simple task when they were informed that they were failing. These results contradict the Drive x Habit theory.

pretation Test. The results showed that there was a reversal of the two motive groups' performance level from the initial to the reversed task, the high IPIT (high M_s) group being superior at the former task and inferior at the latter task (Miles, 1958, pp. 158 ff.). This was the case both among subjects who approached problems in a systematic way (analysers) and among those approaching problems in a more arbitrary way (non-analysers).

Miles interprets these results in terms of Drive x Habit theory, assuming that high achievement imagery scores reflect a high drive level, low scores reflect a low drive level. He emphasizes that it is known that the reversed task is much more difficult than the original task, and therefore " . . . high drive Ss might be expected to do less well relative to low drive Ss on the reversed task than on the standard task" (ibid., p. 161). However, the inference of drive level from achievement imagery scores seems highly curious in the light of the many results showing nAch scores and anxiety (drive) scores to be related to performance in opposite ways. Further, it seems reasonable to assume that the initial pursuitmeter task was not perceived as a very easy one, but more likely as a moderately difficult task (moderate P_s). Since the reversed task was assumed by Miles to be much more difficult, this task should probably represent a relatively low P_s task. The results on the reversed task contradict the predictions which can be derived from Atkinson's model. However, the superiority of the low IPIT (low M_s) group on the reversed, difficult task is quite in accordance with the revised model if our P_s assumption is correct.

The hypothesis of higher motivation for very difficult tasks among $M_s < M_f$ subjects than among $M_s > M_f$ subjects also receives support from an investigation by Gjesme (1971c), concerned with the relationship between achievement-related motives and school performance among girls. Gjesme thinks of the pupil's ability level as a moderator of the perceived difficulty level of tasks. Low ability pupils are presumed to consider their probability of success as relatively low when compared with high ability pupils. This, Gjesme points out, should be all the more conspicuous among girls, since there is a general tendency for girls to underestimate their probability of success (ibid., p. 14). [1] More specifically Gjesme then assumes high IQ girls to have a moderate P_s and low IQ girls to have a very low P_s in the school situation (ibid., p. 15).

Given these assumptions, school performance level (marks in arithmetic,

----

1. The soundness of this assumption is clearly demonstrated by V. C. Crandall (1969, pp. 21 ff.), who found a significantly lower expectancy of success among girls than among boys at a series of tasks.

Norwegian and English) was examined in a sample of 157 girls in the seventh grade. The results showed that among girls with high IQ (moderate P_s) the high TAT nAch/low TASC (high/low) subjects performed better than the low TAT nAch/high TASC (low/high) subjects. However, in the low IQ group (low P_s), which is of particular interest here, the opposite pattern of results was observed, i.e. the low/high group performed better than the high/low group (ibid., p. 58). While Gjesme suggests that the "unexpected" results from the low IQ group might be due to a difference in extrinsic motivation between the two motive groups in favour of the low/high group, the revised theory offers an alternative explanation. If Gjesme's assumption of a very low P_s among low IQ girls is correct, then the results provide support for the hypothesis of higher motivation among $M_s < M_f$ subjects than among $M_s > M_f$ subjects for a very difficult task.

It should also be noted that the results obtained in an earlier study by Spielberger and Weitz (1964), although at first glance ostensibly bewildering, on closer scrutiny are found to represent a parallel to Gjesme's results. Spielberger and Weitz examined the relationship between MAS scores and performance level among male students at Duke University from 1954 to 1960. The investigators point out that although the average ability level of students improved over the years, the average marks awarded to them tended to remain constant. This, the investigators state, indicates that the academic tasks increased in difficulty over the years (ibid., p. 17). As to the anxiety-performance results, anxiety was found to facilitate performance in two cases: Among high ability students from the first years, i.e. from the years where the academic tasks were relatively easy, and among low ability students from the last year, where the academic tasks were relatively difficult (ibid., pp. 15 ff.). Assuming P_s to be inversely related to ability level, the latter group should have a low P_s. From this point of view the higher performance level among high MAS students with low ability is in accordance with the revised theory. Parenthetically speaking, the high ability subjects from the first years should have a high P_s, and then the results from this group in terms of higher performance level among those with high anxiety scores than among those with low anxiety scores are in accordance with the findings by J.P. Denny (1966) and Katahn (1966) referred to previously, and provide further support for the hypothesis of higher motivation among $M_s < M_f$ subjects than among $M_s > M_f$ subjects for easy tasks.

Finally in this chapter we shall pay some attention to a study by C. P. Smith (1966) which is of particular interest since the results obtained are mentioned by Atkinson and O'Connor (1966) as a possible exemplification of the previously discussed (cf. (pp. 104 f.) decrement in performance level because of motivation greater than optimal.

Among other things, Smith examined the relationship between performance level and TAT nAch score, obtained prior to or subsequent to performance. Performance level was measured by 14 minutes of performance on a two-step arithmetic task, where the subject had to write down only his final answer, keeping the intermediate calculations in his mind. The subjects worked under four different conditions, but our interest is restricted to the relationship between nAch scores and performance level under achievement conditions as compared to under multi-incentive conditions, since it is in the latter case that the above optimal motivation phenomenon is most likely to appear. Since there may have been a carry-over effect from the performance situation to the nAch test situation where the test was administered after the arithmetic task, we also restrict our attention to the group where nAch scores were obtained prior to performance. However, the pattern of results was roughly the same under the two nAch test conditions.

The results obtained in a group of 67 male college students revealed a clear inter-action, the mean performance level being the same in achievement and multi-incentive conditions, but the results being quite opposite for the high and low nAch group in the two conditions. The high group performed better than the low group in achievement conditions and worse than the low group in multi-incentive conditions. However, before the negative relationship between nAch score and performance level is ascribed to a possible above optimal motivation level in the multi-incentive conditon, as in-dicated by Atkinson and O'Connor (1966), the two different conditions should be more closely examined.

In the achievement condition the subjects were told that the task required con-siderable concentration and therefore they would be assigned to individual rooms in which to work. The task was said to be similar to various ability tests, and the subjects were asked to solve as many problems as possible in the time allowed. After 14 minutes each subject was stopped and asked to return to the class-room. It seems reasonable to assume that at least for most subjects P_s was within a moderate range under these conditions.

In the multi-incentive condition the subjects were to work in a group. The same orientation was given as in the achievement condition, apart from that about working alone, but in addition the experimenter said: "Since I am interested in seeing your very best performance when you are actually putting out, I am going to award a price of $ 5.00 to the person having the highest score on this test" (op. cit. , p. 283). Throughout the performance of the task the experimenter walked around holding a stopwatch in his hand, and attempting to look concerned about the subjects' performance. It is reported that the procedure was intended to reproduce as nearly as possible the multi-incentive condition in an earlier study by Atkinson and Reitman (1956), and from their report it also appears that the subjects were required to skip an item at the end of each minute and move on to the next one.

These instructions make it quite clear that while an additional incentive was introduced in the multi-incentive condition, there is another and possibly equally important difference between the two conditions. Thus, the emphasis on "very best performance", the procedure of interrupting the subjects before they had finished the item, as well as the disturbances brought about by the experimenter's pacing around, have probably produced a considerably lower P_s under the multi-incentive condition than under the achievement condition. If it is possible that this P_s difference was the most significant difference between the two conditions, then the revised theory offers an alternative explanation of the results: The superiority of the low nAch group in the multi-incentive condition is another example of low M_s individuals being more motivated for difficult tasks than high M_s individuals. This explanation is considerably simpler than that indicated by Atkinson and O'Connor, which, as pointed out at the outset of this chapter, implies a double curvilinearity assumption.

Conclusions

In the preceding pages the results from a selected number of studies have been reinterpreted in light of a revised theory of achievement motivation. This theory has been seen to reconcile apparently bewildering results from the achievement motivation research tradition as well as results obtained within anxiety research. It would, however, be premature to argue that the results considered provide conclusive evidence for the validity of the revised theory. First, the review was started with the reservation that a post hoc arrangement of the tasks on a P_s continuum would necessarily be a risky undertaking, and the reader should once more be reminded of this reservation. Thus, the P_s assumptions made in the review may have been more or less erroneous. Secondly, in some of the reports alternative interpretations have been offered, and where they have not, it is unlikely that the interpretation given in this chapter represents the only possible post hoc interpretation. Thirdly, no attempt has been made to review the whole area of achievement motivation research, and if this was done, it would probably not be difficult to find results that could not be explained in terms of the revised theory.

Yet, despite these reservations the evidence is considered sufficient to animate further work along these lines. This is all the more the case since none of these studies were, of course, designed to test the novel hypothesis of a stronger motivation for very easy and very difficult tasks among $M_s < M_f$ individuals than among $M_s > M_f$ individuals.

GENERAL SUMMARY

In a reconsideration of the achievement motivation theory it has been assumed that moderate stimulation releases positive affects and very low or very high stimulation negative affects. It has further been assumed that as far as the achievement motivation system is concerned, the most stimulating situation is that where the probability of success (P_s) is about .50, the least stimulating that where P_s is near 1.00 or .00. The motive to achieve success (M_s) and the motive to avoid failure (M_f) are thought of as moderators of the stimulation provided by a given situation. M_s-dominated individuals should experience positive affects (moderate stimulation) in situations where P_s is about .50, and should therefore engage in such tasks. P_s near 1.00 or .00 implies very low stimulation, hence negative affects should be released, resulting in resistance towards such situations. M_f-dominated individuals should experience negative affects (very high stimulation) where P_s is about .50, while if they experience any moderate stimulation, and thus positive affects, this should only be where P_s is either very high or very low. This implies that the relationship between M_s strength, or M_f strength, and degree of engagement should vary from positive to negative, depending upon the probability of success in the situation. Results from previous investigations were related to these viewpoints.

CHAPTER 5

OUTLINE OF AN EMPIRICAL INVESTIGATION OF PERSISTENCE

SKETCH OF SITUATIONAL SETTINGS

Since the individual is assumed to be constantly active (Atkinson, 1964, p. 301), the problem of persistence may also, as suggested previously (p. 58), be regarded as that of change from one activity to another. This means, as Feather (1961, p. 553) realized, that when predicting persistence at a task one has to take into account not only the motivation for that task, but also the motivation for possible alternatives. The motivation for the activity in progress and the motivation for an alternative activity may be attributable to the same or to different motivation components. An example of the latter case is where the individual has the choice between continuing to prepare himself for an examination and accepting an invitation to a friend's party. While the achievement motivation should make up an important part of his motivation to prepare himself for the examination, the motivation to join his friends should depend to a considerable extent on the strength of his affiliation motive. On the other hand, if the individual has the choice between for example continuing at a difficult course in mathematics and switching to a somewhat easier one, achievement motivation should be an important component both in the motivation for the activity in progress and in the motivation for the alternative. Since this study is concerned with the problem of achievement motivation and persistence, we shall here restrict our attention to the latter type of situation.

Although after the limitation sketched above we can imagine a number of possible initial/alternative task combinations, it should be sufficient for present purposes to distinguish between a restricted number of situation categories, according to whether the probability of success at either the initial or the alternative task is high, moderate, or low. Then we are left with the combinations shown in Fig. 9.

Let us then, to simplify, assume that an easy task corresponds to $P_s = .95$, a moderately difficult task to $P_s = .50$, and a difficult task to $P_s = .05$. In this connection it should also be recalled that the achievement motivation strength is assumed to be the same for tasks with $P_s = .95$ and tasks with $P_s = .05$ (cf. e.g. p. 116, Fig. 8). Then the initial and the alternative task should be equally

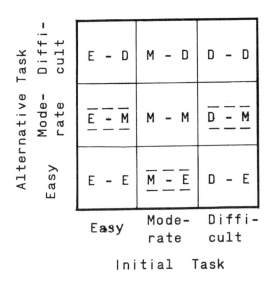

Fig. 9. Possible initial/alternative task combinations according to perceived difficulty level. (The empirical investigation deals with the stippled alternatives.)

attractive (or unattractive) to the individual both with easy/easy, moderate/moderate, difficult/difficult, and with easy/difficult and difficult/easy task combinations. All these combinations seem of little interest, not least because in practice it is probably impossible to establish a situation where the probability of success remains unchanged during work. Change in P_s during work is probably the rule rather than the exception, and this means for example that the moderate/moderate situation should change to an easy/moderate or difficult/moderate situation, depending on whether P_s increases or decreases.

If we exclude situations where the initial and the alternative task are assumed at the outset to be equally attractive or unattractive to the individual, we are left with four situational settings: (1) the moderate/easy, (2) the easy/moderate, (3) the difficult/moderate, and (4) the moderate/difficult. Nevertheless, it should be clear that the problem area is still a comprehensive one. For practical reasons, primarily the time available for the empirical investigation, some further restriction was therefore necessary.

It will be recalled that persistence in situation type (3) has been investigated previously by Feather (cf. pp. 88 ff.). However, his sample consisted of male college students only, and it is of interest to see whether the relationships ob-

served by Feather also hold in a less selected group of individuals. As to situation
(4), passing from a moderately to a very difficult task scarcely represents an
adaptive mode of behaviour. Whether we are concerned with learning situations
or working situations, it does not seem expedient to let the individual turn to a
task at the very limit of, or maybe beyond, his capacities. From a practical point
of view, situation (4) is therefore a rather uninteresting one, so, since a further
restriction of the field of investigation was necessary, it seemed most reasonable
to exclude situation (4).

Thus we are finally left with three initial/alternative task combinations.[1]
Obviously, it is far from unproblematical to establish experimental persistence
situations corresponding to the hypothetical situations sketched here. Catch
phrases like "change in P_s during work", and "individual differences in P_s within
one and the same situation" suffice to demonstrate this. These problems will be
disregarded under the development of hypotheses, but will be considered towards
the end of this chapter.

Turning now to the matter of motivation, in all three situations the total motivation or tendency to engage in the initial task as well as in the alternative task is
considered as made up of motivation attributable to M_s and M_f plus extrinsic
motivation, i.e. motivation attributable to motives other than M_s and M_f. Further,
like Feather (1961, p. 553), we assume that in an experimental situation the
extrinsic motivation to perform the initial task is stronger than the extrinsic
motivation to perform the alternative task, due to the fact that the subject is
asked by the experimenter to start at the initial task, and knows that he is expected to make some attempts at the task.

Since we have previously been concerned with alternative viewpoints on achievement motivation, a few comments are also necessary regarding the theoretical
basis for the investigation.

THEORETICAL BASIS FOR THE INVESTIGATION

In previous chapters we have considered the achievement motivation theory as

----

1. It may be noted that the excluded situation (situation 4) is from an achievement motivation viewpoint functionally equal to situation (1). This is because
the initial tasks are equal and the alternative tasks, either easy or difficult,
are assumed to have the same weighted incentive value (I_{M_s} or I_{M_f}). This
means that the relationships hypothesized for persistence at the initial task in
situation (1) should also apply to situation (4).

developed by Atkinson as well as a proposal for a revised theory of achievement motivation. These theories have been seen to differ completely on certain points, and it would then seem natural to test hypotheses based on the two theories against each other. However, the reader may already have noted that despite the difference, the two theories yield exactly the same hypotheses about differences between motive groups in persistence in situations of the particular kind outlined above, i.e. where the motivation for both the initial and the alternative task contains an achievement motivation component. If this does not appear evident, attention should for a moment once more be paid to Feather's study of persistence at an initial task when an alternative task of moderate difficulty was offered (cf. pp. 88 ff.). Although the $M_s > M_f$ group should be somewhat more strongly motivated for the initial, very difficult (low P_s) task, it was hypothesized that the $M_s < M_f$ group would be most persistent at the initial task. This should be the case because the $M_s > M_f$ group should have a much stronger motivation for the alternative task than the $M_s < M_f$ group. But the same hypothesis would also be proposed on the basis of the revised theory. However, the predicted difference is then thought of as a result of weaker motivation for the initial task and stronger motivation for the alternative task among $M_s > M_f$ subjects than among $M_s < M_f$ subjects. This was what the double explanation of the results obtained by Feather, among others, referred to (cf. p. 98).

By now it should be clear that if a similar analysis were carried out for the other three initial/alternative task combinations to be focused upon, it would show that here too the two theories would yield identical hypotheses. However, since we have seen that the revised theory reconciles a considerable number of results that cannot be explained by the achievement motivation theory as developed by Atkinson, this theory is found preferable as a basis for the hypotheses. Needless to say, this does not mean that a further comparison of the validity of the two theories is considered to be superfluous. Such a comparison will be dealt with in a later part of this work.

Now we are ready to turn to the hypotheses which serve only to outline the main problem area to be investigated in the empirical part of this work. Since the theoretical basis has been thoroughly discussed in a previous chapter, these main hypotheses follow more or less as a matter of course.

MAIN HYPOTHESES

Initial task of moderate difficulty and alternative task of low difficulty

Let us still imagine the moderately difficult task as one where P_s is about .50, and the

easy task as one where P_s is about .95. Then, considering only the influence of the m̶
to achieve success, and placing the initial and the alternative task in the motivation m
in Fig. 6, we can see that there should be a positive motivation or tendency to engage
the initial, moderately difficult task, while the motivation for the alternative, easy ta̶s̶
should be negative. Then, since the strength of the positive motivation for the initial
as well as the negative motivation for the alternative task is presumed to be proportio
to the strength of M_s, the following relationship is expected to emerge:

> Hypothesis 1. When the initial task is of moderate difficulty and the alterna-
> tive task is of low difficulty, there is a positive relationship between M_s stre̶
> and persistence at the initial task.

As regards the motive to avoid failure, we can see from the motivation model in Fig̶
that there should be a negative motivation for, or a tendency to resist, the initial, mo̶
difficult task, while the motivation for the alternative, easy task should be positive.
means that the individual should not work at the initial task at all unless there is some
positive motivation which outweighs and overcomes the tendency to resist. Since the
tendency to resist working at the initial task as well as the positive motivation for the
alternative task is presumed to be proportional to M_f strength, it is predicted:

> Hypothesis 2. When the initial task is of moderate difficulty and the alternat̶i̶
> task is of low difficulty, there is a negative relationship between M_f strength
> and persistence at the initial task.

The resultant achievement motivation or tendency is thought of as the sum of the
motivation due to M_s and that due to M_f, and therefore a combination of hypothesis 1
and 2 should imply a decrease in persistence at the initial, moderately difficult task f̶
an $M_s > M_f$ group via an $M_s \approx M_f$ group to an $M_s < M_f$ group. Needless to say, if hy̶
thesis 1 and 2 hold, we should be able to account for differences in persistence in a m̶
accurate way by taking the strength of both motives into consideration simultaneously

Initial task of low difficulty and alternative task of moderate difficulty

This situation is the reverse of that considered above, and the hypotheses therefore
follow as a matter of course. As regards M_s, there should be a negative motivation ̶
the initial task and a positive motivation for the alternative task, the strength of both
being proportionate to M_s strength. Thus, individuals with a strong M_s should not w̶
at all at the initial task unless there is some other strong motivation which outweighs
and overcomes the M_s-related tendency to resist working at the initial task. It is
predicted:

Hypothesis 3. When the initial task is of low difficulty and the alternative task is of moderate difficulty, there is a negative relationship between M_s strength and persistence at the initial task.

Since M_s and M_f function in opposite ways, it is further predicted:

Hypothesis 4. When the initial task is of low difficulty and the alternative task is of moderate difficulty, there is a positive relationship between M_f strength and persistence at the initial task.

The content of hypothesis 3 and 4 together makes us expect a decrease in persistence at the initial task from an $M_s < M_f$ group via an $M_s \approx M_f$ group to an $M_s > M_f$ group.

Initial task of high difficulty and alternative task of moderate difficulty

As a concrete example of a difficult task, I have used one for which $P_s = .05$. Placing now the initial and the alternative task in the motivation model in Fig. 6 and Fig. 7, we can see that this initial/alternative task combination is functionally equal to that considered above, i.e. to the easy/moderately difficult combination. That is, the alternative task is the same in the two cases, and the initial tasks, although in the one case easy and in the other case difficult, are assumed to have similar weighted incentive values (I_{M_s} or I_{M_f}). This means that the relationships to be hypothesized must also be the same as for the easy/moderately difficult combination:

Hypothesis 5. When the initial task is of high difficulty and the alternative task is of moderate difficulty, there is a negative relationship between M_s strength and persistence at the initial task.

Hypothesis 6. When the initial task is of high difficulty and the alternative task is of moderate difficulty, there is a positive relationship between M_f strength and persistence at the initial task.

Once more we also expect a decrease in persistence at the initial task from an $M_s < M_f$ group via an $M_s \approx M_f$ group to an $M_s > M_f$ group. It will be recalled that this change in persistence from the $M_s < M_f$ group to the $M_s > M_f$ group was also hypothesized by Feather (cf. p. 88).

Inducement of probability of success

Whether one has been concerned with persistence under high or under low P_s conditions, the general paradigm of a persistence situation has, as pointed out in the Introduction (p. 19), been one where an individual is confronted with a very difficult or insoluble task and is free to work at it as long as he wishes. In order to induce a high P_s for the initial task, the individual is instructed that he will find the task an easy one. A moderate P_s should be induced by informing the individual that the chance of success is about 50/50. However, one may ask whether it is possible to induce a moderate, and especially a high P_s in this way. And even if it is, P_s is held to change rapidly during work as a consequence of continuous failure. This change in P_s implies, of course, that one only gets restricted information about persistence under high or moderate P_s conditions. The primary object of interest is in how long the subject would have continued if the probability of success had not changed. To study this question one cannot use tasks which are in fact insoluble. Instead, as far as persistence where P_s is high is concerned, a situation should be established where the initial task is not only said to be, but in fact is a very easy one, though of such a type that the subject can continue to work at it as long as he wishes. Examples of such tasks are drawing rows of simple figures, writing rows of letters, counting buttons, etc. Similarly, persistence where P_s is moderate should be studied in a situation where the subject is confronted with an endless number of tasks at which he has a fair chance of succeeding. This persist situation is, however, a tricky one, since the circumstance that the subject experienc some degree of success very likely implies a change in P_s. The ideal situation, that in which P_s remains constant at about .50 during work, probably exists only on paper The best solution then seems to be to use a task set constructed in such a way that one may be relatively sure in which direction P_s changes during work, for example a set where there is a gradual increase in difficulty.

Within-situation differences in probability of success

When a task is presented to a group of individuals as being of a certain difficulty, one may nevertheless suspect that the perceived difficulty of the task, and thus also its incentive value, varies to a considerable extent from one subject to another. Since the motives M_s and M_f are assumed to manifest themselves in different ways dependi on the perceived difficulty of the task, the variation referred to above implies that, i addition to the general hypotheses presented in this chapter, one could also set forth more differentiated hypotheses. An example in this direction was dealt with in Chapt

(p. 90). However, the modifications to be made in the main hypotheses because of such within-situation differences in P_s are so evident that it seems somewhat superfluous to present them here. Further, such differentiated hypotheses are of interest only insofar as one has any indicator of P_s differences in a persistence situation. Finally, a consideration of the consequences of such within-situation P_s differences would also result in so rich a yield of hypotheses that the main flow of thought would probably be completely lost. All in all, it therefore seems more suitable to postpone the consideration of this matter until we are confronted with data including indicators of such within-situation P_s differences.

The problem of within-situation differences in perceived difficulty of the task may also be considered from another point of view.

Sex differences in perceived difficulty of tasks

The problem of sex differences in persistence was touched upon in connection with the consideration of the individual-oriented approach to persistence (cf. pp. 29 ff.). At that point it was concluded that there was no clear trend as to the influence of sex on persistence. On the other hand, the study by Gjesme (1971c) of sex differences in the relationship between M_s or M_f strength and level of school performance indicates that sex may nevertheless be an interesting variable in this connection.

As will have been noted, most studies of the effects of individual differences in achievement motivation have employed male subjects. As pointed out by Gjesme (1971c, p. 6), the results from the relatively few comparable studies of females have neither shown consistency with the findings among males nor internal consistency with each other. It has, however, already been noted that Gjesme calls attention to the finding that there is a greater tendency for girls than for boys to underestimate their possibility of success at a task (cf. pp. 123 f.). Gjesme also suggests that the divergence in previously obtained performance results is due to a neglect of this sex difference.

Obviously, a sex difference in P_s also has implications for the relationship between M_s or M_f strength and persistence. However, since referring to sex differences in P_s is only another way of approaching the problem discussed in the previous section, i.e. the problem of within-situation differences, it seems expedient to postpone a closer examination of this matter too until the empirical testing of the hypotheses is to be dealt with.

This completes the first part of this work, where the problem of persistence has been considered on the basis of theory and previously obtained empirical results. In the next part we shall deal with an empirical investigation, the primary purpose of which was to test the general hypotheses set forth in this chapter. The present section has, however, made it clear that we were also to look for some differences in the relationships between motive strength and persistence within each of the situational settings.

PART 2

AN EMPIRICAL CONTRIBUTION

CHAPTER 6

GENERAL INFORMATION CONCERNING THE INVESTIGATION

Since the investigation was concerned with how persistence is related to the strength of the motive to achieve success and the motive to avoid failure, the problem of assessment of these motives was a central one. Within the achievement motivation research tradition, as pointed out previously, the motive to achieve success (M_s) has usually been measured by the TAT nAch test, while the strength of the motive to avoid failure (M_f) has usually been inferred from the score on anxiety scales such as the Test Anxiety Questionnaire, the Test Anxiety Scale for Children, or the Manifest Anxiety Scale (cf. pp. 70 ff.). The present work has not followed this tradition, and therefore it is necessary to consider the measurement question in some detail before turning to the investigation proper. Background for and data on the measuring instrument used in this investigation are presented by Nygård (1970), Gjesme and Nygård (1970), Gjesme (1971a), Nygård (1971), and Nygård and Gjesme (1972).[1]

A NEW MOTIVE SCALE

Background

The Motive to Achieve Success (M_s). The frequently used TAT nAch test, as noted previously (p. 70), is a projective test where the subjects are asked to create a story around each of a set of pictures of people in different situations. These stories are scored for a number of empirically validated indices of achievement motivation. Nevertheless, the validity of the projective need achievement tests has been questioned. As an example, Klinger, in a review of achievement motivation studies, points out that the nAch scores had significant positive relationships

----

1. The instrument is also discussed in a recent article by Nygård and Gjesme (1973).

to performance level in only about one half of the studies reported (1966, pp. 295 ff.). In this connection it is, however, important to note that the reasoning presented in Chapter 4 does not imply that there should always be a positive relationship between performance level and scores assumed to indicate the strength of M_s, but that this relationship should vary from positive to negative, depending on the probability of success at the task in question. Thus, the appearance of no or negative relationships between TAT nAch scores and performance level does not in itself prove lacking validity, just as it does not prove the opposite. For a further examination of this question information about the subjects' probability of success at the tasks used in the studies is needed. But, as pointed out previously (p. 118), the probability of success problem has been taken into account only in very few of the achievement motivation studies reported, and the tasks have seldom been of such a kind that they can be confidently arranged post hoc on the probability of success continuum. Yet the reconsideration in Chapter 4 of some previously obtained "unexpected" results indicates that in the face of relationships between nAch scores and performance measures varying from positive to negative one should not too hastily conclude that the test is invalid.

However, apart from this important theoretical problem there are practical objections to such projective instruments. Thus, even for the experienced user the projective procedure is complicated and very time-consuming both as to administration and scoring. This, of course, means that much energy has to be spent in learning the procedure so that it works satisfactorily. Therefore, objective tests characterized by simplicity in administration and scoring would be preferable to projective ones. However, investigations using objective measures of M_s also reveal a somewhat confusing picture as to the validity of such instruments.

According to both McClelland (1958, pp. 25 f.) and Atkinson and Feather (1966, p. 351), objective tests do not work in this connection, and this "... is all the more bewildering in the light of the obvious utility of self-report tests of anxiety" (loc. cit.). Atkinson and Feather, however, base their conclusion on results from studies using the Edwards Personal Preference Schedule (1953) and the Achievement Risk Preference Scale (Atkinson & O'Connor, 1966, pp. 300 ff.). Regardless of the results obtained, it should be noted that both scales are constructed in a way which makes it problematical what to infer from the subjects' scores. Each item consists of two different statements, and by choosing between these two statements the subject indicates which of two motives has higher priority for him. But saying that one motive is stronger than another does not necessarily mean that the first one is a strong motive.

Other results are, however, reported which indicate that Atkinson and Feather's conclusion that objective tests do not work is too strong. Thus, Myers (1965), Furst (1966), and Buxton (1966) all report significant relationships between fairly direct motivation measures (the scores on simple questionnaires or self-rating scales) and important validity criteria such as grade point average and teachers' ratings of motivation. A similar scale was constructed for Norwegian Junior High School students, and the results corresponded very closely to those obtained by the above-mentioned three investigators (cf. Nygård, 1970, pp. 12 ff.). However, the work on the Norwegian scale led to the realization that such scales have a common weakness which from a theoretical point of view makes the obtained relationships to validity criteria rather uninteresting. Thus, the student is asked whether he is eager in the school situation, whether he works harder than others in his class, whether he prepares himself very well for examinations, etc., that is, the scales very often refer to behaviour in an achievement situation. When such scales are used in investigations directed towards relations between motive strength and behaviour, one gets a clear circularity in the research, in that the motive measure assumes all that it was intended to predict: One asks for behaviour in achievement situations, and then uses the answers to predict behaviour in the same situations.

In addition to this weakness the item examples also illustrate another defect of clear significance from a theoretical point of view. The student is asked whether he experiences himself as eager, hardworking, etc., in the school situation. As Gjesme and Nygård realized (1970, p. 5), the answers should in this case be an indicator of the strength of the student's motivation or tendency to engage in the school situation rather than of the strength of his motive to achieve success. It may well be that a student has a strong motive to achieve without reflecting this positively in school behaviour, for example because the school situation does not represent any challenge to him.

Then, to conclude, while scales like those discussed above may be serviceable in certain practical situations where one is interested in charting certain types of behaviour, they are too loaded with weaknesses to be usable within the context of achievement motivation research. This is the reason why work was started on developing a scale more in accordance with achievement motivation theory. But before focusing on this work, we shall for a moment return to the problem of measuring the motive to avoid failure.

The Motive to Avoid Failure (M_f). This motive is regarded as a capacity to anticipate negative affects in achievement situations, i.e. in situations where there
is a considerable degree of uncertainty as to whether the individual will succeed
or not. The test anxiety scales, which are the most frequently used instruments
for the assessment of the strength of M_f, deal with subjects' experiences in terms
of negative affects in achievement situations. Thus, these tests are in accordance
with the theory behind the M_f concept as far as the affective aspect is concerned.
However, in the same way as was the case with the objective tests discussed
above, the items in the test anxiety questionnaires refer, as the names of the
scales indicate, to specific achievement situations, i.e. to test situations. Thus,
as far as they are used to measure M_f, the scales are open to the same criticism
as the objective M_s measures (Gjesme & Nygård, 1970, p. 6). That is, the scores probably reflect strength of avoidance motivation in a particular situation,
more than strength of the student's motive to avoid failure, which may or may
not be aroused in this specific situation. Thus, even for M_f it should be possible
to develop a measuring instrument more in accordance with the underlying motivation theory.

The Achievement Motive Scale (AMS)

Construction. Because of the objections to the use of scales like those discussed
above within achievement motivation research, a new scale was developed (Gjesme
& Nygård, 1970). This project was based on the following two main considerations:

(a) Since the motives M_s and M_f may be characterized as capacities to experience affects in connection with achievement situations, a scale intended to
measure M_s should be loaded with items referring to positive affects, while a
scale intended to measure M_f should be loaded with items referring to negative
affects (ibid., p. 3).

(b) The arousal of the motive is assumed to depend on the perceived possibility of succeeding or failing in the situation in question. Then, since one has to
ask for affects experienced in some situations, differences in motive strength can
be inferred from the answers only if the situations referred to offer the same
chances of success to all the individuals being tested (ibid., pp. 5 f.). If this is
not the case, we have again a measure reflecting differences in motivation strength
rather than in motive strength.

Guided by these considerations, a scale containing 30 items was constructed, the first 15 items intended to measure M_s and therefore referring to positive affects, the second half of the scale intended to measure M_f and accordingly referring to negative affects. The instrument was constructed like a Likert scale (Likert, 1932), and two item examples serve to illustrate its characteristics. The following item is intended to measure M_s: "I feel pleasure when working on tasks that are somewhat difficult for me." The next one is intended to measure M_f: "I become anxious when I meet a problem I don't understand at once." The examples show that: (a) the items refer to positive and negative affects respectively; (b) the items are focused on situations assumed to arouse about the same degree of uncertainty as to the chance of success by referring to tasks being "somewhat difficult for me" and to "a problem I don't understand at once".

The scale is administered as a group test. The items are read aloud by the administrator, and on an answer sheet the subjects mark one of the following alternatives, which are weighted on a four-point scale:

"Is very true of me" ("Passer svært godt") (4)

"Is fairly true of me" ("Passer ganske godt") (3)

"Is partly true of me" ("Passer ikke så verst") (2)

"Is not at all true of me" ("Passer slett ikke") (1)

In the general introduction of the scale to the subjects it is emphasized that there are no right or wrong answers, it is simply a question of how well each of a number of statements applies to them. The subjects are also told that the answers will not be reported to anybody else at the school.

Since an individual may have both a strong motive to achieve success and a strong motive to avoid failure, the general introduction of the scale also contains an instruction to the subjects that if they experience both positive and negative affects in the situations referred to, they are to disregard as far as possible the negative affects when marking items assumed to reflect M_s, and disregard the positive affects when marking M_f items.

The scores on the first 15 items are summarized to a total M_s score, those on the last 15 items to a total M_f score.

Try-Outs. The Achievement Motive Scale (AMS) was first administered under neutral conditions to two junior high school classes in 7th grade, 26 girls and 20 boys, in June 1970. Since the results from the first try-out were regarded as promising, a second try-out was carried out in October 1970, this time on a larger sample, consisting of 460 9th-graders, 246 girls and 214 boys. Further, in order to get an indication of the stability of the scores over relatively long periods of time, the 7th-grade sample was retested after an interval of six months. The results from these try-outs have been presented in detail by Gjesme (1971a), Nygård (1971), and Nygård & Gjesme (1972), and are only reported below in summary. However, the theoretical basis for the analyses of the data is here dealt with somewhat more thoroughly than was the case in the above-mentioned reports.

The basis for the work on the scale was the domain-sampling model (Nunnally, 1967, p. 175), implying a consideration of the M_s items as a random sample of items from the hypothetical domain of items measuring M_s, and those in the M_f part as a random sample of items from the hypothetical domain of items measuring M_f. Empirically this should show itself in a positive correlation between item scores and total scores on each part of the scale. The analyses showed that for the M_s part of the scale the correlations between item score and total test score (results in parentheses referring to the 9th-grade sample) varied from +.22 to +.62 (from +.32 to +.51), the mean correlation coefficient being +.41 (+.40), while the corresponding correlations for the M_f part of the scale ranged from +.34 to +.72 (from +.42 to +.60), the mean correlation coefficient being +.53 (+.53). The results seemed satisfactory in relation to the above-mentioned basis for the work.

Considering the M_s items as a sample from the hypothetical domain of M_s items, and the M_f items as a sample from the domain of M_f items, the reliability of each part of the scale may be estimated by the coefficient alpha (Cronbach, 1951), being the mean of all possible split-half coefficients, and representing the expected correlation of the test with another test of the same length, containing items from the same domain (Nunnally, 1967, pp. 196 f.). Thus, the reliability for the M_s part in terms of the alpha coefficient tells how representative the M_s items are of the whole population of items of this kind measuring the attribute. The alpha coefficient for the M_f part of the scale may be interpreted in a comparable way.

The computations gave $\alpha = .60$ ($\alpha = .80$) for the M_s part of the scale, and $\alpha = .81$ ($\alpha = .88$) for the M_f part. On the basis of the results from the second and most extensive try-out (those given in parentheses) particularly, the scale is judged to have an adequate reliability as long as it is used for the study of problems like those dealt with in the present work, i.e. basic research regarding strength of relationships or differences between groups, which in principle is the same thing (cf. Helmstadter, 1966, pp. 83 f., and Nunnally, 1967, p. 226). On the other hand it should be clear that the reliability of the scale is too low for making important practical decisions for a student, in which case a reliability of .90 should be regarded as a minimum (Nunnally, 1967, p. 226).

The domain-sampling point of departure implies that the characteristics dealt with above are also closely related to the question of the validity of the scale, in that the coefficient alpha can be regarded as a measure of the domain validity (Tryon, 1957, pp. 236 f.), i.e. as an indicator of how validly one can interpret the measures as representative of a certain set of possible measures (Cronbach, Rajaratnam, & Gleser, 1963, p. 157). Another question which also has to do with both reliability and validity is that of the stability of the scores over relatively long periods of time. It will be recalled that the achievement motivation theory assumes the motives to be relatively stable personality characteristics (cf. pp. 59 f.). In this connection the interest is in the results from the retesting of the 7th-grade sample after six months, an interval so long that the retest results are probably very little affected by the first testing. As to the M_s scale results, the scores from the second administration correlated +.71 with those from the first administration, and the mean values from the first and second testing were 48.07 and 47.29. The test-retest correlation for the M_f scale results was +.65, and the mean values 28.26 and 27.75. Thus, not only the relative position, but also the absolute score of the individual tends to remain fairly constant over a relatively long period of time on both parts of the scale. On the assumption that the scores are fairly valid measures of the motives in question, the results lend considerable support to the conception of the motives as relatively stable personality attributes.

In previous research scores assumed to reflect strength of M_s have usually been relatively unrelated to scores assumed to reflect strength of M_f (cf. pp. 73 f.). This question was also considered here, in connection with the try-out of the scale in the 9th-grade sample, where a slight negative correlation between the M_s and M_f scores was obtained ($r = -.20$). Thus, on the assumption that the instrument measures what it was intended to measure, the result supports the viewpoint that the two motives vary in strength relatively independently of each other.

Because of the possibility of sex differences in reactions to instruments of this type, the mean values and standard deviations for girls and boys in the 9th-grade sample were compared. The results for the M_s part of the scale were $\overline{X}_b = 44.35$, $\overline{X}_g = 43.36$, $s_b = 6.15$, $s_g = 6.09$. For the M_f part of the scale the results were $\overline{X}_b = 30.52$, $\overline{X}_g = 31.78$, $s_b = 7.92$, $s_g = 8.01$. The sex differences may be characterized as negligible.

So far we have been only peripherically concerned with the validity question. Focusing now more directly upon this problem, we should once more take into consideration that this is closely related to that of the validity of the underlying theory. Thus, as pointed out by Krause (1967, p. 281), the failure of an instrument to produce results consistent with the derivations from the theory discredits the instrument only if the theoretical propositions are treated as if they were true. This fact implies a clear restriction as to what kind of validity studies are meaningful. Validity examinations have to be based on the least debatable parts of a theory.

In the present case the validity was evaluated by examining the relationship between the scores on the motive test and school performance level, indicated by school marks. To repeat, M_s is assumed to manifest itself by engagement in achievement situations, while M_f is assumed to manifest itself in resistance towards such situations. In an unselected group of pupils there should therefore be a positive relationship between M_s scores and performance level, and a negative relationship between M_f scores and performance level. On the other hand, since performance is assumed to be determined by several variables other than the motives M_s and M_f, such as other aroused motives, ability level, and so forth, the strength of these relationships was expected to be only moderate.

Analyses of the data from the 7th-grade sample revealed correlations between M_s scores and standpoint marks in the subjects Norwegian, English, and mathematics varying from +.20 to +.54, and correlations between M_f scores and the same marks varying from -.36 to -.63. The results were quite similar for girls and boys.

As to the 9th-grade sample the motive scores were correlated with the results on achievement tests in Norwegian, English, and mathematics. Here too, all correlations were in the expected direction, but on the whole they were weaker, most M_s-related correlations being about +.20, and the M_f-related ones between -.10 and -.20. In this connection it should, however, be noted that the criterion in terms of results on common achievement tests for all pupils in 9th grade was a problematical one. Thus, the pupils had followed courses in the subjects in question at various levels of scope and difficulty, and therefore they were very differently qualified for the achievement tests. Under such conditions high correlations would have caused more surprise than the low ones obtained.

Since motives are considered as relatively stable personality characteristics, they are expected not only to influence performance in the present and future, but also to have influenced the pupils' performance in the past. Hence the scale, to be satisfactory, should also be applicable in postdictions. Therefore the motive scores for the 9th-grade sample were correlated with marks obtained at the end of the 7th grade. The correlations were rather low, but they were all in the expected direction, i. e. the M_s-related ones were positive and the M_f-related ones negative.

Then, to sum up, the results obtained in the two try-outs referred to above were all in the expected direction, and quite similar for boys and girls. Since school performance level is assumed to be influenced by several variables other than the motives M_s and M_f, it seems reasonable to emphasize this consistency in the results more than the size of the correlations obtained. From this point of view, the relationships revealed are found to provide a satisfactory basis for using the scale in subsequent achievement motivation studies.

SAMPLE

Sample size

Within behavioural research one important and difficult question to be considered before carrying out an investigation is that of the size of the sample to be used. Other things being equal, the larger the sample, the more precise the obtained information. The difficulty lies in the degree of insecurity we are willing to accept. Thus, given (1) the risk of mistakenly rejecting the null hypothesis when it is true (α risk), (2) the risk of mistakenly not rejecting the null hypothesis when it is false (β risk), and (3) the limits for what is regarded as a zero relationship in the population from which the sample stems, the sample size is also determined. These problems were considered prior to the carrying through of the investigation, where we abided by an α risk of .05, a β risk of .20, and a lower limit of .20 for the population correlation of interest, which implied that we had to aim at a sample of minimum 153 subjects. However, the next section will show that when it came to the point, we could not get a random sample from a defined population, and the risks referred to above apply only to the case of a random sample. Since we do not know to what extent the characteristics of our sample deviated from those of a random one, it is thus of little interest to go into any more detail here with respect to these problems. However, the questions considered here are judged to be very central ones within behavioural research, and yet for some reason only very rarely considered. An account of the procedure for determining the size of the sample, although not of much interest in connection with this particular investigation, may therefore nevertheless be of some general value. A somewhat detailed description of the determination of the size of the sample is therefore given in Appendix A, to which the interested reader is referred.

Subjects

Ultimately, our interest is in how persistence in different situations is related to all possible values of the motive variables. In other words, our farthest interest is in a hypothetical population of individuals of today and of the future with all potential values of motive strength. In sampling from such a population there is no possibility of listing the elements for random assignment to the sample. In such cases the sample of individuals has to be selected in a more or less "haphazard" way, depending on the practical possibilities, which are often very limited.

In the present case practical considerations made it desirable to restrict the investigation to pupils at one and the same grade level. Since there seemed to be no reason why the relationship between motive strength and persistence should vary with age level, this was found to be a justifiable approach. On the other hand, to maximize the probability of getting the whole range of possible motive strengths represented in the sample, one had to focus upon a grade level where the selection mechanisms within the educational system have not played a decisive role. This should be the case in the compulsory school. Since the Achievement Motive Scale (AMS) had been tried out only in the upper grades of the compulsory school (grades 7 and 9) we had also to choose one of these grade levels.

Another consideration which influenced the selection of subjects had to do with the problem area itself. It will be noted that the problem of persistence in a situation where the individual is confronted with a task of a certain difficulty and is free to cease working at it and turn to some alternative task whenever he wishes, is relatively closely related to problems encountered when using self-instructional materials in the school. In such work situations, where pupils are under far less control than in the more traditional school situation, their achievement-related motives are expected to be of clearer importance for for example persistence at work than in the more teacher-controlled situation. These problems will not be further discussed in the present report, but by carrying out the investigation in school classes where such self-instructional material was employed, the motive measures obtained could be used in subsequent studies of the relationship between motive strength and various aspects of behaviour in self-instructional learning situations.

Considering these circumstances the National Council for Innovation in Education (Forsøksrådet for skoleverket) gave permission for the investigation to be carried out among 7th graders participating in the IMU project, a project where self-instructional material in mathematics was tried out. To prevent, as far as possible, participation in the IMU project itself from influencing the results, it was decided to carry out the investigation at the beginning of the school year, i.e. at a period when the pupils had had only limited experience with the self-instructional material.

Within these limits the final selection was influenced by the available resources in terms of time and grants for the project. First, it was decided to use the same subjects in all three persistence situations to be examined (cf. pp. 128 ff.), thus reducing the expense connected with the assessment of the independent variables to a minimum. In this connection it should also be mentioned that if one were to use different subjects in the three different situational settings, the variability in persistence might to some extent be due to differences between the samples existing prior to the investigation. By using the same subjects, this problem was avoided. On the other hand, when the same subjects are used in different conditions, one has to be aware of possible carry-over effects from one condition to another.

A second consequence of the restricted resources was that the data collection had to be limited to the Oslo area. At the same time it had to be taken into account that many schools within this area, and especially the schools within the City of Oslo itself, are frequently burdened with research and development work of various kinds, and pupils from such schools ought therefore, if possible, not to be included in the sample. Further, to prevent communication between the pupils in the breaks from influencing the results, it was found desirable to include only one class from each school in the sample. [1]

Prior to the investigation it had been estimated that the sample should include at least 153 subjects (cf. pp. 147 f.). To ensure getting a sample of at least this size it was calculated with a mean class size of only about 20 pupils, which meant that we had to employ eight classes, i.e. one class from each of eight different schools.

Earlier (p. 148) the importance of including the whole range of possible motive strengths in the sample has been emphasized. Previous investigations have demon-

----

1. Another class from each school participated in an investigation concerning the relationship between motive strength (M_s and M_f) and performance level at tasks of different difficulty. This investigation is not dealt with in the present report.

strated a relatively clear relationship between social background and strength of the motives M_s and M_f (Nygård, 1967, pp. 65 ff; 1968, pp. 7 ff; 1969, pp. 226 ff.). Therefore, by selecting pupils from a very wide range of social backgrounds there seemed to be rather good reason to assume that virtually the whole range of possible motive strengths were represented in the sample.

These considerations, together with the fact that only a restricted number of schools participated in the IMU project, meant that there was in fact no real choice as to which schools the sample could be taken from. Finally we were left with three classes from urban districts (Strømmen, Lillestrøm, Lørenskog), three classes from mixed urban and rural areas (Skedsmokorset, Kløfta, Bingsfoss), and two classes from more typically rural areas (Høland, Gjerdrum), a total of 174 subjects, 90 boys and 84 girls, i.e. a sample somewhat larger than what had been aimed at. The subjects represented a very wide range of social backgrounds, and despite the fact that they were not selected in any random fashion, they were judged to be fairly representative of 7th graders in general, at least in eastern Norway.

The persistence tasks were administered in three sessions, and three of the 174 subjects participating in the moderately difficult/easy persistence situation were absent from their classes during the administration of the easy/moderately difficult task set, while four subjects were absent during the administration of the difficult/moderately difficult task set. This is the reason why the results reported in the next chapter are based on varying numbers of subjects.

The problem of significance testing

At the beginning of the previous section (p. 148) it was underscored that ultimately our interest is in how persistence in different situations is related to all possible values on the motive variables. Practical circumstances made it necessary to restrict the attention to motive measures obtained from individuals at one and the same grade level. This was found to be a justifiable approach, since there was no reason to believe that the motives would work in different ways at different age levels. However, it appears from the foregoing that although the subjects were selected in a way ensuring a wide range in M_s and M_f strength, they did not constitute a random sample from the population of individuals with all potential values of M_s and M_f strengths. The question therefore arose whether it would be legitimate to apply tests of significance in this case.

Stated conventionally, significance testing means examining the probability that the observed relationship between the variables in question could have occurred in a random sample if the true population relationship were zero. Stated otherwise, the sample serves as a basis for generalizing to a specified population. The α and β risks discussed in the section on sample size also refer only to cases of randomly selected samples. Thus, although the M_s and M_f strengths of our subjects were thought to be fairly representative of the strengths of these motives in general, the use of a selection procedure like the one scheduled above precludes the use of significance testing as a basis for generalizing. That is, from a conventional point of view the answer as to the legitimacy of significance testing in this case should be no.

However, following a line of reasoning similar to that presented by Gold (1969, pp. 42 ff.), Winch and Campbell (1969, pp. 142 f.), among others, we may make a roundabout approach, stating the problem somewhat differently: We are interested in the relationship between for example M_s strength and persistence at a particular task. We examine this problem in a group not asserted to constitute a random sample from the population of possible M_s strengths. To make the idea clear, let us assume that the subjects are divided into a low (score 1), a moderate (score 2), and a high (score 3) M_s group. Following the reasoning of Winch and Campbell (ibid., p. 142), let us further assume that these three motive groups constitute a single homogeneous set with respect to persistence at the task in question, i.e. that there is no correlation between motive score and persistence score. This is our null hypothesis, and our plan is to examine the plausibility of this assumption.

This examination can be done by randomly assigning the values 1, 2, and 3 to the subjects in such a way that we get three new subgroups of the same size as the three motive groups, and correlating these values with the persistence scores. This procedure is repeated until we get a large distribution of correlation coefficients, which represents the sampling distribution of correlation coefficients. Then we are permitted to ask the question: Is our M_s variable one that orders the data into subgroups in such a way that its correlation with persistence scores is well within the sampling distribution obtained in this way, or did it produce a quite unusual correlation? This is what the significance test tells us. We ask what the probability is that dividing the set into three subsets on the basis of a variable which really does not correlate with persistence would result in a relationship as strong as that observed between M_s scores and persistence scores. The result then tells us how likely the relationship would appear by chance alone. In other words, we try to interpret our observed data by relating them to a model, that of a random process model. Within this way of reasoning, Winch and Campbell argue, there is every justification to run a test of significance (ibid., p. 143). They argue that on the whole the social scientist is better off for using the significance test than for ignoring it, since "... it does provide a relevant and useful way of assessing the relative likelihood that a real difference exists and is worthy of interpretive attention, as opposed to the hypothesis that the set of data could be a haphazard arrangement" (ibid. , p. 140).

However, it should be clear, as also pointed out by Winch and Campbell (ibid. , p. 143), that the establishment of a statistically significant relationship is only one step towards establishing an interpretation of the relationship, that of excluding the hypothesis of chance. The other steps involve examining a list of other possible threats to internal as well as external validity, such as for example the possibility that the resulting differences in persistence are not due to motive differences per se, but to some bias in the selection of subjects from each of the motive levels. The important point in this connection is, however, that the test of significance indicates the degree to which there is any point in going about the task of examining the possibility of such threats to validity.

Thus, what seems unreasonable is to base a high degree of confidence in a single significant result, without considering possible threats to validity. And even if no such validity threats can be demonstrated, a significant result does not, of course, prove a theory, but only probes it. Therefore, as also pointed out by Peaker (1968, p. 207), a significant result encourages us to look for the same relationship once more under similar circumstances, and if the strength of the relationship is strikingly significant we may even be encouraged to look for it not only under closely similar, but also under rather different circumstances.

Finally, since a great deal of attention has been paid to the problem of significance testing, it has also to be underscored that statistical significance is a minimum and only one criterion against which the results should be evaluated. Statistical significance should not be confused with the strength of an association. The latter, which has very often been disregarded within social sciences, ought to be another central theme in the evaluation process.

MATERIAL AND GENERAL PROCEDURE

Assessment of motives and test-taking attitudes

The strength of the motive to achieve success (M_s) and that of the motive to avoid failure (M_f) were inferred from the scores on the Achievement Motive Scale (AMS), described in detail previously in this chapter. Since this scale is of the self-report kind, it was also of interest to get an indication of the extent to which the answers

obtained were affected by tendencies on the part of the subjects to give false
and misleading information about themselves. Therefore, following the administration of AMS, 10 items either similar or identical to those in the lie
scale developed by S. B. Sarason and his co-workers (1960, pp. 108 ff.) were
read aloud to the subjects, and on an answer sheet the subjects had to circle
one of the alternative answers "yes" or "no". These items referred to experiences assumed to be so universal that if the subjects were able and willing
to report their experiences without distortion, they should answer "yes" to
all or nearly all of the items (e. g. "Are you ever sorry about something you
have done?", "Do you ever worry that you won't be able to do something you
want to do?"). Thus, the number of "noes" circled on the answer sheet was
held to be an approximate indicator of the strength of the subject's tendency
to provide misleading information.

Tasks employed in the persistence situations

The hypotheses concern relationships between M_s or M_f strength and persistence
at the initial task in three different situations, with respect to the difficulty level
of the initial and the alternative task. It was therefore crucial to find tasks of
clearly differing difficulty levels. As far as the initial task was concerned, this
demand was satisfied by using an anagrams task, a simple figure-drawing task,
and an unsolvable labyrinth task as the initial one in the moderately difficult/
easy, easy/moderately difficult, and difficult/moderately difficult situations
respectively. A more complete description of these tasks is given in Chapter 7,
where each of the three persistence situations is dealt with more specifically.

The alternative tasks were of little interest in this connection, since the problem to be examined was that of persistence at the initial task under different
conditions, i. e. since we were not here concerned with what happened after the
individual left the initial task and turned to the alternative one. Therefore,
there seemed to be no need to spend much effort on the working out of alternative
tasks. A more or less arbitrary selection resulted in a set of easy arithmetic
tasks, a set of crossword puzzles, and a set of moderately difficult arithmetic
tasks as the alternative in the moderately difficult/easy, easy/moderately difficult,
and difficult/moderately difficult situations respectively. The subjects did not
get any information beforehand as to what kind of task the alternative was, but
were only told that it was easier or more difficult than the initial one. Therefore, the kind of alternative should not affect persistence at the initial task.

Some Comments on the Tasks Used. The brief description given above shows that the tasks used in the three persistence situations varied not only in difficulty, but also in kind. There were several reasons why no attempt was made to work out task sets varying only in difficulty level. First, since the same subjects were to be used in all three persistence situations, the possible carryover effects from one persistence situation to another had to be considered. The use of tasks of the same kind, varying only in difficulty level, under the different persistence conditions would probably increase rather than reduce the likelihood of such carryover effects. Secondly, the problem of holding all factors except difficulty level constant from one situation to another is in itself a far from simple one. The criteria of equality might themselves be highly problematical, especially since the investigator's criteria would not necessarily coincide with the subject's own criteria of equality.

Further, variation not only in difficulty level, but also in kind of task from one persistence situation to another should be of no significance insofar as the interest is only in the relative position of the subjects with respect to persistence under different difficulty conditions. To exemplify, the relationship between M_s strength and persistence at an initial task was hypothesized to be positive when the initial task was a moderately difficult one and the alternative task an easy one, and negative when the inital task was an easy one and the alternative a moderately difficult task. This should be the case whether or not the two initial tasks were of the same kind (e.g. both anagrams tasks), i.e. varying only in difficulty level. We have made no reservations that the relationships hypothesized should hold for only particular kinds of tasks.

Taking these circumstances into account, there did not seem to be obvious advantages connected with the use of tasks in the three persistence situations varying only in difficulty level. The initial/alternative task combinations briefly described above were assumed to satisfy the demand for combinations in which the hypotheses set forth could be tested.

However, while the motives M_s and M_f are assumed to affect persistence in different ways depending on the difficulty level of the tasks, persistence is not, of course, thought to be determined by this particular personality by situation interaction alone. It may well be that task characteristics other than difficulty level influence persistence in an independent way or, what is more likely, through some kind of interaction with personality characteristics other than M_s and M_f. Therefore, if one goes beyond the problem area outlined by the hypotheses and looks for changes in absolute persistence level from one situation to another as a function of M_s and/or M_f strength, then all factors but difficulty level should be held constant. Only under such conditions should also the change in <u>absolute</u> persistence be due to the M_s and M_f by task difficulty interaction or to some main effect of difficulty level. However, the present investigation cannot shed light on these questions.

General procedure

The three sets of persistence tasks used in the investigation were tried out in the last part of the spring term of 1971 in three classes of 7th graders. A booklet containing the initial task and an envelope with another booklet containing the alternative task were passed out to each subject. The subjects were instructed that they were free to quit the initial task and turn to the alternative one whenever they wished.[1] A stop clock was placed on the administrator's desk in such a way that it could not be seen by the subjects, and the time for each subject's turning over to the alternative task was noted. The tasks were group-administered (class-administered), and even though some subjects looked at what their class-. mates did before they gave up the initial task and switched to the alternative one, the main impression was that the procedure worked satisfactorily, most subjects changing task relatively independently of each other. It was therefore found justifiable to use this group procedure in the investigation proper.

The investigation was carried out by the author in the autumn term of 1971. For each class there were three school periods of 45 minutes each for the investigation, the first one at the very beginning of the school year (August). The Achievement Motive Scale (AMS) and the items intended to reflect test-taking attitudes were administered at the beginning of the first period. After that the moderately difficult/easy persistence task set was administered. The other two persistence task sets followed at intervals of two weeks. Half of the classes got the easy/moderately difficult set as the second one, and the other half the difficult/moderately difficult set as the second one.

<u>Some Comments on the General Procedure</u>. The fact that only three school periods were allotted for the investigation created certain problems which have to be commented on.

----

1. The instructions for the persistence tasks are presented in Appendixes B, C, and D.

Ideally, to prevent the measuring of the motives from influencing persistence at the tasks in question, or the opposite, to prevent participating in the persistence situations from affecting the motive measures, the AMS should be administered quite independently of the persistence tasks. However, in the present case the motive measurement had to be carried out in connection with one of the persistence tasks, and here the best solution seemed to be to administer the AMS prior to the first persistence task set. As the AMS was followed by the test-taking attitude items and subsequently by the distribution of the booklets containing the persistence task set, there was at least a small interval between the motive measurement and the administration of the persistence task.

The AMS and the subsequent test-taking attitude items took a little more than 15 minutes. Thus, there was at the very best only about 25 minutes left of the school period for the administration of the first persistence task, as compared with an entire session of 45 minutes for the two subsequent tasks. However, on the basis of the results from the try-out of the tasks, a period of 25 minutes was held to be fairly adequate, since only a very few subjects worked for more than 20 minutes at the initial task.

We have previously touched on the problem of carryover effects from one persistence situation to another. The fact that there was an interval of two weeks between each task set was thought to reduce the likelihood of such effects. It would nevertheless be of interest, especially with a view to possible future investigations, to get an indication of whether such effects were present. One way to obtain this information would be to administer the task sets in a counterbalanced sequence, and compare the results at each task set for those having it as the first, the second, and the third set. However, since less time was available for the first persistence situation, such a procedure would imply that even if some subjects in the two subsequent persistence situations spent the entire school session at the initial task, the highest attainable persistence score could not exceed that corresponding to the time limit for the first persistence session. It was in order to prevent loss of information in this way that all subjects were given one and the same task set, i.e. the moderately difficult/easy set, as the first one. Since half of the classes got the easy/moderately difficult set as the second one, and the other half got it as the last one, some information about possible carryover effects would nevertheless be obtained. While even more information might have been obtained if all three task sets had been administered in a counterbalanced sequence, it should on the other hand be clear that counterbalancing does not in itself remove carryover effects, but only serves to spread these effects over the various situational conditions. In this way it may also to some extent mask those effects which are of main interest. Counterbalancing is therefore a double-edged tool, and it is not too obvious that we would have been much better off with a complete counterbalancing, even if there had been no time limit problems to take into account.

METHOD OF ANALYSIS

Single motive measures and persistence

In the previous chapter linear relationships, either positive or negative, were hypothesized between strength of the motives M_s and M_f on the one hand and persistence on the other. That is, it was predicted that persistence would increase or decrease in a linear fashion with increase in motive strength. Since it is clear in this case which are the independent or predictor variables and which is the dependent one, the hypotheses may be said to deal with regression problems (Hays, 1963, pp. 492 f.). Therefore, the data related to the hypotheses were examined by analysis of regression, which is an analysis of variance adapted to problems of this kind. Like the usual analysis of variance it rests, as far as significance testing is concerned, on the assumption that at each level of the independent variable (X) the scores on the dependent variable (Y) are normally distributed, and that the variances of Y scores are the same at all levels of X. It has, however, been repeatedly shown that F and t tests are very robust statistics (e.g. Baker, Hardyck, & Petrinovich, 1966, pp. 301 ff; Boneau, 1960, pp. 53 ff.; Norton, 1952, cited by Lindquist, 1953, pp. 78 ff.), so that unless there are serious deviations from normality, there is little reason to worry about the assumptions.

Let us then consider the application of this method to those persistence problems with which we are concerned. Exemplifying by the relationship between M_s scores and persistence scores, the regression equation reads $Y' = a + bX$, where Y' = predicted persistence score, $X = M_s$ score, b = the coefficient for linear regression of Y on X, giving the slope of the regression line or telling how many units the persistence score increases or decreases for every increase of one unit in the M_s score, and a = a constant determining the general level of the regression line. The ratio (F) of the variance accounted for by this regression line to the residual variance (or the within-group variance) tells whether the slope of the regression line has to be regarded as significantly different from zero.

This method of analysis, however, provides answers not only to the question of whether there is a linear trend in the results, but also to whether there are significant deviations from linearity, i.e. whether the means of the observed Y's for the arrays of X's deviate significantly from the linear regression line (Draper & Smith, 1966, pp. 26 ff.). The presence of such deviations is indicated by a lack of correspondence between the sum of squares accounted for by the regression line and the total between-groups sum of squares. The ratio (F) of the variance representing this lack of correspondence to the within-group variance tells whether the deviations should be regarded as significantly different from zero. The possibility of such deviations should be considered, since if they are present, it means that a straight line does not represent a good fit to the data.

A particular problem was encountered in connection with the dependent (persistence) variable in the moderately difficult/easy situation. This variable took the two values 0 and 1 only. When employing parametric techniques, such as for example analysis of regression, the dependent variable is usually a continuous one. This does not, however, mean that parametric techniques cannot be used in cases where the dependent variable takes only two values. Rather, it is recommended that parametric methods be used as an approximation in preference to χ^2 methods even where the data are ones and zeroes only (Cochran, 1950, p. 262; see also Cochran, 1954, p. 441, and Cohen, 1965, pp. 111 ff.). The special case of using analysis of regression under such conditions is illustrated by Armitage (1971, pp. 336 ff.) and by Guilford (1965, pp. 381 f.), and is also proposed by Cohen in his article on regression analysis as a general data-analytic system (1968, p. 427). The regression function obtained in this case with the dependent variable taking the values 0 and 1 only can be shown to yield the same result as the linear discriminant function, which is used to classify observations into groups on the basis of known measurements (Armitage, 1971, p. 336). In the case of persistence in the moderately difficult/easy situation, using discriminant analysis would mean to decide on the basis of the motive scores whether an individual should be expected to belong to the group with a low persistence score (score 0) or to that with a high persistence score (score 1). However, since regression analysis had to be used in the analysis of the data from the other two persistence situations dealt with, we also preferred this method in connection with the dichotomous data from the moderately difficult/easy situation.

Having assigned the value 0 to the group which is low in persistence and 1 to that which is high in persistence, we may use the regression equation $Y' = a + bX$, where Y' = predicted persistence score, and X = motive score, to estimate whether the most likely outcome for an individual with a particular motive score is a high

or a low persistence score. If the predicted score exceeds .50 it means that
the probability is above .50 that the individual is a high persister, i.e. the most
likely outcome is a high persistence score. From the regression equation it
should then be possible to estimate the probability of a high persistence score
at any motive score level. One should, however, be aware that the regression
equation may give predictions outside the possible range, i.e. greater than 1.00
or less than .00, owing to the fact that the restriction of the predicted scores to
the range zero to one is not included in the calculating routine. Thus, a strict
interpretation of the predicted values in terms of probabilities cannot be made.
Rather, as proposed by H.T. Amundsen (in Retterstøl,. 1966, p. 194), negative
estimates should be interpreted as practically zero, while estimates above one
should be interpreted as practically one.

Hitherto we have been concerned only with the very simplest kind of regression
problem, that with only one predictor variable. The theoretical part deals, however, with two main predictor variables, the motive to achieve success and the
motive to avoid failure, and therefore their joint effect on persistence is also
of interest.

The combination of motive measures

Since M_s and M_f measures have been combined in different ways, some attention
should initially be paid to the methods used in previous achievement motivation
research.

One of these methods has.been to subtract the standard score on the instrument
used to measure M_f from the standard score on that used to measure M_s (Moulton,
1965, p. 402; O'Connor, Atkinson, & Horner, 1966, p. 236; C.P. Smith, 1964,
p. 525; among others). This procedure has as its basis the assumption made in
the theory of achievement motivation that the motives M_s and M_f have diametrically opposite effects. If this is correct, it should be sufficient to focus upon the
difference between their strengths only, disregarding the strength of each of the
motives. However, such a procedure does not give the reader any opportunity to
evaluate the validity of the assumption made. To exemplify, consider the possibility that subjects with a high M_s and a high M_f score are getting the highest scores
on a dependent variable, while subjects with a low M_s and a low M_f score are getting the lowest scores on the dependent variable. In this case the difference method
gives both groups of subjects a resultant motive score near zero ($M_s \approx M_f$) and the
mean score on the dependent variable for these subjects may very well fall between

the means for those with a clearly positive $(M_s > M_f)$ and those with a clearly negative $(M_s < M_f)$ resultant motive score, thus fitting in nicely with the theory. Nevertheless the results from this hypothetical case give a very misleading picture of the true relationships. Therefore, this method should not be used before the stage in the validation of the theory is reached where there is no doubt at all that the motives work in the assumed way. It does not seem too clear that we are at this stage yet.

Another usual procedure has been to compare the results relating to the motive groups obtained when the score distributions on the instruments used to measure the motives are dichotomized at the median. Very often, however, only the results for the high M_s/low M_f and the low M_s/high M_f groups have been compared, without any attention at all being paid to the other two possible motive constellations, i. e. to the high M_s/high M_f and the low M_s/low M_f groups (Feather, 1961, p. 555; 1963, pp. 605 ff.; 1965, pp. 205 f.; Littig, 1963, p. 419; Litwin, 1966, p. 104; among others). Theoretically, the results for the high M_s/high M_f group and the low M_s/low M_f group should fall somewhere between the results for the more clear-cut motive groups, but when the results are not reported, the reader is not offered any opportunity to evaluate this theoretical supposition. Rather, he is left with an unanswered question, and this is all the more the case since the reports in which the results for all four motive groups are presented do not always show the results from the high M_s/high M_f group and the low M_s/low M_f group to fall between those for the extreme motive groups (cf. for example Atkinson & Litwin, 1960, p. 57; Gjesme, 1971b, p. 93; 1971c, pp. 105 ff., and Raynor & Rubin, 1971, p. 39). Thus, one should not use the median split procedure without reporting the results for all groups. However, apart from the circumstance that do dichotomize variables that take on a range of values means to throw away information, there is also another problem connected with a usual analysis of variance approach. Thus, a factorial analysis of variance presupposes an equal number of subjects in the cells, i. e. uncorrelated independent variables. But a condition of no correlation between non-experimental variables, as the motives are, does rarely exist, and to orthogonalize the variables by means of subject selection or by some statistical adjustment then implies a distortion of reality. It does therefore seem more appropriate also to approach the problem of the joint influence of M_s and M_f by analysis of regression, by extending it to a multiple analysis (Draper & Smith, 1966, pp. 104 ff.), a method which does not presuppose orthogonality among the independent variables.

Multiple regression analysis is used to express the values of the dependent variable on the basis of the values on a set of predictor variables. In our case the regression equation reads $Y' = a + b_1X_1 + b_2X_2$, where Y' = predicted persistence score, $X_1 = M_s$ score, $X_2 = M_f$ score, b_1 and b_2 = coefficients for linear regression on each of the motive variables, and a = the constant determining the level of the line. By this equation one may find the most likely persistence score for any combination of M_s and M_f scores. Thus, this method takes better care of the information and therefore gives a much more complete picture of the relationships than that obtained by the above-mentioned classification of subjects into four motive groups only. If one nevertheless prefers to think in terms of motive groups, there is no difficulty in doing this on the basis of the regression equation.

Interaction effects

Hitherto in the account of the method of analysis, persistence in a given situation has been considered as a result of additive motive effects. However, one ought also to be aware of the possibility that some interactional effects are present. First, the effect of M_s on persistence may be different at different levels of M_f strength and vice versa. That is, M_s and M_f may have a joint effect on persistence over and above their separate additive effects. Secondly, in connection with the development of hypotheses we also touched upon the possibility that when a group of individuals is confronted with a persistence task said to be of a certain difficulty, there may nevertheless be considerable within-group differences in the perceived probability of success, and, as a consequence, differences in the relationship between motive strength and persistence. That is, the relationship between motive strength and persistence should be different for subjects with a relatively high and subjects with a relatively low probability of success. The same line of reasoning implies that if it is correct that girls as a group estimate their probability of success to be lower than do boys (cf. p. 135), then the relationship between motive strength and persistence should be different for boys and girls. In these cases probability of success and sex, the latter indirectly reflecting probability of success, may be regarded as "moderators" of the motive effect (Saunders, 1956, p. 209), which means that we have an interaction problem.

A usual way of analysing such problems in cases where the various independent variables have been more or less correlated has been to carry out the analyses within each of the subgroups, and then to compare the results of the analyses from each of the groups. Thus, we might for example examine the relationship between motive scores and persistence scores within the high and low probability of success group and afterwards compare the results. This is, of course, a somewhat cumbersome way of estimating the interaction effect, and, what is more serious, the partitioning into subgroups results in a drastic loss of the power of the data, due to the reduction in degrees of freedom. The loss of power can be avoided, however, by an alternative method of analysis, by drawing on the flexibility of the multiple regression analytic system, and analysing the interactional effects within this system. In a multiple regression analysis the joint effect of, for instance, M_s and M_f, over and above their separate effects, is carried by a third variable, defined by the product of the individual's M_s score and M_f score (cf. for example Cohen, 1968, p. 436, and Draper & Smith, 1966, pp. 222 ff.). Similarly, the interactional effect of motives and probability of success is carried by a variable which is the product of motive score and probability of success score. The squared partial correlations between these new variables and persistence scores gives the proportion of the variance in the persistence variable due to interaction (e. g. , M_s x M_f, M_s x P_s).

Since the principles for forming interaction variables also hold for nominal variables and for mixtures of variables (Cohen, 1968, p. 437), the question of sex differences in the relationship between motive strength and persistence may be considered in a similar way. The subjects' sex may be represented by a dummy variable (Cohen, 1968, p. 428; Draper & Smith, 1966, p. 134), by assigning an arbitrary number, e.g. 0, to all boys, and another arbitrary number, e.g. 1, to all girls. The interaction between motive strength and sex is then carried by a variable which is the product of motive score and the value on the dummy variable representing the subjects' sex, and its contribution to the variance in the persistence variable may then be determined.

Separate or combined analyses

The hypotheses deal with the relationship between motive strength and persistence in three different situations, and in the account of the method of analysis we have also referred to the data from each of the situations separately. However, it should be clear that the prediction of different relationships between motive strength and persistence under different situation conditions is simply a way of predicting motive by situation interactions. From this point of view it would seem appropriate to analyse all persistence data within one single, and, since the same subjects participated under all conditions, repeated measures design. Such an analysis would provide more statistical information than what can be obtained when the data from each of the persistence situations are treated separately. Furthermore, the treatment of the data as repeated measures would possibly also make the analysis more sensitive because of the extraction of possible systematic subject variance from the error variance.

However, despite the advantages referred to above it was found preferable to analyse the results from each of the three persistence situations separately, leaving an overall evaluation for the final discussion. One reason was that if the data from all three persistence situations were to be treated within one and the same multiple analysis of regression, this would be a very complex and un-surveyable analysis. Among other things, to be able to extract the systematic variance due to subjects (reflected in the repeated measures) a large number of dummy variables had to be used. Thus, to identify N subjects one needs N - 1 dummy variables, no matter how coded (Cohen, 1968, p. 428). However, the main reason for preferring the more simple procedure of analysing the data from each persistence situation separately lies in the nature of the data. It has already been mentioned that in the case of the moderately difficult/easy situation the dependent variable was a very crude one, taking the values 0 and 1 only. In the other two cases it was possible to use finer units of measurement. If, however, the data from all three persistence situations were to be analysed within one and the same design, then the same crude (equivalent) units of measurement had to be used in all three persistence situations, thereby squandering a considerable amount of information. This weakness is here judged not to be compensated by the fact that an overall analysis would provide additional statistical information (based only on crude data!) concerning possible main effects of the situational conditions themselves as well as motive by situation interaction effects.

The problem of class variance

As has been pointed out earlier in this chapter (p. 149) the sample consisted of pupils from eight school classes, and in such cases one has to be aware of the possibility of variance in the dependent variable due to differences be-tween the classes which from the study's theoretical point of departure may be considered as irrelevant (cf. Lindquist, 1940, pp. 21 ff.). Thus, in a study of persistence it is for example natural to think of differences between the classes in working habits as one such possible source of irrelevant variance, some classes probably being more accustomed than others to such independent work as is needed in the persistence situation. Another example is possible instructions given by the teacher before the persistence session. Thus, even though the pupils in the present case should not have been prepared in any way for the persistence sessions, the administrator nevertheless heard one of the classes being requested to work hard and behave well before it was left by the teacher! This well-meant piece of acvice, may, to put it mildly, have created a somewhat different condition to that intended by the administrator.

The two examples mentioned above represent sources of variance over which one does not have any control beforehand, and which are expected to more or less mask the relationships in which one is interested. Another possible source of variance was in the present case connected with the procedure itself, Thus, as pointed out previously, the persistence task sets were group-administered (class-administered), and persistence in group situations may well be affected by the performance of other members of the group. While the try-out of the task sets indicated that most subjects turned from the initial set to the alternative one without being much influenced by what their class-mates did, it was nevertheless necessary to be aware that such comparison effects might have been at work in the investigation proper. One had to be especially aware of the occurrence of such comparison effects among girls, since, as pointed out by Gjesme (1971c, p. 13) research indicates that they are more responsive to peers and show more group conformity than do boys (Crutchfield, 1955, p. 196; McCandless, Bilous, & Bennett, 1961, p. 515; Patterson & Anderson, 1964, p. 958). If such comparison effects were at work, one would for example expect the first subject's shift of task set to release a series of other shifts too. Thus, if the first subject turned to the alternative task after only a short time, the mean persistence score of the class would probably be relatively low. On the other hand, if it took a long time before the first shift in a class, the mean persistence score of this class would of course be high.

Thus far we have recognized that a considerable part of the variance in the dependent variable might be due to various irrelevant class differences. If a large number of such effects were present, then it would not seem unreasonable to assume that on the whole they should neutralize each other, and under such conditions there should not be any systematic distortion of the relationship between motive strength and persistence, but only a reduction in the strength of this relationship. On the other hand, if only one or very few such differences were influencing the results, one would expect them to cause systematic differences in the classes' mean score on the dependent variable, and thus distortions of the relationship between motive strength and persistence unless the variance due to these differences is removed or controlled in some way or other. The following discussion will show, however, that at least in the present case the removal of such irrelevant variance is a far from simple matter.

What is said above may seem to imply that the classes' mean persistence scores might be taken as an indicator of whether irrelevant class effects were present. It should, however, be recalled that to ensure having virtually the whole range of possible motive strengths represented in the sample, the classes were taken from schools assumed to represent rather different social environments (cf. pp. 149 f.). Thus, we would expect differences among the classes in mean motive strength. The class variance in persistence due to such differences in motive strength should not, of course, be removed, representing as it does a part of that variance in which we are interested. What should be removed, if possible, is only that part of the class variance in persistence scores which cannot be traced back to the motive variables focused upon. Technically, on the assumption that the regression of persistence scores on M_s scores and M_f scores respectively was the same in all classes, this irrelevant variance could be removed in a somewhat roundabout way, by first using the common within class regression to estimate the mean persistence score of each class. The differences between these estimated mean values and the observed mean values of the classes would show how much the scores within each of the classes had to be adjusted upwards or downwards in order to eliminate the irrelevant class variance.

Unfortunately, however, one can in theory be quite sure in advance that the assumption of an equal regression of persistence scores on motive scores in all classes will not be fulfilled. This assertion demands a few comments. First, the relationship between M_s or M_f strength and persistence should be strongest when persistence is influenced by these motives alone. When the motivation due to M_s and M_f makes up only a small part of the total motivation, persistence should, needless to say, be only weakly related to the strength of M_s and M_f. Secondly, differences in the classes' mean persistence scores other than those due to M_s and M_f effects have to be accounted for in terms of differences in extrinsic motivation of one kind or another. From these circumstances one can conclude that to the extent that there were irrelevant class differences in persistence, there should also be class differences in the regression of persistence scores on motive scores, all the more so because there were probably also changes in the expectancy of success during work, which were greater within a class which, for some reason, worked for a long time at the initial task. From a methodological point of view, of course, this conclusion is a troublesome one.

Thus, to sum up, there did not a priori seem to be any good basis for a correction of the persistence scores for irrelevant class differences. At the very best, the basis seemed so dubious that a correction would hardly be worth the effort needed. Therefore, it was decided to carry out the analyses without previous correction of the persistence scores, and instead take this problem into consideration when evaluating the results.

This completes our consideration of some important questions related to the empirical investigation. In the next chapter we shall present the results of the investigation.

CHAPTER 7

RESULTS

In the first main section of this chapter we shall consider some general results pertaining to the motive variables. After that, we shall in due course examine the results relevant to the hypotheses concerning persistence in the moderately difficult/easy, easy/moderately difficult, and extremely difficult/moderately difficult stiuations.

GENERAL RESULTS PERTAINING TO THE MOTIVE VARIABLES

In Chapter 6 some general results from previous try-outs of the Achievement Motive Scale (AMS) were reported. In the following we shall consider the general results of the AMS obtained in the sample used in the present investigation.

Raw score distributions, item-test correlations, and reliabilities

Although pains were taken to ensure that all the items on the Achievement Motive Scale (AMS) were answered, in a few cases some items were left blank (3 on the M_s part and 4 on the M_f part). In these cases the subjects were simply assigned scores on the blank items corresponding to their most frequent score on the marked items.

Since the AMS contains 15 items assumed to reflect M_s and another 15 items assumed to reflect M_f, and the score on each of the items can vary from 1 to 4, the theoretically possible range of M_s as well as M_f raw scores is from 15 to 60. The results given in the upper halves of Figs. 10 and 11 show that the M_f score distribution obtained in our sample covered practically the whole possible range, while there was a considerably smaller variation in the M_s scores. Means and standard deviations for boys and girls and for the sample as a whole are presented in Table 6. For some reason the means on both the M_s and the M_f part of the scale were somewhat higher than those from the try-outs (cf. p. 145). Further, it can be seen that girls scored lower than boys on the M_s part of the scale, while there was practically no sex difference in the scores on the M_f part of the scale.

The correlations between item scores and sum scores are presented in Table 7,

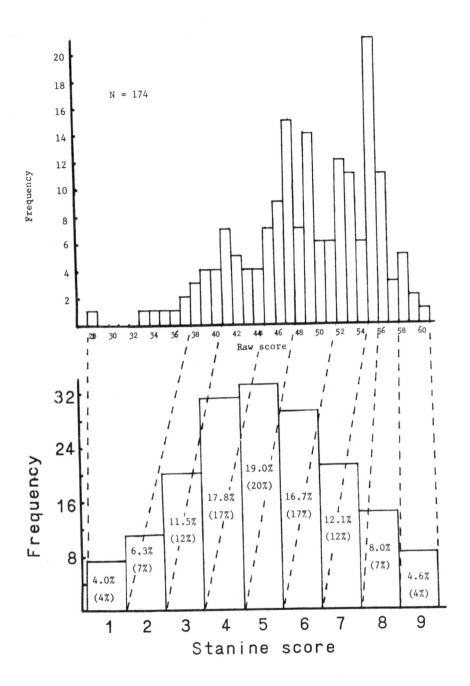

Fig. 10. Frequency distribution of M_S raw scores and M_S stanine scores.
(Ideal percentages in parentheses.)

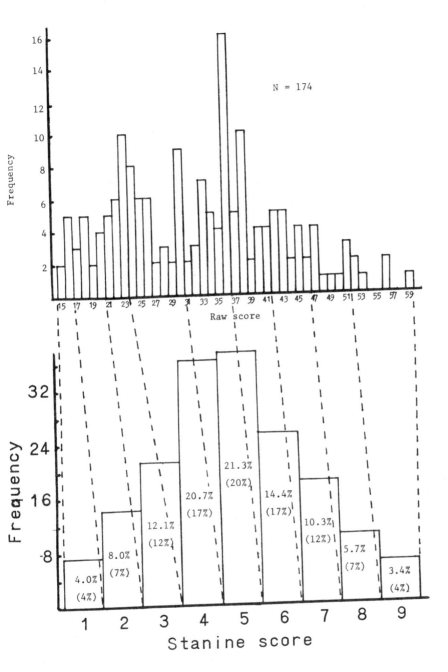

Fig. 11. Frequency distribution of M_f raw scores and M_f stanine scores.
(Ideal percentages in parentheses.)

Table 6. M_s and M_f mean scores for boys, girls, and total sample

	M_s scores			M_f scores		
	Boys	Girls	Total	Boys	Girls	Total
N	90	84	174	90	84	174
$\overline{X}$	50.22	47.60	48.95	32.30	32.57	32.43
s	5.13	6.85	6.15	10.13	10.04	10.06
D	-2.62			-.27		
t	-2.88			-.17		
p	<.005			>.10		

Table 7. Correlations between item scores and sum scores* on the M_s and M_f part of the Achievement Motive Scale

Item no.	1	2	3	4	5	6	7	8	9	10	11	12	13	14	15
M_s part	.44	.48	.18	.34	.37	.49	.14	.48	.24	.49	.49	.25	.39	.55	.46
M_f part	.38	.58	.51	.66	.65	.69	.54	.64	.57	.59	.66	.53	.59	.58	.59

* Corrected values, the item score excluded from the sum score.

which shows that for the M_s part of the scale most correlations are about .40, while for the M_f part most of them are about .60. The reliability in terms of alpha coefficients corresponds roughly to that obtained in the try-outs referred to previously (cf. p. 144). Thus, for the M_s part α = .79, and for the M_f part α = .90. Separate analyses for girls and boys gave for the M_s part α = .81 and α = .73 respectively, and for the M_f part α = .91 and α = .90.

The relationship between M_s scores and M_f scores

To get an indicator of the relationship between the M_s and M_f scores in the present case, the correlation coefficient was computed, giving r = -.11 (N = 174, p >.10) for the sample as a whole and r = -.16 (N = 90, p >.10) and r = -.08 (N = 84, p >.10) for boys and girls respectively. Thus, the results from the present study, too, support the idea referred to previously (cf. pp. 73 f., 145) of M_s and M_f as two relatively independent personality characteristics.

The negligible relationship between M_s and M_f scores also implies a practical advantage as far as the hypotheses testing is concerned, in that the M_f variable may be disregarded while testing the M_s-related hypotheses, and vice versa. If there had been any clear association between M_s and M_f scores, one motive variable ought to have been controlled while the hypotheses related to the other motive variable were being tested.

Motive scores and test-taking attitude scores

As will be recalled, a scale consisting of 10 items assumed to reflect test-taking attitudes was administered after the AMS. To get at least a crude indicator of to what degree test-taking attitudes had affected the answers to the AMS, the sum scores on the test-taking attitude items were correlated with the M_s and M_f scores. The results are presented in Table 8, which shows that all correlations but one are of a negligible size, and the correlation between M_f scores and test-taking attitude scores for girls is not alarmingly high either. Thus, insofar as the test-taking attitude items reflect tendencies on the part of the individual to provide false information about himself, this does not seem to have been a serious problem in the present investigation. On the basis of these results it was found justifiable to ignore this problem in connection with the data analyses.

Table 8. Correlations between motive scores and test-taking attitude scores for boys, girls, and total sample

	Boys (N = 90)	Girls (N=84)	Total (N=174)
M_s scores	- .03	+. 09	+. 08
M_f scores	.00	-. 20*	-. 09

* $p < .10$

Transformation of raw scores to stanine scores

The causation behind the motive to achieve success as well as the motive to avoid failure is assumed to be a rather complicated one, i.e. the motives are assumed to be determined by several relatively independent factors, such as for example how stimulating the home and wider environment is, what restrictions are placed on the child's behaviour, at what age the child is allowed to be independent, etc. Relying on this assumption of an interaction between a number of factors, it seems reasonable to expect the strength of the motives to be normally distributed in the population. It was therefore found convenient to transform the raw scores to stanine scores for internal use in the persistence project. While the 7th graders participating in the investigation were not thought to deviate to any significant extent from 7th graders in general with respect to motive strength, the fact that we did not have a random sample of 7th graders means that the norms should not automatically be considered as valid outside the sample.

The results of the transformations can be seen in Figs. 10 and 11. The deviations of the distributions of the transformed scores from the ideal stanine score distribution are held to be of no practical significance.

INITIAL TASK OF MODERATE DIFFICULTY AND ALTERNATIVE TASK OF LOW DIFFICULTY

The task set

The initial set consisted of a booklet with 21 sets of jumbled letters. The subject was to rearrange each group of letters so that they made a meaningful Norwegian word. For each of the problems there was ample space for trials.

In connection with the development of hypotheses the moderately difficult/easy situation was described as a somewhat tricky one (p. 134), because of the problems of changes in probability of success during work. It was taken for granted that such changes would occur. Therefore, it was decided to use a set of items which increased in difficulty. The first ones were simple, three-letter problems (words from a primer), the last one an 18-letter anagram which was in fact insoluble. By this method one could be relatively sure in which direction P_s would change during work.

The task set was worked out in an A and B form, each part containing the same number of three-letter anagrams, four-letter anagrams, and so forth. Apart from this restriction the anagrams were randomly distributed on the two forms.

The alternative task set, which is of little interest in this connection, consisted of a number of very simple arithmetic problems.

Procedure

The booklets containing the initial task set were passed round together with an envelope with the alternative task set. To reduce the chance of cheating, every other row of pupils got the A form of the initial set, and every other row the B form. The instructions for the persistence test are presented in their entirety in Appendix B. Here only the main points will be summed up.

The subjects were instructed that the envelope contained a set of tasks so easy that they could all manage it, and that the task set in the booklets was a moderately difficult one. To concretize what moderate difficulty meant, they were told that only about half of the pupils usually managed these tasks. After being given an example from the initial set, the subjects were requested to indicate their expectancy of success at the test on a 20-point rating scale with "Quite sure I'll manage them" at one end and "Quite sure I won't manage them" at the other.

Before the subjects were allowed to start working at the initial task set, they were instructed that they were free to leave the initial set and turn to the alternative, very easy one, whenever they wished. This was repeated, in order to ensure that it was perceived by all subjects.

The time for each subject's switching over to the alternative task set was noted.

General results

Results Related to the Probability of Success Assumptions. While the initial task was presented as being of moderate difficulty, the crucial point in this connection is whether the individual himself perceived the task as one where his probability of success was within the moderate range. Unless this was the case, a testing of the hypotheses related to the moderately difficult/easy situation became meaningless.

As appears from the section above, an attempt was made to obtain a measure of the subject's expectancy of success at the initial task. As pointed out by Vroom (1964, pp. 25 f.), self-report measures of probability of outcomes have not received enthusiastic support from decision theorists, but have nevertheless been found to carry meaningful information in studies within social and personality psychology (cf. Diggory & Ostroff, 1962, pp. 94 ff.; Diggory, Riley, and Blumenfeld, 1960, pp. 43 ff.; Rotter, Fitzgerald, & Joyce, 1954, pp. 113 f.). Therefore, the subjects' reported expectancies of success in the present case were held to be a passable indicator of whether our assumptions about P_s were correct.

The subjects' own estimates of probability of success given prior to the work at the initial task are shown in Fig. 12. Four subjects had not given any estimate, and to avoid getting a different number of subjects in the analyses where the P_s variable was included, they were randomly distributed on the two values closest to the median (13 and 14).

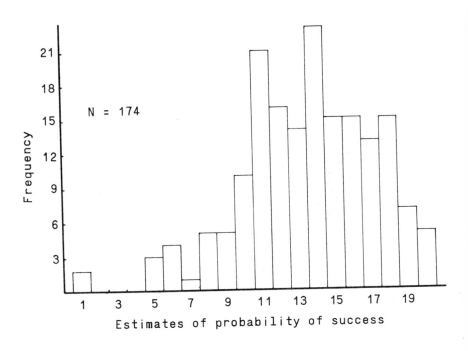

Fig. 12. The subjects' estimates of probability of success at the initial task in the moderately difficult/easy situation. (1 = "Quite sure I won't manage them", 20 = "Quite sure I'll manage them".)

The figure reveals a considerable variation in the estimates, but most of them may nevertheless be said to fall within the moderate range. Accordingly the data should provide a satisfactory basis for testing the main hypotheses about motive effects on persistence at the initial task in a moderately difficult/easy situation. On the other hand, the variation indicates that the data should also be usable for testing hypotheses about differences in the motive effects due to within-situation differences in probability of success.

The Persistence Results. From the general information section (pp. 155 f.) it will be recalled that the moderately difficult/easy task set was administered after the motive measurement. This meant that the time limit for the persistence task itself, exclusive of the instruction for it, had to be set to 20 minutes. The sample's persistence results are shown in Fig. 13. While only a very few subjects worked at the initial task for more than twenty minutes under the try-out

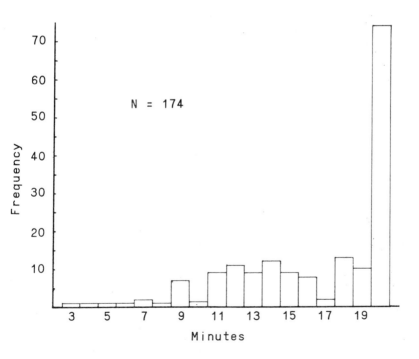

Fig. 13. Persistence in minutes at the initial task in the moderately difficult/easy situation.

of the task set, the figure shows that this was for some reason not the case in the investigation proper, where almost half of the subjects worked until they had to be interrupted. Thus, there is a skewness in the results which might have been avoided or at least reduced by the subjects having more time at their disposal for this persistence situation.

Even though it seems reasonable to consider persistence as a normally distributed variable, the skewness in the results obtained in the present case is so extreme that it was not even possible to transform the results into an approximately normal distribution. Therefore the persistence results were reduced to scores 1 and 0 only, according to whether they were above or below the median. Thus, subjects working 19 minutes or more at the initial task were given the score 1, those working less than 19 minutes were given the score 0. However, as pointed out earlier (p. 158), the fact that we were left with a very crude dependent variable did not make it necessary to deviate from the planned method of analysis, since the regression analysis is also applicable in cases where the dependent variable is only a dichotomous one.

Empirical testing of hypotheses

In the analyses to be presented the following basic variables appear:

Y = Persistence score (0 = low, 1 = high)
X_1 = M_s stanine score
X_2 = M_f stanine score
X_3 = P_s score (0 = low, 1 = high)
X_4 = Sex (0 = boys, 1 = girls)

The intercorrelations between these variables are given in Table 9.

Table 9. Intercorrelations between the variables related to the moderately difficult/easy persistence situation

Variable	Variable			
	X_1	X_2	X_3	X_4
X_1 (M_s)				
X_2 (M_f)	−.14			
X_3 (P_s)	+.14	−.10		
X_4 (Sex)	−.18	+.02	−.11	
Y (Persistence)	+.15	+.01	+.19	+.19

In addition we shall also introduce several interaction variables, i.e. variables which are products of the variables mentioned above.

<u>The Overall Relationship Between Motive Score and Persistence.</u> Hypothesis 1 asserted a positive relationship between M_s strength and persistence at the initial task when the initial task is one of moderate difficulty and the alternative is a task of low difficulty, while hypothesis 2 stated that the corresponding relationship between M_f strength and persistence should be negative. The basic data relevant to these hypotheses are presented in Fig. 14 together with the mean persistence scores for each M_s and M_f score group.

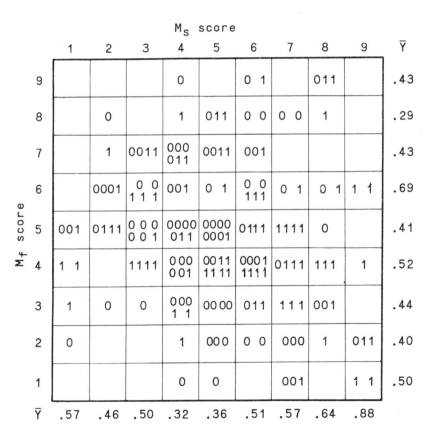

Fig. 14. Persistence scores in the moderately difficult/easy situation in relation to M_s and M_f scores.

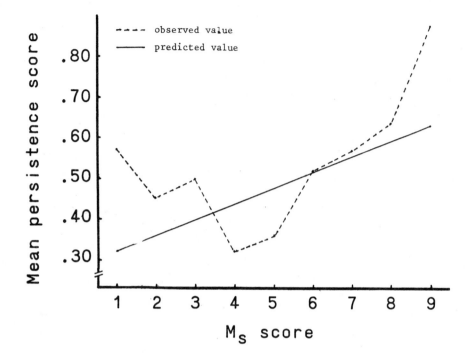

Fig. 15. Observed and predicted persistence scores in the moderately difficult/easy situation in relation to M_s score.

The regression line for persistence scores on M_s scores is described by the equation

$$Y' = .2856 + .0388X_1,$$

where Y' = predicted persistence score, and $X_1 = M_s$ stanine score. Thus, the regression is seen to be positive, as expected. The linear regression line for the data is shown in Fig. 15 together with the observed mean values. A further analysis of these results, presented in Table 7, shows the positive linear regression of persistence scores on motive scores to be significant. The deviations of the observed mean values from the regression line are insignificant, and this means that there is no need to pay any further attention to the slight curvilinear trend in the data. Thus, hypothesis 1 is confirmed.

However, the strength of the relationship between M_s score and persistence score is a rather modest one, corresponding to $r_{pb} = +.15$. This was held to be partly due to the effect of other variables, such as the M_f variable, which according to hypothesis 2 should have a negative influence on persistence in the moderately difficult/easy situation. However, the results presented in Fig. 14 make it quite clear without further analysis that there is no overall systematic relationship between M_f strength alone and persistence in our sample. Thus, the results do not so far provide any evidence in favour of hypothesis 2.

This also implies, as shown in Table 10, that there is no significant increase in the explained persistence score variance when the M_f measure is added to the M_s measure in the regression analysis. A new variable was also introduced into the analysis, i.e. the product of the individuals' M_s and M_f score. This variable

Table 10. Analysis of regression for persistence scores in the moderately difficult/easy situation (a) on M_s scores, (b) on M_s and M_f scores

Source	SS	df	MS	F	p
Total	43.4483	173	.2511		
(a)					
Linear regression					
M_s	1.0384	1	1.0384	4.21	<.025*
Residual	42.4099	172	.2466		
Deviation from linear regression	2.0843	7	.2978	1.22	>.10
Within M_s scores	40.3256	165	.2444		
(b)					
Linear regression	1.1210	3	.3737	1.50	>.10
M_s	1.0384	1	1.0384	4.17	<.025*
M_f	.0478	1	.0478	–	
M_s x M_f	.0348	1	.0348	–	
Residual	42.3273	170	.2490		

* One-tailed test.

The variables in (b) were introduced into the analysis in the same sequence as they appear in the table.

takes care of possible interaction effects of the two motive variables on persistence. The analysis shows that there were no such interaction effects. This means that when the sample is considered as a whole the previously noted positive relationship between M_s strength and persistence held regardless of M_f strength, and that the lacking relationship between M_f strength and persistence held regardless of M_s strength. Thus, knowledge about the individual's M_f score does not result in a more precise prediction of persistence score in the moderately difficult situation than that based on M_s score alone.

It has been mentioned that the relative weakness of the relationship between M_s score and persistence might be due to the effect of other variables on persistence. It might also be that the lacking overall relationship between M_f strength and persistence is due to such hitherto neglected variables. In the following we shall therefore make some more detailed analyses of the relationship between motive score and persistence.

Within-Situation Differences in the Relationship between Motive Score and Persistence: The P_s and Sex Variable.

The persistence situation dealt with here has been considered as one where the subject starts working at the initial task, regarding his probability of success as moderate. Hitherto the sample has been considered homogeneous with respect to probability of success. However, the probability estimates given at the beginning of the persistence situation have been seen to vary considerably (cf. p. 174, Fig. 12). In the following this variation will be taken into account. However, since there was no basis for a more thorough-going evaluation of the probability of success measure, it was found unreasonable to include this variable in the analyses in a finely graded form like that shown in Fig. 12. Rather, it was found sufficient to distinguish between a high and a low group as to probability of success, according to whether the score was above or below the median. Thus, subjects with estimates of 13 or lower were considered to constitute a relatively low P_s group, those with estimates above 13 to make up a relatively high P_s group. While the probability of success measure obtained might be considerably loaded with errors, it is nevertheless assumed that there was a clear P_s difference between the two groups we have arrived at in this way.

It will be recalled that the initial task set consisted of items of increasing difficulty, the very last item being in fact insoluble. It is assumed that this implies a decrease in P_s during work. Then, considering a group with a relatively high P_s (i.e. $P_s > .50$) the unsuccessful attempts should first, as far as M_s is concerned, result in an increase in the motivation to perform until P_s passes .50, followed by a decrease (cf. p. 112, Fig. 6). The amount of this initial increase should be proportional to the M_s strength. If, however, initial P_s is relatively low, (i.e. $P_s < .50$), there should be a decrease in motivation from the very beginning. Thus, M_s should have a less positive effect here than when P_s is relatively high. In other words, hypothesis 1 may be further specified as follows:

Hypothesis 1, modification a:

There is a stronger positive relationship between M_s strength and persistence among subjects with a high P_s than among subjects with a low P_s.

The basic data for testing this prediction are presented in Table 11. Since the number of observations within some of the M_s/P_s combinations is very small, less emphasis should be placed on the mean persistence score for each M_s/P_s combination than on the overall trends in the results revealed by analysis of regression. However, a preliminary inspection of the results shows the relative frequency of 1's, i.e. of high persistence scores, to be highest in the upper right-hand part of the table, i.e. in that part representing high M_s strength and high P_s value, a result which is in accordance with the prediction.

To get more precise information concerning the trends in the results a new variable was constructed by multiplying the subject's motive score and probability of success score. This variable carries the interaction effect of M_s and P_s dealt with above. The regression lines for the persistence scores are now described by the equation

$$Y' = .3827 + .0000X_1 - .1395X_3 + .0612X_1X_3,$$

Table 11. Persistence scores in the moderately difficult/easy situation in relation to M_s and P_s scores

P_s	Persistence score	\(M_s \) score									Total
		1	2	3	4	5	6	7	8	9	
High	1	1	1	6	6	10	9	9	6	5	53
	0	2	3	3	11	8	5	5	2	1	40
Low	1	3	4	4	4	2	6	3	3	2	31
	0	1	3	7	10	13	9	4	3	0	50
Total		7	11	20	31	33	29	21	14	8	174

where Y' = predicted persistence score, $X_1 = M_s$ score, $X_3 = P_s$ score, and $X_1 X_3 = M_s$ score x P_s score. The regression lines based on this equation are shown in Fig. 16, and are seen to be in accordance with the prediction. Expressed in terms of correlation coefficients the relationship between M_s score and persistence score within the high P_s group corresponds to $r_{pb} = .24$, while there is no correlation between M_s score and persistence score within the low P_s group ($r_{pb} = .00$). But it may also be seen from the figure that the null correlation within the low P_s group hides observed mean values falling far from the regression line, pointing in the direction of a curvilinear regression. However, the impression of such a curvilinear regression is weakened considerably when taking into consideration that the mean values farthest from the regression line, those for M_s scores 1 and 9, are based on only four and two observations respectively. A further analysis, presented in Table 12, shows that the deviations from linear regression are also insignificant. Hence, we may concentrate on the main trends in the results without offering these deviations further attention.

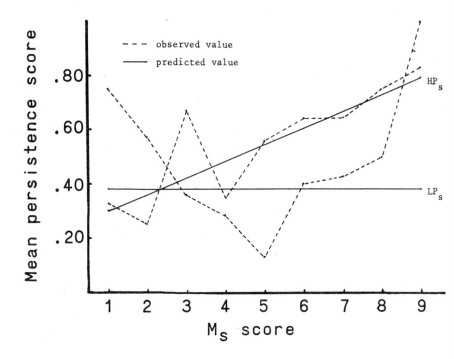

Fig. 16. Observed and predicted persistence scores in the moderately difficult/easy situation for the various M_s/P_s combinations.

Table 12. Analysis of regression for persistence scores in the moderately difficult/easy situation on M_s and P_s scores

Source	SS	df	MS	F	p
Total	43.4483	173	.2511		
Linear regression	2.8854	3	.9618	4.03	< .01
M_s	1.0384	1	1.0384	4.35	< .025*
P_s	1.2103	1	1.2103	5.07	< .05
$M_s \times P_s$	.6367	1	.6367	2.67	≈ .05*
Residual	40.5629	170	.2386		
Deviation from linear regression	3.6430	14	.2602	1.10	> .10
Within M_s/P_s scores	36.9199	156	.2367		

* One-tailed test.
The variables were introduced into the analysis in the same sequence as they appear in the table.

As to the findings of primary interest here, those carried by the M_s by P_s interaction variable, they are seen to signify a fair basis for rejection of the null hypothesis of no interaction effect over and above the separate M_s and P_s effects. This $M_s \times P_s$ effect reflects the difference in the slope of the regression lines shown in Fig. 16. Thus, the result lends relatively clear support to the prediction of a stronger relationship between M_s strength and persistence within the high P_s group than within the low P_s group.

Some attention should also be paid to the findings of a main effect of the P_s variable on persistence. When this result is related to Fig. 16, it is seen to mean that on the whole those with a high P_s score are more persistent than those with a low P_s score, regardless of motive score. The only exception is at extremely low M_s scores, but this reversal is negligible in relation to the positive P_s effect among individuals with high M_s scores. This P_s effect will be taken up again later on.

While in the preceding pages we have been directly concerned with the P_s

variable, in the following we shall be concerned with this variable from a some-what other point of departure, turning to the problem of sex differences in the relationship between M_s strength and persistence. This problem was touched upon in the theoretical part of this work, where attention was called to the greater tendency among girls than among boys to underestimate their probability of success (cf. p. 135). To the degree such a difference in the estimation of probability of success exists, there should also, according to the reasoning related to the P_s variable, be a sex difference in the relationship between M_s strength and persis-tence. More precisely, since a stronger relationship between M_s strength and persistence within a high P_s than within a low P_s group has been predicted, hypo-thesis 1 may also be amplified as follows:

Hypothesis 1, modification b:

There is a stronger positive relationship between M_s strength and persistence among boys than among girls.

The assumption behind this prediction, that of a sex difference in perceived probability of success, is checked in Table 13. The table shows that the direction of the results is in accordance with the expectation, with a somewhat higher fre-quency of high P_s scorers among boys than among girls. However, the difference is only a modest one, implying that the basis for the prediction above is not a very strong one.

Table 13. Sex difference in P_s score for the initial task in the moderately dif-ficult/easy situation

P_s score	Boys	Girls	Total	χ^2	df	p
1 (high)	53	40	93			
				2.22	1	< .10*
0 (low)	37	44	81			

* One-tailed test.

The data for testing the prediction are given in Table 14. The most striking feature in this table is the higher frequency of high persistence scores among girls than among boys, while there seems to be only a negligible difference, if any, between the sexes in the relationship between M_s score and persistence. However, for a more thorough evaluation of the results a further analysis was performed.

Table 14. Persistence scores in the moderately difficult/easy situation in relation to M_s score and sex

Sex	Persistence score	M_s score 1	2	3	4	5	6	7	8	9	Total
Girls	1	4	4	8	7	5	7	3	6	5	49
	0	2	3	6	8	8	5	2	1	0	35
Boys	1	0	1	2	3	7	8	9	3	2	35
	0	1	3	4	13	13	9	7	4	1	55
Total		7	11	20	31	33	29	21	14	8	174

To take care of the interaction effect of M_s and sex in this analysis, boys were assigned 0's and girls 1's, and an interaction variable was constructed by multiplying the subjects' M_s score and sex "score". The regression lines for the persistence scores may then be described by the equation

$$Y' = .0204 + .0608X_1 + .3880X_4 - .0309X_1X_4$$

where Y' = predicted persistence score, $X_1 = M_s$ score, X_4 = Sex, and $X_1X_4 = M_s$ x Sex score. The regression lines based on this equation can be seen in Fig. 17 along with the observed mean values, and the analysis of the results is presented in Table 15. The relationship between M_s strength and persistence expressed in terms of correlation coefficients corresponds to $r_{pb} = .24$ for boys, and $r_{pb} = .16$ for girls. While the direction of this result is as expected, the table makes it clear that the difference has to be considered as negligible.

There is, however, a highly significant unpredicted main effect of sex on persistence level. This difference in favour of girls is remarkable in the light of the previously noted somewhat lower P_s among girls than among boys together with the positive relationship between P_s level and persistence. In other words, in spite of the fact that girls as a group consider their probability of success as somewhat lower than do boys, they are nevertheless more persistent than boys in the moderately difficult/easy situation.

So far we have dealt with the question of differences in the relationship between M_s strength and persistence as a function of differences in probability of success,

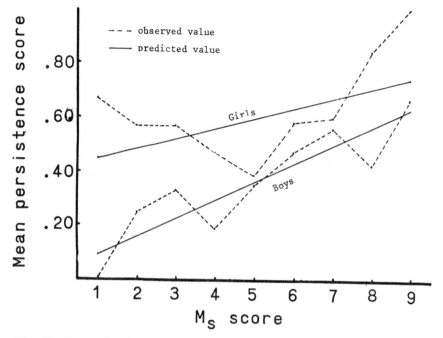

Fig. 17. Observed and predicted persistence scores in the moderately difficult/easy situation for the various M_s/sex combinations.

Table 15. Analysis of regression for persistence scores in the moderately difficult/easy situation on M_s scores and sex

Source	SS	df	MS	F	p
Total	43.4483	173	2511		
Linear regression	3.4150	3	1.1383	4.83	<.005
M_s	1.0384	1	1.0384	4.41	<.025*
Sex	2.2202	1	2.2202	9.43	<.005
M_s x Sex	.1564	1	.1564	–	
Residual	40.0333	170	.2355		
Deviation from regression	2.1485	14	.1535	–	
Within M_s/Sex	37.8848	156	.2429		

* One-tailed test.
The variables were introduced into the analysis in the same sequence as they appear in the table.

as well as the very closely related question of sex differences in this relationship. Previously we have observed that there is no overall relationship between M_f score and persistence. Nevertheless it is of interest to take a look at the relationship between M_f score and persistence within the subgroups considered above, i.e. within the high and low P_s group, as well as within each of the sexes, to see whether there are any trends deserving further attention. But first, let us take a look at the theoretical implications of differences in probability of success for the relationship between M_f strength and persistence.

Considering a group with a relatively high P_s (i.e. $P_s > .50$), the unsuccessful attempts should first, as far as M_f is considered, result in an increase in the tendency to resist working at the task, followed by a decrease (cf. p. 114, Fig. 7). This tendency to resist is proportional to the motive strength. When initial P_s is relatively low (i.e. $P_s < .50$), there should be a decrease in the tendency to resist from the very beginning. Hence, hypothesis 2 might have been further elaborated in the following way:

Hypothesis 2, modification a:
There should be a stronger negative relationship between M_f strength and persistence within the high P_s group than within the low P_s group.

Regarding boys as a relatively high P_s group and girls as a relative low P_s group, the hypothesis might also have been elaborated as follows:

Hypothesis 2, modification b:
There should be a stronger negative relationship between M_f strength and persistence among boys than among girls.

However, the lacking support for the hypothesis of an overall negative relationship between M_f strength and persistence also implies lacking support for these more specified predictions. The direction of possible differences is nevertheless of interest.

The relevant data concerning the P_s groups are given in Table 16. According to these data the relationship between M_f score and persistence within the high P_s group corresponds to $r_{pb} = .01$, and that within the low P_s group to $r_{pb} = .05$. Since the size of these correlations is negligible, no significance should be attached to this result, although the direction of the difference is as expected. Further, since the mean values for the various M_f/P_s combinations do not reveal any other systematic trends, there is no need for additional analysis, and it may be concluded that the lack of relationship between M_f strength and persistence found in the overall analysis (cf. pp. 178 ff.) also holds for each of the two subgroups considered here.

Let us then consider the question of sex differences in the relationship between M_f strength and persistence.

Table 16. Persistence scores in the moderately difficult/easy situation in relation to M_f and P_s scores

P_s	Persistence score	\multicolumn{9}{c}{M_f score}	Total
		1	2	3	4	5	6	7	8	9	
High	1	1	2	6	21	9	8	3	2	1	53
	0	3	5	6	3	6	10	5	2	0	40
Low	1	2	2	3	4	6	5	5	2	2	31
	0	1	5	6	8	16	2	5	4	3	50
Total		7	14	21	36	37	25	18	10	6	174

Table 17. Persistence scores in the moderately difficult/easy situation in relation to M_f score and sex

Sex	Persistence score	\multicolumn{9}{c}{M_f score}	Total
		1	2	3	4	5	6	7	8	9	
Girls	1	2	2	2	14	9	9	5	3	3	49
	0	0	8	5	3	10	3	4	2	0	35
Boys	1	1	2	7	11	6	4	3	1	0	35
	0	4	2	7	8	12	9	6	4	3	55
Total		7	14	21	36	37	25	18	10	6	174

Table 17 gives the basic data. The table shows a surprisingly different relationship between M_f strength and persistence for boys and girls. The regression lines for the persistence scores are described by the equation

$$Y' = .5896 - .0421X_2 - .2439X_4 + .0911X_2X_4,$$

where Y' = predicted persistence score, $X_2 = M_f$ score, and $X_2 X_4 = M_f$ x Sex score. The lines are shown in Fig. 18 together with the observed mean values for each M_f/sex combination. A further analysis of these results is given in Table 18, and

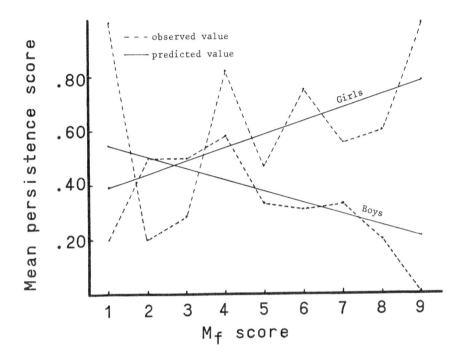

Fig. 18. Observed and predicted persistence scores in the moderately difficult/easy situation for the various M_f/sex combinations.

shows the M_f by sex interaction effect to be clearly significant. Thus, while the first analysis related to the hypothesis of a negative relationship between M_f strength and persistence in the moderately difficult/easy situation did not provide any evidence in favour of the hypothesis, the present analysis revealed such a negative relationship among boys, but not among girls. Since no M_f by P_s interactions were found (cf. p. 188) this sex difference cannot be explained in terms of probability of success differences alone. Other possible causes will be considered later on.

Thus far we have related the persistence scores to M_s scores, M_f scores, P_s scores, and sex, as well as to various combinations of these variables (inter-

Table 18. Analysis of regression for persistence scores in the moderately difficult/easy situation on M_f scores and sex

Source	SS	df	MS	F	p
Total	43.4483	173	.2511		
Linear regression	2.9588	3	.9863	4.14	< .01
M_f	.0043	1	.0043	–	
Sex	1.6424	1	1.6424	6.90	< .01
M_f x Sex	1.3121	1	1.3121	5.51	< .025
Residual	40.4895	170	.2382		
Deviation from regression	5.0805	14	.3629	1.60	< .10
Within M_f/Sex	35.4090	156	.2270		

The variables were introduced into the analysis in the same sequence as they appear in the table.

action variables). Not all of these variables turned out to be significantly related to persistence. To sum up the main trends in the results, an analysis was therefore performed where the main variables and only those interaction variables which had been observed to be significantly related to persistence, were included. The regression lines for the persistence scores based on these variables are described by the equation

$$Y' = .2759 + .0176X_1 - .0220X_2 - .0648X_3 + .0499X_1X_3 - .1443X_4 + .0792X_2X_4,$$

where Y' = predicted persistence score, $X_1 = M_s$ score, $X_2 = M_f$ score, $X_3 = P_s$ score, $X_1X_3 = M_s$ x P_s score, X_4 = Sex, and $X_2X_4 = M_f$ score x Sex.

The relationships hidden behind this somewhat complex regression equation are spelled out in Fig. 19, and the corresponding analysis of regression is presented in Table 19. Since M_s, M_f, and P_s are the variables of primary interest in this connection, they are the first ones introduced into the analysis. As can be seen, this analysis did not reveal anything new, compared with those presented previously. However, the independent variables which have been considered were more or less correlated, and therefore the effect ascribed to each of them has to some extent depended on the stage at which they were introduced into the analysis. A final control analysis was therefore carried out. In this analysis the first order interaction variables which were not included in the summing up analysis (M_s x M_f,

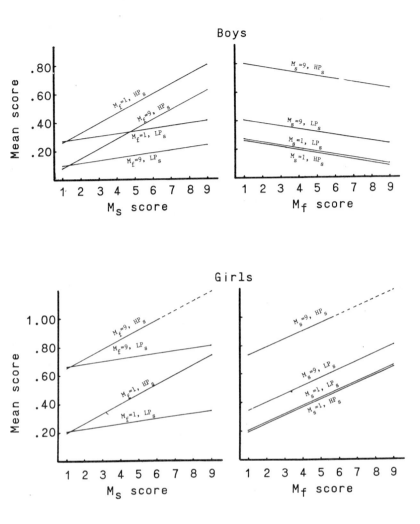

Fig. 19. Predicted persistence scores for boys and girls in the moderately difficult/easy situation in relation to M_s, M_f, and P_s scores.

$M_f \times P_s$, $M_s \times$ Sex, and $P_s \times$ Sex) were introduced one by one subsequent to the set of variables which appear in Table 19. The persistence scores were not significantly related to any of these variables. Finally, the $M_s \times P_s \times$ Sex variable and the $M_f \times$ Sex $\times P_s$ variable were included. The first one was included in order to see whether there was any significant sex difference in the M_s by P_s

Table 19. Analysis of regression for persistence scores in the moderately difficult/easy situation on M_s scores, M_f scores, P_s scores and sex

Source	SS	df	MS	F	p
Total	43.4483	173	.2511		
Linear regression	6.3912	6	1.0652	4.80	<.001
M_s	1.0384	1	1.0384	4.48	<.025*
M_f	.0478	1	.0478	-	
P_s	1.2644	1	1.2644	5.70	<.025
$M_s \times P_s$	.6864	1	.6864	3.09	<.05*
Sex	2.2811	1	2.2811	10.28	<.005
$M_f \times$ Sex	1.0731	1	1.0731	4.84	<.05
Residual	37.0571	167	.2219		

* One-tailed test.
The variables were introduced into the analysis in the same sequence as they appear in the table.

interaction which had been observed, and the second in order to find out whether there was any significant difference between the two P_s groups in the M_f by sex interaction. None of these interaction variables turned out to be of significance. The remaining higher-order interaction variables were of no interest.

Discussion

The results summed up in Fig. 19 and Table 19 make up a rather mixed case for evaluation. To take the most conspicuous outcome first, the variables dealt with in the foregoing account for only a modest part of the variance in the persistence results. Thus, as appears from Table 19, the variables which are significantly related to persistence capture together no more than 15 per cent of the variance in persistence scores. This indicates that in the present study we have oversimplified the persistence problem, or, in other words, it indicates that persistence is also influenced by variables other than those considered in the present study. With this self-evident fact in mind, let us consider the findings more closely, and let us first pay attention to that part of the results bearing directly on the predictions set forth.

Hypothesis 1:

There is a positive relationship between M_s strength and persistence.

A positive relationship between M_s score and persistence score was observed in the sample as a whole (main effect of M_s). Thus, hypothesis 1 was supported by the data. Since the relationship observed did not cover up any clear M_s by sex interaction, the prediction is considered as verified for both sexes.

Hypothesis 1, modification a:

There is a stronger positive relationship between M_s strength and persistence among subjects with a high P_s than among subjects with a low P_s.

An M_s by P_s interaction in this direction was observed, thus providing support for hypothesis 1-a. Since this interaction did not cover up any M_s by P_s by sex interactions, the prediction is regarded as verified for both sexes.

Hypothesis 1, modification b:

There is a stronger relationship between M_s strength and persistence among boys than among girls.

This hypothesis was based on the assumption that boys could be considered as a high P_s group and girls as a low P_s group. As will be recalled, a check on this assumption revealed a sex difference in P_s in the expected direction, but this difference was only a modest one. Thus, the basis for the hypothesis was a rather shaky one. An insignificant sex difference in the relationship between M_s score and persistence score in the expected direction was observed (cf. p. 186, Fig. 17). Because of the weak basis for the hypothesis a further discussion of this result has no interest.

Hypothesis 2:

There is a negative relationship between M_f strength and persistence.

No overall relationship between M_f score and persistence score was observed (no main effect of M_f). However, a further analysis of the data revealed a negative relationship among boys and a positive relationship among girls. Thus the hypothesis received support from the data on boys, but not from those on girls.

Hypothesis 2, modification a:

There is a stronger negative relationship between M_f strength and persistence among subjects with a high P_s than among subjects with a low P_s.

There was no evidence in favour of this hypothesis.

Hypothesis 2, modification b:

There is a stronger negative relationship between M_f strength and persistence among boys than among girls.

The lack of support for hypothesis 2-a implies lack of support for hypothesis 2-b too, since these hypotheses simply represent two ways of expressing the same idea.

From this brief recapitulation of the hypotheses and some of the results we can

193

13

see that as far as only boys are concerned, all hypotheses except that of a stronger relationship between M_f strength and persistence among high P_s subjects than among low P_s subjects received support. In this connection it should also be of some interest to note the pattern for the motive combination groups. We may, since these combinations appear directly from Fig. 19, focus on the M_s/M_f score combinations 9/1 and 1/9 as representing $M_s > M_f$ and $M_s < M_f$ respectively, and the combinations 1/1 and 9/9 as representing $M_s \approx M_f$. Turning now to the best fitting straight lines in Fig. 19, the following pattern appears for boys: The $M_s > M_f$ group had a higher predicted persistence score than the $M_s < M_f$ group. The superiority of the $M_s > M_f$ group over the $M_s < M_f$ group was most conspicuous among boys with a high P_s score. The $M_s \approx M_f$ groups' predicted scores fell between those for the $M_s > M_f$ group and the $M_s < M_f$ group both for those with a high and those with a low P_s score. Since we here have focused upon the most extreme motive score combinations, it is worth noting that exactly the same pattern would appear if we had concentrated on less extreme combinations, such as 7/3 and 3/7, as representatives for $M_s > M_f$ and $M_s < M_f$. Thus, the trends for the motive combination groups turned out completely as expected for boys. Taking this circumstance into account, there seems to be no reason to discuss the lack of an M_f by P_s interaction any further. It seems more reasonable to wait and see whether this result is replicable. It is, in fact, a belief in such an interaction that provides the basis for the hypothesis of a positive relationship between M_f strength and persistence in the other two persistence situations to be considered.

Then, to conclude, the results as far as only boys are concerned provide satisfactory support for the theorizing.

Turning now to the group of girls, we are faced with a more tangled pattern. On the one hand, hypothesis 1 as well as its variant 1-a received support, while on the other hand the results contradicted hypothesis 2. A consideration of motive combination groups throws this inconsistency even more clearly into relief. True enough, the difference between the predicted scores for the $M_s > M_f$ group and the $M_s < M_f$ group is in the expected direction among those subjects where the clearest difference was expected, i.e. among subjects with a high P_s score. However, the $M_s \approx M_f$ groups' predicted scores did not fall between those for the $M_s > M_f$ group and the $M_s < M_f$ group, the low/low group having the highest score, and the high/high group the lowest score. The latter results, of course, simply reflect the fact that the persistence scores correlated positively both with M_s and M_f scores.

While no intuitively compelling explanation of this partly unexpected result appears immediately, a cause may possibly be found in the class variance phenomenon. It was pointed out in the previous chapter that irrelevant class variance might obscure the relationships of interest. A two-fold question then arises, namely, whether the expected as well as the unexpected findings could be due to some irrelevant class effect. To get an indication of whether this could be the case, the correlation between M_s as well as M_f score and persistence was computed for each class. Mean within class correlation coefficients could then be computed by first transforming the r's to Fisher's z coefficients, next weighting each of these coefficients for its number of degrees of freedom to account for the fact that the number of subjects differed from one class to another, and finally transforming the mean z back to its corresponding r (cf. Guilford, 1965, pp. 348 f.). For boys this gave a mean correlation between M_s score and persistence of +.21, and a mean correlation between M_f score and persistence of -.16. These results are very close to those presented previously (r = +.24, and r = -.16), and indicate that as far as boys are concerned the relationships have not been seriously distorted because of irrelevant differences between the classes. As to the girls, the results are more problematical. Here the mean coefficients were +.07 and -.13 respectively. The first one is in the same direction as that obtained in the overall analysis (r = +.16), and strengthens our belief in the previously presented result. The circumstance that the within-class correlation coefficient is a very low one is not surprising when recalling that much of the M_s score variance is excluded by this procedure (cf. p. 165). However, the M_f-related mean correlation coefficient turned out to be in the opposite direction from the coefficient from the overall analysis, where a correlation of +.24 was obtained. Post hoc reasoning should not be carried too far, but there is one outstanding fact which makes us lean towards the view that this inconsistency is at least partly a reflection of the higher group conformity among girls pointed out previously (p. 164). This higher conformity should result in less variation in persistence scores within the classes among girls than among boys. This is clearly illustrated by the fact that in one of the classes none of the girls turned to the alternative set, and in another class there was only one low persister (persistence score 0) among the girls. At the same time the mean M_f scores for the girls in these two classes were higher than those in the other classes. While we cannot, of course, disregard the possibility that the very high persistence of the girls in these two classes might just be due to their high M_f level, it is of some interest to note that when these two groups of girls were excluded from the analysis, the overall correlation between M_f score and persistence changed from +.24 to -.06. The size of this negative coefficient is too low to be of any interest, but the change indicates at least that the positive regression for girls of persistence scores on M_f scores reported previously is an unreliable one. [1] For the moment, there does not seem to be any point in discussing this problem any further. Conclusions should not be drawn before this result has been seen to be replicable.

In addition to the results directly relevant to the hypotheses, the analyses also revealed two other outstanding results. First, a main effect of P_s on persistence was observed, i.e. the relatively high P_s group was on the whole more persistent than the relatively low P_s group. As will be recalled, a similar result has been reported by Feather (cf. p. 92). It was pointed out during the discussion of Feather's result that the achievement motivation theory does not assume any main effect of P_s. This also holds for the revised theory presented in Chapter 5. The result obtained in the present investigation as well as in Feather's might indicate that P_s has an independent positive main effect. However, before drawing any conclusions in this direction, it should also be taken into consideration that the absence of a main P_s effect should be observed only in samples where the average M_s and M_f strength is the same (cf. e.g. p. 116, Fig. 8). It has been argued that Feather's finding, which refers to college students, may reflect that on the average M_s is stronger than M_f in a selected group like college students. The finding in the present investigation may possibly indicate that this is the case even in an unselected group of subjects like pupils in 7th grade.

The final result to be considered is that of the significantly higher persistence among girls than among boys. In fact, of the variables considered, the sex variable is the one most clearly related to persistence, accounting for a little more than 5 per cent of the persistence score variance when it is introduced into the analyses after the motive variables (cf. p. 192, Table 19). There are no indications of sex differences in motive strength which should produce this persistence difference (cf. p. 170, Table 6). Then it seems necessary and reasonable to account for this result in terms of a sex difference in extrinsic motivation, i.e. in motivation due to motives other than M_s and M_f. In this connection it is natural to call attention to the demonstrated greater social orientation among girls than among boys (see for example Anastasi, 1958, pp. 478 ff.). A greater sensitivity on the part of girls to the administrator's request to start working at the initial task may have created a difference in extrinsic motivation to perform this task. Thus, it may very well be that among girls such extrinsic motivation has made up a main part of the total motivation to perform the initial task, at least during the first part of the persistence period. The dominance of such extrinsic motivation may also to some extent explain why the results related to the hypotheses were not as clear

----

1. The exclusion of the two groups resulted in a positive correlation between M_s score and persistence of +.13.

among girls as among boys. It remains to be seen whether the sex difference demonstrated here also applies to other persistence situations. Some evidence concerning this matter is presented in the next section.

Summing up

In short, the main findings from the moderately difficult/easy persistence situation are:

(a) There was an overall positive relationship between M_s score and persistence score (main effect of M_s).

(b) There was no overall relationship between M_f score and persistence score (lack of main M_f effect).

(c) Subjects with a high P_s score were on the whole more persistent than subjects with a low P_s score (main effect of P_s).

(d) Girls were more persistent than boys (main effect of sex).

(e) The positive relationship between M_s score and persistence score held across M_f levels, and the lacking relationship between M_f score and persistence score held across M_s levels (no M_s x M_f effect).

(f) The overall relationship between M_s score and persistence score masked a stronger positive relationship in the high P_s group than in the low P_s group (M_s x P_s effect).

(g) There was no significant sex difference in the relationship between M_s score and persistence score (no significant M_s x Sex effect). This was the case irrespective of P_s group (no M_s x P_s x Sex effect).

(h) The lack of relationship between M_f score and persistence score held for both P_s groups (no M_f x P_s effect).

(i) The lack of relationship between M_f score and persistence score masked a negative relationship among boys and a positive relationship among girls (M_f x Sex effect). This was the case irrespective of P_s group (no M_f x P_s x Sex effect).

Focusing on motive combination groups, the best-fitting straight lines give the following:

(j) Among boys the $M_s > M_f$ group was more persistent than the $M_s < M_f$ group. The superiority of the $M_s > M_f$ group was most conspicuous among boys with a high P_s score. The $M_s \approx M_f$ groups' results fell between those for the $M_s > M_f$ group and the $M_s < M_f$ group, both for those with a high and those with a low P_s score.

(k) Among girls the $M_s > M_f$ group was more persistent than the $M_s < M_f$ group as regards girls with a high P_s score, but not as regards those with a low P_s

score. The $M_s \approx M_f$ groups' results did not fall between those for the $M_s > M_f$ group and the $M_s < M_f$ group, the low/low group being the least persistent, and the high/high group being the most persistent.

INITIAL TASK OF LOW DIFFICULTY AND ALTERNATIVE TASK OF MODERATE DIFFICULTY

The task set

To create a very high probability of success at the initial task the subjects were confronted with a very simple drawing task, that of drawing a row of simple figures. The row of figures to be drawn was presented to the subjects in a booklet of five pages. It was printed at the top of each page, which had 15 empty lines to be filled in.

The alternative, moderately difficult task set consisted of arithmetic problems.

Procedure

The instructions for the persistence test are presented in their entirety in Appendix C. Here only the main points will be given.

After the initial and the alternative task set had been passed round, the subjects were instructed that the envelope contained a set of tasks of moderate difficulty, i.e. so difficult that only about half of the pupils would normally manage them. They were further informed that the booklet contained a task which was very, very easy, so easy that all the pupils would manage it. After the subjects had been made acquainted with the drawing task, instructions were given that the drawing might be continued ɪor as long as they wished, but that they could also leave that task and turn to the alternative, moderately difficult one whenever they wished.

The most essential part of the instruction was repeated, and after that the subjects were asked to start working.

The time for each subject's switch to the alternative set was registered.

Comments regarding the probability of success assumptions

In connection with the hypotheses to be tested, the crucial point is not so much that the initial task was presented as one of low difficulty but more how the subjects perceived the task, i.e. how they regarded their possibility of success. It will be recalled that in connection with the moderately difficult/easy situation a direct attempt was made to let the subjects indicate their perceived possibility of success on a 20-point scale before they started the work. In the present case, however, it was found meaningless to make a corresponding attempt, because of the routine character of the task. For most of the subjects the drawing of rows of simple figures must of necessity have been a task offering no challenge in terms of uncertainty as to whether they would manage it, i.e. the probability of success should be extremely high in this case. We cannot, however, exclude the possibility that some of the subjects have primarily focused upon whether they would manage to fill in the whole figure drawing booklet. In that case a lower expectancy of success (expectancy of getting through the whole booklet) would probably have resulted. However, none of the observations made indicated that this was a general problem.

General results

The Persistence Results. For the easy/moderately difficult persistence situation one school session of forty-five minutes was allotted. Since the instruction for the task set took a few minutes, the time limit for the persistence situation itself was set to thirty-five minutes.

The sample's persistence results in terms of minutes spent at the initial task are shown in the upper part of Fig. 20. This figure reveals a conspicuously skewed distribution, 22 subjects working for less than one minute before turning to the alternative task, while only two subjects worked at the initial task until interrupted. Since this skewness in the persistence results would be problematical in connection with the data analyses to be performed, the question of whether it would be legitimate to transform the results to an approximately normal distribution had to be considered.

In connection with the transformation question attention should again be directed towards the motivation model upon which this study was based (cf. e.g. p. 116, Fig. 8). From this model it should be clear that some subjects, i.e. those with a strong motive to achieve success and a weak motive to avoid failure, should, unless extrinsically motivated, actually show resistence towards working at tasks where the probability of success is very high. In other words, it seems psychologically meaningful to conceive of the persistence variable as varying from strongly negative to strongly positive, the negative part implying resistance towards the task, the positive part implying attraction towards the task. From this point of view those turning to the alternative task at once may be conceived of as revealing resistance towards the task, and should, if possible, have scored negatively on the persistence variable.

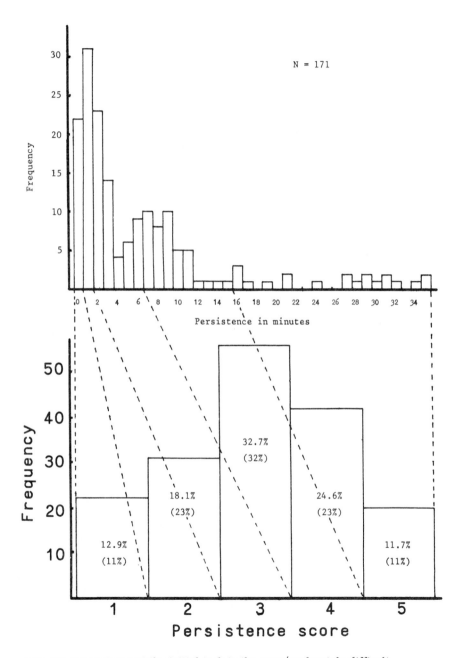

Fig. 20. Persistence at the initial task in the easy/moderately difficult
situation. Observed and transformed data.

Thus, the skewness in the results is regarded as a technical matter, an artifact due to the way persistence is measured. Therefore, a transformation of the results to a distribution approaching a normal one as closely as possible was not only justifiable, but also to be recommended.

However, the accumulation of subjects persisting less than one minute at the initial task placed a clear restriction upon the kind of transformation that could be carried out. Inspection indicated that one would come closest to a normal distribution by converting the data to a five-point scale with intervals corresponding to .80 standard deviation units on the base line of the unit normal curve. In this way, the data would be compressed within a distance from - 2.00 to + 2.00 standard deviation units. Further, it meant that score 3, the middle one, should cover the interval from -.40 to +.40 in standard deviation units, within which approximately 32 per cent of the area of the normal curve falls. Score 4 should cover the interval from +.40 to +1.20 in standard deviation units, corresponding to about 23 per cent of the area, and so forth.

Even though the chosen transformation is a coarse one, and thus only gives an approximate normalization, it was nevertheless held to be sufficiently refined for the purpose of this study.

The result of the transformation is shown in the lower part of Fig. 20 along with the ideal frequencies in per cent.

Carryover Effects. The problem of carryover effects from one persistence setting to another was dealt with in the general information chapter (p. 156). It will be recalled that all subjects were confronted with the moderately difficult/easy persistence situation first. However, half of the classes got the easy/moderately difficult task set as the second one and the extremely difficult/moderately difficult set as the third one, while the other half had the order of the last two sets reversed. By this procedure one would obtain some information concerning possible carryover effects.

The mean persistence score for the subjects faced with the easy/moderately difficult set as the second one and for those confronted with this set as the third one are given in Table 20. This table does not provide any clear-cut evidence (p > .05), but points in the direction of somewhat lower persistence among those given the easy/moderately difficult task set as the last one. One ought to be aware that to the extent that such effects have been present, they have also increased the persistence score variance, and thus resulted in a lowering of the relationship between motive scores and persistence scores.

Table 20. Mean persistence score in the easy/moderately difficult situation for subjects confronted with this situation in second and third place in the series

| | Easy/moderately difficult set as | | Total |
	no. 2	no. 3	
N	85	86	171
$\overline{X}$	3.21	2.87	3.04
s	1.06	1.29	1.19
D		.34	
t		1.88	
p		<.10	

Empirical testing of hypotheses

In the analyses the following basic variables appear:

$Y =$ Persistence score
$X_1 =$ M_s stanine score
$X_2 =$ M_f stanine score
$X_4 =$ Sex (0 = boys, 1 = girls)

The intercorrelations between these variables are presented in Table 21.

Table 21. Intercorrelations between the variables related to the easy/moderately difficult persistence situation

| Variable | Variable | | |
	X_1	X_2	X_4
X_1 (M_s)			
X_2 (M_f)	−.15		
X_4 (Sex)	−.18	+.02	
Y (Persistence)	−.28	+.22	+.34

The Overall Relationship Between Motive Score and Persistence. According to hypothesis 3 there should be a negative relationship between M_s strength and persistence at the initial task when the initial task is one of low difficulty and the alternative is a task of moderate difficulty, while, according to hypothesis 4, the corresponding relationship between M_f strength and persistence should be positive. The basic data relevant to these hypotheses are presented in Fig. 21, where the mean persistence score for each M_s and M_f score category is also given. These mean scores are seen to reveal trends in the expected direction, and the trends are further analysed below.

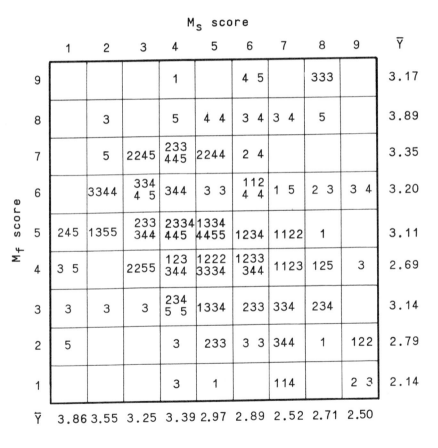

Fig. 21. Persistence scores in the easy/moderately difficult situation in relation to M_s and M_f scores.

The regression line for persistence scores on M_s scores is described by the equation

$$Y' = 3.8929 - .1682X_1,$$

where Y' = predicted persistence score and $X_1 = M_s$ score. The regression line for the data is shown in Fig. 22 along with the observed mean values. A further analysis of these results, presented in Table 22a, demonstrates that the linear regression is significant. The observed means are so close to the regression line that further analyses of their deviations are unneccessary. Then, since Fig. 22 has shown the regression to be negative, hypothesis 3 is regarded as confirmed.

Table 22. Analysis of regression for persistence scores in the easy/moderately difficult situation (a) on M_s scores, (b) on M_f scores, (c) on M_s and M_f scores

Source	SS	df	MS	F	p
Total	240.7135	170	1.4160		
(a)					
Linear regression					
M_s	19.4256	1	19.4256	14.84	< .001*
Residual	221.2879	169	1.3094		
(b)					
Linear regression					
M_f	11.5302	1	11.5302	8.50	< .0025*
Residual	229.1833	169	1.3561		
Deviation from linear regression	8.6826	7	1.2404	–	
Within M_f scores	220.5007	162	1.3611		
(c)					
Linear regression	27.9228	3	9.3076	7.30	< .001
M_s	19.4256	1	19.4256	15.25	< .001*
M_f	7.7510	1	7.7510	6.08	< .01*
$M_s \times M_f$	.7462	1	.7462	–	
Residual	212.7907	167	1.2742		

*One-tailed test.
The variables in (c) were introduced into the analysis in the same sequence as they appear in the table.

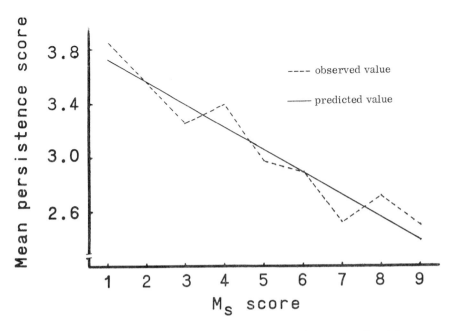

Fig. 22. Observed and predicted persistence scores in the easy/moderately difficult situation in relation to M_s score.

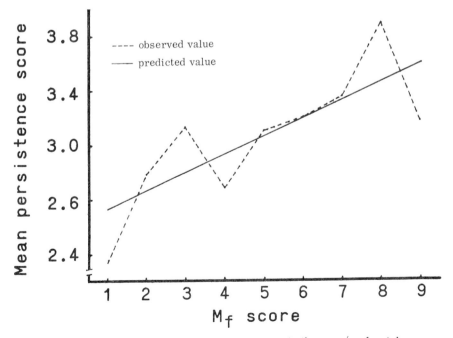

Fig. 23. Observed and predicted persistence scores in the easy/moderately difficult situation in relation to M_f score.

Turning to the M_f variable, the regression line for persistence scores on M_f scores is expressed by the equation

$$Y' = 2.3878 + .1365X_2,$$

where Y' = predicted persistence score, and $X_2 = M_f$ score. The regression line can be seen in Fig. 23 along with the observed mean values. The corresponding analysis of variance, presented in Table 22b, shows the linear regression to be significant. The table also indicates that there should be no reason to pay further attention to the deviations of the observed means from the regression line. Since the regression has been shown to be positive, hypothesis 4 is also confirmed.

It has been shown that there is only a very weak relationship between M_s and M_f scores (cf. e.g. Table 21), and the results reported above were therefore thought to imply a significant increase in the explained persistence score variance when the M_f variable was added to the M_s variable in the regression analysis. In this connection it would also be of interest to see whether there was any M_s by M_f interaction effect, i.e. any effect above the separate M_s and M_f effects on persistence. Such interaction effects are taken care of by the variable which is the product of the M_s and M_f scores.

When these three variables are considered simultaneously, the regression lines for the persistence scores are described by the equation

$$Y' = 3.8121 - .2429X_1 + .0000X_2 + .0194X_1X_2,$$

where Y' = predicted persistence score, $X_1 = M_s$ score, $X_2 = M_f$ score, and $X_1X_2 = M_s \times M_f$ score. The implications are given in Fig. 24 and in Table 22c. The interaction variance in the table emerged by finding the difference between the variance accounted for by all three variables and that accounted for by only the M_s and M_f variables together.

Table 22c makes it clear that there is a significant increase in the explained persistence score variance when the M_f variable is added to the M_s variable. Further, it should be noted that the M_s by M_f interaction, which shows itself in the different slopes of the regression lines in Fig. 24, is too small to be given any significance, i.e. the slope differences are so small that they should be regarded as within the range of chance fluctuations.

The persistence scores in the easy/moderately difficult situation have been seen to be systematically related to the M_s and M_f variable, but it should also be noted that these two variables together account for no more than about 11 per cent of the persistence score variance ($R = .34$). In the following we shall, however, be somewhat concerned with another variable which in connection with the data from the moderately difficult/easy situation turned out to be clearly related to persistence.

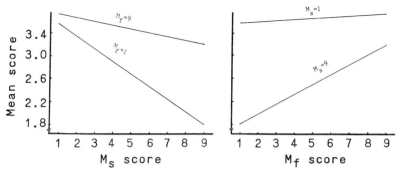

Fig. 24. Predicted persistence scores in the easy/moderately difficult situation in relation to M_s and M_f scores.

The Sex Variable. In connection with the data pertaining to the moderately difficult/ easy situation we considered the question of differences in the relationship between motive strength and persistence due to differences in probability of success. A related problem was that of sex differences in the relationship between motive strength and persistence, which was approached from the point of view that girls as a group consider their probability of success to be lower than do boys. In the present case, however, the initial task was of such a kind that the probability of success was assumed to be extremely high, and it therefore seemed meaningless to let the subjects rate their perceived chance of success before starting their work. Under these extreme conditions there seems also to be little reason to expect any sex difference in the probability of success. Therefore, neither does there seem to be any basis so far for expecting any sex difference in the relationship between motive strength and persistence.

However, the incentive value of the alternative task also has to be taken into account in this connection. In the present case this task was presented as being of moderate difficulty. But even if we assume that boys perceive their probability of success at the alternative task as higher than do girls, this circumstance alone does not determine which group should be most strongly motivated for the alternative task. To exemplify, if boys and girls perceive their probability of success at the alternative task to be about .70 and about 30 respectively, motivation for the alternative task should be equal for boys and girls with the same motive strength

Table 23. Persistence scores in the easy/moderately difficult situation in relation to M_s score and sex

Sex	Persistence score	M_s score 1	2	3	4	5	6	7	8	9	Total
	5	3	3	3	2	2	1	0	2	0	16
Girls	4	1	1	3	6	4	4	1	1	1	22
	3	2	3	3	6	5	4	2	2	2	29
	2	0	0	5	1	2	2	2	2	2	16
	5	0	0	0	3	0	0	1	0	0	4
Boys	4	0	1	2	4	5	4	4	0	0	20
	3	0	2	3	4	6	5	3	3	1	27
	2	1	0	1	3	4	3	1	1	1	15
	1	0	1	0	2	4	4	7	3	1	22
Total		7	11	20	31	32	27	21	14	8	171

(cf. e.g. p. 116, Fig. 8). Therefore, a consideration of the role of the alternative task is not a basis either for expecting sex differences in the relationship between motive strength and persistence. However, since the sex variable turned out both to have a main effect and to interact with one of the motive variables in an unexpected way in the moderately difficult/easy situation, it is of some interest to see whether this is the case even in the persistence situation considered in this section.

The relevant data as far as the M_s variable is concerned are given in Table 23. Here, as in the moderately difficult/easy situation, the most outstanding feature is the higher frequency of high persistence scores among girls than among boys. Actually, the lowest persistence score, score 1, does not appear at all among girls.

The sex difference in persistence is also spelled out in Fig. 25, showing the regression lines for persistence scores on M_s scores for boys and girls, along with the observed means. The regression model underlying this figure is expressed by the equation

$$Y' = 3.4951 - .1563X_1 + .5377X_4 + .0336X_1X_4,$$

where Y' = predicted persistence score, $X_1 = M_s$ score, X_4 = Sex (boys = 0, girls = 1), and $X_1X_4 = M_s \times$ Sex.

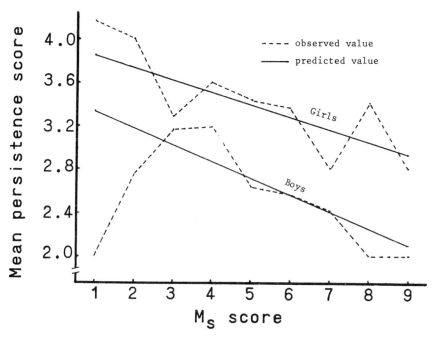

Fig. 25. Observed and predicted persistence scores in the easy/moderately difficult situation for the various M_s/sex combinations.

In this connection it should first be noted that the most striking deviation from the regression lines, that for boys with M_s score 1, is based on one observation only. The other observed mean values are seen to be located fairly close to the regression lines, a fact which also comes through in Table 24, which shows the deviations from regression to be insignificant.

The analysis of regression presented in the table also shows that the sex difference in persistence level is significant, as was the case in the moderately difficult/easy situation too. Further, as shown in the table and also in Fig. 25, there is no M_s by sex interaction effect, i.e. the relationship between M_s score and persistence score is the same for both boys and girls. Calculation of the correlation between M_s score and persistence score within each of the sex groups gave $r = -.23$ for boys, and $r = -.26$ for girls.

As to the M_f variable, the basic data are given in Table 25. The regression lines for these data are described by the equation

$$Y' = 2.0357 + .1294X_2 + .7646X_4 + .0064X_2X_4,$$

Table 24. Analysis of regression for persistence scores in the easy/moderately difficult situation on M_s scores and sex

Source	SS	df	MS	F	p
Total	240.7135	170	1.4160		
Linear regression	40.5362	3	13.5121	11.27	< .001
M_s	19.4256	1	19.4256	16.21	< 001*
Sex	20.8458	1	20.8458	17.39	< .001
M_s x Sex	.2648	1	.2648	-	
Residual	200.1773	167	1.1987		
Deviation from linear regression	9.4794	14	.6771	-	
Within M_s/Sex	190.6979	153	1.2464		

* One-tailed test.

The variables were introduced into the analysis in the same sequence as they appear in the table.

Table 25. Persistence scores in the easy/moderately difficult situation in relation to M_f score and sex

Sex	Persistence score	M_f score									Total
		1	2	3	4	5	6	7	8	9	
Girls	5	0	1	0	3	6	1	2	2	1	16
	4	0	1	1	3	6	7	2	2	0	22
	3	1	6	6	6	4	2	1	1	2	29
	2	1	2	0	5	3	2	3	0	0	16
Boys	5	0	0	2	0	0	1	1	0	0	4
	4	1	1	3	2	4	2	4	2	1	20
	3	1	0	5	5	5	7	1	2	1	27
	2	0	1	3	5	3	0	3	0	0	15
	1	3	2	1	6	6	3	0	0	1	22
Total		7	11	20	31	32	27	21	14	8	171

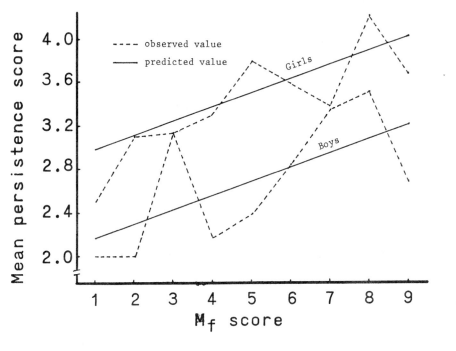

Fig. 26. Observed and predicted persistence scores in the easy/moderately difficult situation for the various M_f/sex combinations.

where Y' = predicted persistence score, S_2 = M_f score, X_4 = Sex, and X_2X_4 = M_f x Sex. The correspondence between this model and the observed means is seen in Fig. 25, and the analysis presented in Table 26 shows that the deviations from the regression lines are of no further interest.

As will be recalled, a clear M_f by sex interaction effect was observed in the study concerned with persistence in the moderately difficult/easy situation, where the correlation between M_f score and persistence score was negative for boys and positive for girls. In the present case, however, no such interaction effect appeared, i.e. there was no evidence that the relationship between M_f score and persistence was different for boys and girls. In terms of correlation coefficients, computed within each sex group, the relationship corresponds to $r = +.20$ for boys and $r = +.25$ for girls.

The persistence scores from the easy/moderately difficult situation had now been related to M_s scores, M_f scores, and their combinations, as well as to M_s scores

Table 26. Analysis of regression for persistence scores in the easy/moderately difficult situation on M_f scores and sex

Source	SS	df	MS	F	p
Total	240.7135	170	1.4160		
Linear regression	38.7308	3	12.9103	10.67	<.001
M_f	11.5302	1	11.5302	9.53	<.0025*
Sex	27.1765	1	27.1765	22.47	<.001
M_f x Sex	.0241	1	.0241	–	
Residual	201.9827	167	1.2095		
Deviation from linear regression	19.3995	14	1.3857	1.16	>.10
Within M_f/Sex	182.5832	153	1.1934		

*One-tailed test.

The variables were introduced into the analysis in the same sequence as they appear in the table.

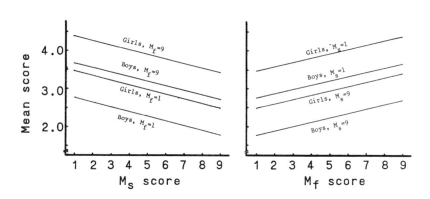

Fig. 27. Predicted persistence scores in the easy/moderately difficult situation in relation to M_s score, M_f score, and sex.

and sex, and M_f scores and sex. To sum up the main trends in the data, an anal-ysis was also carried out where the persistence scores were simultaneously re-lated to M_s scores, M_f scores, and sex, i.e. to the variables which had been ob-served to make significant contributions to the variation in persistence scores. This analysis yielded a model described by the equation

$Y' = 2.7653 - .1208X_1 + .1135X_2 + .7093X_4$,

where Y' = predicted persistence score, $X_1 = M_s$ score, $X_2 = M_f$ score, and $X_4 =$ Sex (0 = boys, 1 = girls). This model is made concrete in Fig. 27, and the corre-sponding analysis of regression is presented in Table 27.

Table 27. Analysis of regression for persistence scores in the easy/moderately difficult situation on M_s scores, M_f scores, and sex

Source	SS	df	MS	F	p
Total	240.7135	170	1.4160		
Linear regression	48.0946	3	16.0315	13.90	<.001
M_s	19.4256	1	19.4256	16.84	<.001*
M_f	7.7510	1	7.7510	6.72	<.01*
Sex	20.9180	1	20.9180	18.14	<.001
Residual	192.6189	167	1.1534		

*One-tailed test.

The variables were introduced into the analysis in the same se-quence as they appear in the table.

Since there was some correlation between the independent variables, the effect ascribed to each of them would vary to some extent according to the stage at which they were included in the analysis. Therefore, although the first-order interaction variables, i.e. the $M_s \times M_f$, $M_s \times$ Sex, and $M_f \times$ Sex variables, did not turn out to be of any significance according to the previous analysis, they were included in a final control analysis. In this analysis each of them was introduced subsequent to the variables in the summing up analysis presented above. However, no inter-action effects were observed.

Discussion and summing up

According to hypothesis 3 there should be a negative relationship between M_s strength and persistence at the initial task in the easy/moderately difficult situation, and according to hypothesis 4 there should be a positive relationship between M_f strength and persistence in this situation. The data have been seen to lend support to both hypotheses. If we focus upon the best fitting straight lines in Fig. 24 and the M_s/M_f score combinations 9/1 and 1/9 as representing $M_s > M_f$ and $M_s < M_f$ respectively, and the combinations 1/1 and 9/9 as representing $M_s \approx M_f$, this further implied, as can be seen from Fig. 24, that the predicted score for the $M_s < M_f$ group was higher than that for the $M_s > M_f$ group, while the score for the $M_s \approx M_f$ groups fell somewhere between these extreme motive groups. It has also been demonstrated that the relationship between motive score and persistence score was roughly the same for both sexes, i.e. there were no indications of motive by sex interactions, in contrast to what was the case in the moderately difficult/easy situation, where an M_f by sex interaction appeared. In this connection it seems natural to focus once more upon the P_s variable, since it appears reasonable to assume that the P_s condition for the initial task was clearer in the easy/moderately difficult situation than in the moderately difficult/easy situation. In the present case the initial task was a very simple one, a task managed by all subjects. P_s has therefore probably been very high for most subjects. Since there seemed to be no reason for a sex difference in P_s in this extreme situation, there was not reason to expect a sex difference in the relationship between motive score and persistence score, either.

While the results turned out in the expected direction, it must also be noted that the M_s and M_f variables do not jointly account for more than about 11 per cent of the variance in persistence scores (R = .34, cf. Table 27). Thus, persistence has obviously been strongly influenced by variables other than M_s and M_f. Although the relationship between motive score and persistence score was the same for boys and girls, girls were as a group clearly more persistent than boys. As appears from Table 27, the sex variable alone accounts for about 9 per cent of the variance when it is introduced into the analysis subsequent to the motive variables. It will be recalled that a similar sex effect was observed in the moderately difficult/easy situation too. Thus, the results from the easy/moderately difficult situation strengthen the view presented in the discussion of the results from the moderately difficult easy situation that girls as a group are more extrinsically motivated than boys.

Before we leave the results from the easy/moderately difficult situation, their validity should be examined from the point of view that irrelevant class differences might have distorted the relationships. Following the same procedure as

214

in connection with the data from the moderately difficult/easy situation, we obtained a mean within-class correlation between M_s score and persistence score of $-.29$, while that between M_f score and persistence score was $+.14$. Thus, this simple control analysis shows that the directions of these mean within class correlations correspond to those from the overall analyses presented previously (p. 202), and this is thought to indicate that irrelevant between-class differences have not represented any serious source of error in the present case.

The persistence findings from the easy/moderately difficult situation may then be summed up as follows:

(a) There was an overall negative relationship between M_s score and persistence score (main effect of M_s).

(b) There was an overall positive relationship between M_f score and persistence score (main effect of M_f).

(c) Girls were more persistent than boys (main effect of sex).

(d) The negative relationship between M_s score and persistence score held across M_f levels, and the positive relationship between M_f score and persistence score held across M_s levels (no $M_s \times M_f$ effect).

(e) There was no sex difference in the relationship between M_s or M_f score and persistence score (no $M_s \times$ Sex or $M_f \times$ Sex effect).

If we consider the motive combination groups, the following findings may be added:

(f) The $M_s < M_f$ group was more persistent than the $M_s > M_f$ group. The $M_s \approx M_f$ groups' results fell between those of the $M_s < M_f$ group and the $M_s > M_f$ group. This was the case both for boys and girls.

INITIAL TASK OF HIGH DIFFICULTY AND ALTERNATIVE TASK OF MODERATE DIFFICULTY

The problems to be treated in this section are much the same as those dealt with in the persistence study by Feather (1963), considered previously (cf. pp. 88 ff.), and therefore this study may to a certain extent be regarded as a replication of the Feather study.

The task set

In the present case, as in the Feather study (1963), a situation had to be created where the initial task would be perceived as an extremely difficult one. For this purpose Feather used a diagram task where all the lines of the diagram had to be traced without lifting the pencil and without drawing any line twice. In the present case a modified version of the task used by Feather was chosen, which was more suitable in a group situation.

The initial task set consisted of a booklet with in all 33 identical labyrinths. The task consisted of drawing an unbroken line through all the passages in the labyrinth in such a way that the line already drawn was never crossed. This task was in fact insoluble.

The alternative task set, to which further attention will not be paid here, consisted of a set of small crossword puzzles.

Procedure

From the instructions, presented in their entirety in Appendix D, it is seen that the booklets containing the initial task were passed round together with an envelope containing the alternative task set. The subjects were told that the envelope contained tasks of moderate difficulty, i.e. so difficult that only about half the pupils normally managed them. Further, they were instructed that the initial task was very, very difficult, so difficult that hardly more than one out of a hundred pupils usually managed it. After they had been instructed what to do by examining an example and had taken a look at the labyrinth task to be solved, the subjects were asked to indicate their expectancy of success at the task on a 20-point scale identical to that used in the moderately difficult/easy situation.

As in the two persistence settings considered previously in this chapter, instructions were given that the subjects were free to work for as long a time as they wanted at the initial task, and that they could turn to the alternative, moderately difficult task set whenever they wished.

The time before each subject turned to the alternative task set was registered.

General results

Results Related to the Probability of Success Assumptions. In the present case the initial task was presented as one of very high difficulty, by informing the subjects that less than one in a hundred pupils would be able to solve it. The question is then whether the subjects themselves perceived the task as intended, i.e. as an extremely difficult one. As mentioned earlier, they were asked, as in the moderately difficult/easy situation, to estimate their chances of solving the problem. The answers may be taken as at least a rough indicator of whether the purpose was achieved.

The results are shown in Fig. 28, which includes three subjects who had not reported any expectancy of success and who were randomly distributed on the two values closest to the median (7 and 8). The figure reveals a considerable spread in the reported chances of success. Thus, the answers vary from 1, which means "Quite sure I won't manage the task", to 16, which indicates that the subject perceived his chance of success to be fairly high. Obviously, the task is perceived as more difficult than the initial one in the moderately difficult/easy situation (cf. p. 174, Fig. 12), but, as far as the subjects' own estimates can be trusted, only a small part of the sample regarded the task as an extremely difficult one. In other words, a considerable number of subjects seem to have regarded the initial task as being one of only moderate difficulty. A similar tendency to over-estimate low probabilities of success has been reported by other investigators too (e.g. Feather, 1963, p. 607; Preston & Baratta, 1948, pp. 187 f.), indicating that the results obtained in the present case reflect a general tendency.

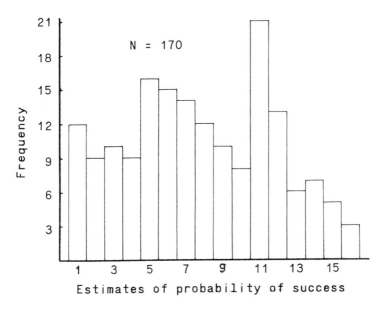

Fig. 28.   The subjects' estimates of probability of success at the initial task in the extremely difficult/moderately difficult situation. (1 = "Quite sure I won't manage the task", 20 = "Quite sure I'll manage the task".)

Thus, to put it mildly, there seems to have been a certain lack of correspondence between the situation assumed in the hypotheses and that from which the data were obtained. This discrepancy should be kept in mind when turning to the analyses of the persistence results.

The Persistence Results. As in the easy/moderately difficult situation there was one school session available for the extremely difficult/moderately difficult persistence situation and the time limit was set at thirty-five minutes.

The results in terms of minutes spent at the initial task are presented in the upper part of Fig. 29. They are approximately normally distributed, so that no transformation was necessary because of the shape of the distribution before the analyses were carried out. However, a one-digit variable is easier to handle, and since the data from the easy/moderately difficult situation had been transformed into a 5-point scale and since such a scale was regarded as sufficiently refined for the purpose of the study, it was found convenient to use the same scale in the present case.

The transformed persistence results are presented in the lower part of Fig. 29.

Carryover Effects. It has previously been pointed out that half of the classes got the easy/moderately difficult tasks as the second set and the extremely difficult /moderately difficult ones as the third set, while the other half had the two sets in reversed order. The mean persistence scores for subjects confronted with the extremely/moderately difficult tasks as the second set and for those having them as the third set are presented in Table 28, which shows the means to be almost identical. Thus, insofar as these results may be taken as an indicator of whether carryover effects from one persistence situation to another were present, there is no evidence at all that the data from the extremely/moderately difficult situation are influenced by such effects.

Empirical testing of hypothesis

In the analyses to be reported the following basic variables are included.

Y = Persistence score

X_1 = M_s stanine score

X_2 = M_f stanine score

X_3 = P_s score (0 = low, 1 = high)

X_4 = Sex (0 = boys, 1 = girls)

The intercorrelations between these variables are shown in Table 29.

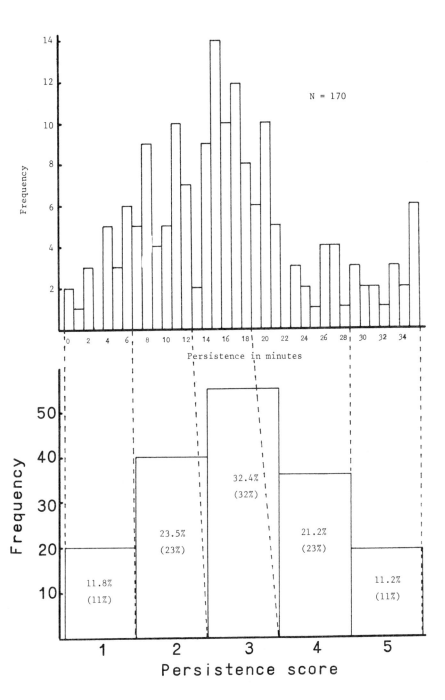

Fig. 29.   Persistence at the initial task in the extremely difficult/moderately
difficult situation. Observed and transformed data.

Table 28. Mean persistence score in the extremely difficult/moderately difficult situation for subjects confronted with this situation in second and third place in the series

| | Extremely/moderately difficult set as | | Total |
	no. 2	no. 3	
N	83	87	170
$\overline{X}$	2.93	3.00	2.96
s	1.19	1.16	1.17
D		.07	
t		.40	
p		>.10	

Table 29. Intercorrelations between the variables related to the extremely difficult/moderately difficult persistence situation

| Variable | Variable | | | |
	X_1	X_2	X_3	X_4
X_1 (M_s)				
X_2 (M_f)	-.14			
X_3 (P_s)	+.18	+.10		
X_4 (Sex)	-.18	+.04	-.15	
Y (Persistence)	+.11	.00	+.05	+.03

The Overall Relationship between Motive Score and Persistence. Hypothesis 5 states that when the initial task is perceived as being of very high difficulty and the alternative task as being of moderate difficulty, the relationship between M_s strength and persistence at the initial task should be negative. According to hypothesis 6 the corresponding relationship between M_f strength and persistence should be positive.

The data concerning these predictions are presented in Fig. 30, where the mean persistence scores for the various M_s and M_f score categories are also given.

As far as the M_f variable is concerned, these means do not reveal any systematic trend at all, the relationship corresponding to $r = .00$. Turning to the M_s variable, the means indicate the opposite of what was predicted, i.e. higher persistence among those with high M_s scores. However, this relationship is too weak to deserve any further attention here ($r = .11$, $p > .10$). Neither do the data reflect any M_s by M_f interaction.

Thus, to conclude, there is thus far not the least evidence in favour of the hypotheses. This fact should, however, be considered in the light of the circumstance mentioned above, that there seems to be a rather weak correspondence between the situation dealt with in the hypotheses and that from which the data were obtained. The data should therefore be examined somewhat more thoroughly, to see whether there is any indication that the lack of results in the expected direction might be due to this possible failure to establish an extremely/moderately difficult persistence situation.

	M_s score									
M_f score	1	2	3	4	5	6	7	8	9	Ȳ
9				5		3 5		234		3.67
8		1		4	233	3 4	3 5	5		3.30
7		4	1135	112 3 4	1123	1 2				2.19
6		2234	223 3 4	234	4 5	122 2 5	3 5	1 2	2 5	2.92
5	123	2344	124 455	1234 444	2222 2333	1345	1335	5		3.00
4	3 3		3455	223 444	1223 3334	2233 4444	135	235	3	3.17
3	3	3	3	223 3 3	2233	233	224	344		2.81
2	3			1	2 3	4 4	234	3	345	3.15
1				1	4		133		3 4	2.71
Ȳ	2.57	2.91	3.25	2.83	2.59	3.04	3.05	3.29	3.63	

Fig. 30. Persistence scores in the extremely difficult/moderately difficult situation in relation to M_s and M_f scores.

Within-Situation Differences in the Relationship between Motive Score and Persistence: The P_s and Sex Variable. The probability of success estimates indicated that a majority of the subjects held the task to be only moderately difficult. It might then be that both the initial and the alternative task were regarded as moderately difficult. In such a case no systematic relationship between motive strength and persistence can be expected, since the motivation for the initial and the alternative task should be about the same.

Another, probably more reasonable guess, is that the overestimation of probability of success also applied to the alternative task. If this were the case, the setting intended to represent an extremely/moderately difficult persistence situation has probably been experienced as a moderately difficult/easy situation by a considerable number of the subjects.

However, even in such a case one would not expect any clear overall relationship between motive strength and persistence. Thus, the positive relationship which should exist between M_s strength and persistence among subjects experiencing the situation as a moderately difficult/easy one should to some extent be counterbalanced by a negative relationship among those experiencing the situation in the intended way, i.e. as an extremely/moderately difficult situation. A corresponding line of reasoning should apply to the relationship between M_f strength and persistence.

Based on these considerations the analyses were brought one step further, by comparing subjects who had indicated a very low probability of success at the initial task with those with a higher probability of success. To be relatively confident that the first group really did perceive the initial task as an extremely difficult one, only subjects with estimates of probability of success (see p. 217, Fig. 28) below 5, i.e. the lowest third, were included here (P_s score = 0), the rest of the sample making up the high P_s group (P_s score = 1).

The persistence data for the low and high P_s groups are related to the M_s scores in Table 30. This table does not reveal any clear relationship. However, the number of observations within several of the M_s/P_s combinations is very small, and therefore focus should be upon possible trends revealed by an analysis of regression, rather than upon the particular means. According to such an analysis the relationships are described by the equation

$$Y' = 3.0156 - .0374X_1 - .4956X_3 + .1287X_1X_2,$$

where Y' = predicted persistence score, $X_1 = M_s$ score, $X_3 = P_s$ score, and $X_1X_3 = M_s \times P_s$ score. This regression equation gives the regression lines shown in Fig. 31, which indicates an interaction between M_s and P_s in accordance with the reasoning above. In terms of correlation coefficients the relationship between

Table 30. Persistence scores in the extremely difficult/moderately difficult situation in relation to M_s and P_s scores

P_s	Persistence score	M_s score									Total
		1	2	3	4	5	6	7	8	9	
High	5	0	0	3	0	1	2	4	2	2	14
	4	0	2	2	8	3	7	2	2	2	28
	3	4	3	3	6	10	7	8	4	2	47
	2	0	1	3	3	7	6	3	2	1	26
	1	1	1	3	2	3	2	3	0	0	15
Low	5	0	0	2	1	0	1	0	1	0	5
	4	0	2	2	2	0	1	0	1	0	8
	3	1	0	2	1	3	0	0	0	1	8
	2	1	2	0	4	5	1	0	1	0	14
	1	0	0	0	3	0	1	0	1	0	5
Total		7	11	20	30	32	28	20	14	8	170

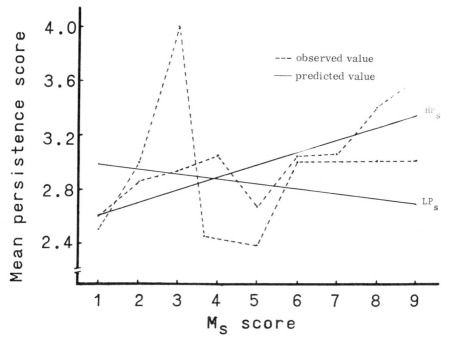

Fig. 31. Observed and predicted persistence scores in the extremely difficult/moderately difficult situation for the various M_s/P_s combinations.

M_s score and persistence score within the high P_s group corresponds to r = +.16, while that within the low P_s group corresponds to r = -.06. The analysis presented in Table 31 shows, however, that the interaction reflected in the difference between these two correlations is well within the limits of what might be regarded as chance fluctuations.

Turning to the M_f variable, the reasoning presented at the outset of this section implies that the null correlation between M_f score and persistence found in the sample as a whole might cover up a positive relationship within the low P_s group and a negative relationship within the high P_s group. The data pertaining to this expectation are presented in Table 32.

Table 31. Analysis of regression for persistence scores in the extremely difficult/moderately difficult situation on M_s and P_s scores

Source	SS	df	MS	F	p
Total	231.7882	169	1.3715		
Linear regression	5.1689	3	1.7230	1.26	>.10
M_s	3.0132	1	3.0132	2.21	>.10
P_s	.2782	1	.2782	-	
M_s x P_s	1.8775	1	1.8775	1.38	>.10*
Residual	226.6193	166	1.3652		
Deviation from linear regression	15.1931	13	1.1687	-	
Within M_s/P_s scores	211.4262	153	1.3819		

*One-tailed test.

The variables were introduced into the analysis in the same sequence as they appear in the table.

When we consider only the direction of the relationships between M_f score and persistence, the data are in accordance with the expectation, in that within the high P_s group r = -.03, while r = +.09 within the low P_s group. However, the difference between the correlations is even less than it was in connection with the M_s variable, so that further analyses of this result have no interest. Obviously, no significance can be attached to this result alone.

Since we have not been able to reveal any clear change in the relationship between persistence score and each of the variables M_s scores and M_f scores from the high

Table 32. Persistence scores in the extremely difficult/moderately difficult situation in relation to M_f and P_s score

P_s	Persistence score	M_f score									Total
		1	2	3	4	5	6	7	8	9	
High	5	0	1	0	2	4	3	1	2	1	14
	4	2	4	2	6	6	4	1	2	1	28
	3	2	5	8	10	8	5	3	4	2	47
	2	0	1	4	3	5	8	3	1	1	26
	1	2	0	0	2	4	1	5	1	0	15
Low	5	0	0	0	2	1	1	0	0	1	5
	4	0	0	1	3	3	0	1	0	0	8
	3	1	0	3	3	1	0	0	0	0	8
	2	0	1	3	4	4	2	0	0	0	14
	1	0	1	0	0	1	1	2	0	0	5
Total		7	13	21	35	37	25	16	10	6	170

to the low P_s group, it might be of some interest to see whether persistence was more clearly related to a combination of the two motive measures and P_s score. However, there was practically no increase in the multiple correlation when the predictors M_f and M_f x P_s were added to the predictor variables referred to in Fig. 31 and Table 31 (R = .150, and R = .154), so that no further analyses were carried out regarding this point.

In the data from the moderately difficult/easy persistence situation as well as those from the easy/moderately difficult situation a clear sex difference in persistence was revealed, girls being more persistent than boys. Further, the question of differences in the relationship between motive strength and persistence has been dealt with, based on the viewpoint that when comparing the sexes, girls may be regarded as a low and boys as a high P_s group. To get more information on these questions, they should be considered further here.

The assumption of a sex difference in P_s for the initial task is checked in Table 33, and the direction of the result is in accordance with that of the result from the moderately difficult/easy situation (cf. p. 184, Table 13), as there is a higher frequency of high P_s scores among boys than among girls. But contrary to what was the case in the moderately difficult/easy situation, we are here faced with a clearly significant difference. This difference should from a theoretical point of

Table 33. Sex difference in P_s score for the initial task in the extremely difficult/moderately difficult situation

P_s score	Boys	Girls	Total	χ^2	df	p
1 (high)	72	58	130			
0 (low)	15	25	40	3.92	1	<.025*

*One-tailed test.

view imply that the relationship between motive score and persistence score should be somewhat different for boys and girls. However, no clear interaction between M_s and P_s or between M_f and P_s has been demonstrated in the analyses presented above, and accordingly no clear interaction effect of motive strength and sex on persistence could be expected. The data pertaining to the M_s variable are given in Table 34, and the means on the persistence variable for each M_s/sex combination are shown in Fig. 32 along with the regression lines for the persistence scores.

Table 34. Persistence scores in the extremely difficult/moderately difficult situation in relation to M_s score and sex

Sex	Persistence score	M_s score									Total
		1	2	3	4	5	6	7	8	9	
	5	0	0	3	0	0	1	0	2	0	6
	4	0	2	3	7	0	4	1	1	2	20
Girls	3	5	2	5	3	8	3	2	2	2	32
	2	1	2	1	3	4	3	2	1	1	18
	1	0	1	2	2	0	1	0	1	0	7
	5	0	0	2	1	1	2	4	1	2	13
	4	0	2	1	3	3	4	1	2	0	16
Boys	3	0	1	0	4	5	4	6	2	1	23
	2	0	1	2	4	8	4	1	2	0	22
	1	1	0	1	3	3	2	3	0	0	13
Total		7	11	20	30	32	28	20	14	8	170

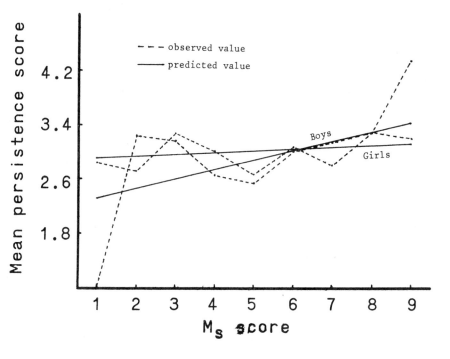

Fig. 32. Observed and predicted persistence scores in the extremely difficult/moderately difficult situation for the various M_s/sex combinations.

These regression lines are described by the equation

$$Y' = 2.1802 + .1388X_1 + .6899X_4 - .1112X_1X_3,$$

where Y' = predicted persistence score, $X_1 = M_s$ score, X_4 = Sex (boys = 0, girls = 1), and $X_1X_4 = M_s$ score x Sex. The corresponding analysis of regression is presented in Table 35.

Focusing first upon the sex variable, the mean persistence score for boys is 2.93 and that for girls 3.00, i.e. a difference in the same direction as that observed in the moderately difficult/easy as well as the easy/moderately difficult persistence situation. However, in contrast to what was the case in the other two persistence situations, the difference is here negligible.

Since boys, according to the probability of success estimates, regarded their chances of success as being higher than girls did, they should to a greater extent than girls have perceived the persistence situation with which we are concerned here as being a moderately difficult/easy one. Hence, it would be of interest to see whether the slight overall positive relationship between M_s score and persis-

Table 35. Analysis of regression for persistence scores in the extremely difficult/moderately difficult situation on M_s scores and sex

Source	SS	df	MS	F	p
Total	231.7882	169	1.3715		
Linear regression	5.5629	3	1.8543	1.36	> .10
M_s	3.0132	1	3.0132	2.21	> .10
Sex	.6027	1	.6027	–	
M_s x Sex	1.9470	1	1.9470	1.43	> .10
Residual	226.2253	166	1.3628		
Deviation from linear regression	14.7991	14	1.0571	–	
Within M_s/Sex	211.4262	152	1.3910		

The variables were introduced into the analysis in the same sequence as they appear in the table.

tence score was mainly due to a positive relationship among boys. A tendency in this direction is also revealed by Fig. 32, but the analysis presented in Table 35 shows this sex difference in the relationship between M_s score and persistence score, expressed through the M_s x Sex variable, to be far from significant.

Turning now to the question of sex difference in the relationship between M_f strength and persistence, the circumstance that boys to a greater extent than girls are presumed to interpret the situation as a moderately difficult/easy one poses the question of whether the null correlation observed in the sample as a whole covers up a negative relationship between M_f score and persistence score among boys and a positive relationship between these variables among girls. The basic data concerning this matter are given in Table 36, and the main trends are illustrated in Fig. 33. The regression lines are here described by the equation

$$Y' = 2.5879 + .0726X_2 + .8103X_4 - .1540X_2X_4,$$

where Y' = predicted persistence score, X_2 = M_f score, X_4 = Sex (boys = 0, girls = 1), and X_2X_4 = M_f score x Sex. These regression lines reveal trends in quite the opposite direction to that expected, i.e. a positive relationship between M_f score and persistence score among boys, corresponding to $r = +.11$, and a negative relationship among girls, corresponding to $r = -.15$. The analysis in Table 37 shows, however, that this sex difference, like all other differences or relationships

Table 36. Persistence scores in the extremely difficult/moderately difficult situation in relation to M_f score and sex

Sex	Persistence score	M_f score									Total
		1	2	3	4	5	6	7	8	9	
Girls	5	0	0	0	3	0	11	1	1	0	6
	4	1	4	1	2	8	1	2	1	0	20
	3	1	2	5	10	6	3	1	2	2	32
	2	0	2	1	2	4	6	2	0	1	18
	1	0	1	0	0	1	1	3	1	0	7
Boys	5	0	1	0	1	5	3	0	1	2	13
	4	1	0	2	7	1	3	0	1	1	16
	3	2	3	6	3	3	2	2	2	0	23
	2	0	0	6	5	5	4	1	1	0	22
	1	2	0	0	2	4	1	4	0	0	13
Total		7	13	21	35	37	25	16	10	6	170

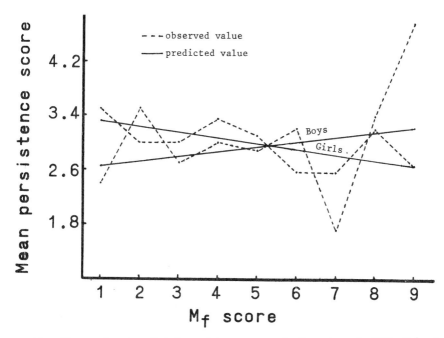

Fig. 33. Observed and predicted persistence scores in the extremely difficult/moderately difficult situation for the various M_f/sex combinations.

Table 37. Analysis of regression for persistence scores in the extremely difficult/moderately difficult situation on M_f scores and sex

Source	SS	df	MS	F	p
Total	231.7882	169	1.3715		
Linear regression	3.8477	3	1.2826	–	
M_f	.0000	1	.0000	–	
Sex	.2086	1	.2086	–	
M_f x Sex	3.6391	1	3.6391	2.65	>.10
Residual	227.9405	166	1.3731		
Deviation from linear regression	28.7253	14	2.0518	1.57	≈.10
Within M_f scores	199.2152	152	1.3106		

The variables were introduced into the analysis in the same sequence as they appear in the table.

analysed in this section, is insignificant. It should nevertheless be noted that this is the only difference of those considered hitherto with a direction opposite to what is expected on the basis of the theory.

To sum up the main trends in the results from the moderately difficult/easy and the easy/moderately difficult situation, a final analysis was performed, including all independent variables which had been observed to contribute significantly to the variation in persistence scores. In the present case, however, all the relationships have been seen to be very weak ones. Under these circumstances an encompassing summing up analysis was found pointless, since it would mean a very great capitalization on chance.

Discussion

The main hypotheses which guided the research reported above were that in the extremely/moderately difficult situation persistence at the initial task should be negatively related to M_s strength and positively related to M_f strength. The overall results reported did not provide any support at all for these hypotheses. This also means that we were not able to replicate the findings reported by Feather from a similar study (cf. pp. 88 ff.). It was, however, pointed out at the beginning that the subjects' own estimates of probability of success indicated a rather clear discrepancy between the situation referred to in the hypotheses and that actually established. Another possible source of error is that of irrelevant class differences, to which some attention has been paid. However, a check of the mean within-class correlations between motive score and persistence score does not indicate that such effects have played a decisive role. The mean within-class correlation between M_s score and persistence score was +.19, and that between M_f score and persistence score +.02, while the corresponding correlations from the overall analyses were +.11 and .00 respectively. Thus the within-class results do not turn out more favourably in relation to the hypotheses, rather the contrary.

Suspecting that a majority of the subjects perceived the initial task in a way that was not intended, i.e. as being of moderate difficulty, we carried out more thorough analyses of the data, where a distinction was made between subjects reporting a high and a low expectancy of success. However, the results demonstrate that, throughout the whole series of analyses, no trend at all was revealed which, from a statistical point of view, can be considered as a relatively reliable one. Yet the pattern of the relationships which appeared, weak though they are, perhaps deserves some further attention.

To take the M_s variable again first, it was expected that the low positive relationship revealed by the overall analysis masked a negative relationship within the low P_s group. As can be seen from Fig. 31 (p. 223), the directions of the best-fitting straight lines based on the analysis of regression correspond exactly to this expectation.

With respect to the M_f variable, the expectation was that the overall null correlation between this variable and persistence scores should hide a positive relationship among subjects with a low P_s and a negative relationship among subjects with a high P_s. The correlations were +.09 and -.03 respectively (cf. p. 224).

Obviously, each of the changes in the relationship between motive score and persistence score from the high to the low P_s group separately is far too small to be trusted, but taken together their pattern is a sufficient basis for the question of what the relationship would be in an even more extreme P_s group than that considered here. A final check was therefore made, where only those 12 subjects with the most extreme probability of success estimates, i.e. probability of success estimates of 1 (cf. p. 217, Fig. 28), were included. The results from this analysis in terms of correlation coefficients are presented in Table 38 along with the various correlation coefficients for the groups referred to above.

Although based on a very small number of subjects, the results from the very

Table 38. Correlations between motive scores and persistence scores in the extremely difficult/moderately difficult situation for the high, low, and extremely low P_s group

		High P_s (N = 130)	Low P_s (N = 40)	Extremely low P_s (N = 12)
	Boys	+.23	-.12	.00
M_s scores	Girls	+.09	-.02	-.41
	Total	+.16	-.06	-.10
	Boys	+.05	+.40	+.39
M_f scores	Girls	-.18	-.10	+.53
	Total	-.03	+.09	+.43

extreme P_s group are on the whole seen to underscore the trends in the data referred to in the foregoing. The relationships between motive score and persistence score observed within this group correspond very well to the hypothesized relationships. Thus, while the results from the first analyses of the data, where the subject's own estimate of probability of success was disregarded, did not reveal anything at all in favour of the hypotheses, the more thorough-going analyses have to a certain extent modified this impression. The changes in the correlations referred to above do not, of course, constitute any conclusive evidence, but they may be taken as at least a modest indication that the hypotheses of a negative relationship between M_s strength and persistence and a positive relationship between M_f strength and persistence in extremely/moderately difficult situations may still be valid.

Two additional results should finally be observed. First, while girls turned out to be more persistent than boys both in the moderately difficult/easy and in the easy/moderately difficult situations, the difference in favour of girls was only negligible here. The differences in the two previously considered persistence situations were explained in terms of stronger extrinsic motivation among girls than among boys. This line of reasoning also implies that there was not the same difference in extrinsic motivation in the present case. One may wonder whether this pattern of results reflects a sex role difference. Thus it may be that girls, when compared with boys, experience relatively less pressure to master the task as its difficulty increases.

Lastly, it will be recalled that in the moderately difficult/easy situation a clear positive main effect of P_s was observed, but in the present case no considerable P_s effect has been demonstrated. During the discussion of the P_s effect in the moderately difficult/easy situation it was pointed out that such an effect should occur in samples where the average strength of M_s exceeds that of M_f (provided that we find ourselves in the left-hand part of the motivation model, p. 116, Fig. 8). It was suggested that a difference in the average strength of the two motives in this direction might be present in our sample. However, the very weak relationship between P_s score and persistence score observed in this latter persistence situation indicates that no firm conclusions should be drawn at this point.

Summing up

According to hypothesis 5 a negative relationship should exist between M_s strength and persistence at the initial task in the extremely/moderately difficult situation, and according to hypothesis 6 the relationship between M_f strength and persistence in this situation should be a positive one. The data did not lend any clear support to these hypotheses, either for boys or for girls. However, some indications that the hypotheses may nevertheless be valid were found in the changes in the correlations between motive scores and persistence scores from the sample as a whole via a subgroup with relatively low reported expectancies of success to the small group with the very lowest expectancy of success.

Contrary to what was found in the moderately difficult/easy persistence situation, no positive main effect of P_s on persistence was observed, and contrary to the findings in both of the previously considered persistence situations, no clear difference in persistence in favour of girls was observed here.

THE THREE SETS OF FINDINGS IN PERSPECTIVE

The relatively detailed presentation of results in the last sections may to a certain extent have obscured the main points. In the following, therefore, instead of summarizing all the findings, an attempt will be made to gather up the main threads from the three persistence situations, which have been considered relatively isolated from each other in this chapter.

The empirical investigation had as its main aim the testing of a set of hypotheses which originated in a conception of persistence as the result of a personality by situation interaction. The results, although not always equally clear-cut, have provided considerable support for this point of view. We shall, however, initially return for a moment to where we started out, i.e. to the two simpler traditions of studying persistence problems which were discussed in Chapter 1, of which one is primarily personality-oriented, and the other primarily situation-oriented. Although the present investigation was not designed to test the separate contributions of personality and situation characteristics to persistence, some of the findings may nevertheless be related to these traditions.

First, a comparison of the raw data from the three persistence situations described in the foregoing sections indicates a clear situation effect. Thus, if we concentrate on the time spent by the sample on the initial task, we find a variation from Mdn $\approx$ 18 minutes for the moderately difficult/easy situation (cf. p. 175, Fig. 13), via Mdn $\approx$ 3 minutes for the easy/moderately difficult situation (cf. p. 200, Fig. 20), to Mdn $\approx$ 15 minutes for the extremely/moderately difficult situation (cf. p. 219, Fig. 29). Needless to say, differences between situations or tasks have several dimensions. Achievement motivation theory actually deals with only one such dimension, that of (perceived) task difficulty, which is assumed to determine the incentive value of the task. In the present case there were differences between the initial tasks not only in difficulty, but also in kind. Since it is not possible to untangle the effects of difficulty and kind, and the present work has mainly dealt with only one aspect of the very complex task acceptance problem, the differences in persistence from one situation to another will not be interpreted any further. This also means that these results are of very restricted interest.

The results referred to above lend a certain support to the situation-oriented research tradition, but should not, of course, on that account be interpreted to mean that persistence is independent of the characteristics of the individuals involved. One could in fact equally well regard the results as lending some support to the personality-oriented research tradition. This tradition emphasizes the possibility of predicting who will and who will not be high persisters on the basis of knowledge about individual differences. From this point of view the observed sex difference in persistence should be underscored. As will be recalled from Chapter 1 (pp. 29 ff.), previous research has not revealed any clear pattern with respect to sex differences in persistence. Naturally, males have been observed to be more persistent than females at tasks requiring physical strength, while somewhat higher persistence among girls than among boys has occasionally been observed at tasks where physical strength is of little importance. The tasks used in the present investigation belong to the latter group, and in the analyses girls have turned out more persistent than boys. Thus, in the moderately difficult/easy as well as in the easy/moderately difficult situation girls were clearly more persistent than boys, and in the extremely/moderately difficult situation too, where the difference was only a very slight one, the direction was the same.

The finding of a sex difference in persistence is also of some significance within an achievement motivation context. Thus, this difference has to be conceptualized as a reflection of stronger extrinsic motivation, i.e. motivation due to motives other than M_s and M_f, among girls than among boys, possibly because of a greater sensitivity on the part of the girls to the administrator's request to start working at the initial task first. We have previously called attention to Gjesme's suggestion that the repeatedly observed less clear relationship between M_s or M_f scores and performance criteria among girls than among boys is due to a lower expectancy of success among girls. Some evidence in favour of Gjesme's assumption of a sex difference in expectancy has also been obtained in the present investigation (cf. p. 184, Table 13, and p. 226, Table 33). However, in the present case these within-situation sex differences in expectancy of success did not bring about any clear differences in the relationship between motive scores and persistence scores, possibly because they were too weak. Disregarding this matter, the sex difference in extrinsic motivation referred to above may indicate an additional cause for the frequently observed weaker relationship between M_s or M_f scores and behaviour criteria among girls. Thus, if girls generally have a stronger extrinsic motivation than boys in performance situations like those dealt with in achievement motivation research, it also seems reasonable to expect a weaker relationship between M_s or M_f strength and behaviour criteria among girls. This should be so because the motivation due to M_s and M_f should make up a smaller fraction of the total motivation to engage in the task in question among girls than among boys.

Hitherto this section has dealt with findings which fit in with a situation-oriented or an individual-oriented approach to the problem of persistence. However, by concentrating on the results directly related to achievement motivation theory, one is faced with findings that can be explained neither within the situation-oriented tradition alone nor within the individual-oriented tradition alone. Instead, they illustrate very well the governing idea behind the present study, which is that not only do individuals with different motive constellations react in opposite ways to the same situation, but also individuals with the same motive constellation react in opposite ways to different situations. To underscore and illustrate this fact the findings that were considered in detail in the foregoing sections have been boiled down to differences between the four motive constellation groups which appear on the basis of a median split on each of the two motive variables. Because no curvilinear relationships between motive score and persistence score have been revealed through the previous analyses, this was found to be a justifiable way of summing up the main trends in the results. For the sake of simplicity the groups obtained by this split will later on be referred to as the $M_s > M_f$ group, the $M_s < M_f$ group, and the $M_s \approx M_f$ groups.

The mean persistence scores in the three different persistence situations for each of these groups are given in Fig. 34. Although, on the basis of the more refined analyses presented previously, some of the values in Fig. 34 are known to mask underlying differences due to within-situation variations in perceived probability of success, they nevertheless serve to throw the most important relationships into relief.

The differences in reactions to the same situation are reflected in the relationships between motive constellation and persistence score within each of the three persistence situations. True enough, not all of these relationships were equally clear-cut but they suffice to accentuate the influence of the motives M_s and M_f. Recalling that the mean scores for the moderately difficult/easy situation are based on 0's and 1's only, and therefore give the percentages of high persisters, we observe that in this situation there is, as far as the boys are concerned, a majority of high persisters among the $M_s > M_f$ subjects, while the percentage of high persisters is very low in the $M_s < M_f$ group. Concerning girls, the results are more ambiguous. While the difference between the $M_s > M_f$ group and the $M_s < M_f$ group is in the expected direction, it is a very small one, and since the pattern in this crude summing up does not correspond exactly to the trends revealed by the analysis of regression, these results should not be given any significance. We have previously pointed out that the unclear results from the group of girls might be due to for example a higher group conformity among girls than among boys (cf. p. 195).

In accordance with expectation a markedly different pattern was observed in the easy/moderately difficult situation. Here the $M_s < M_f$ subjects had the highest mean persistence score and the $M_s > M_f$ subjects had the lowest mean persistence score. This was the case both among boys and girls.

Finally, the results from the extremely/moderately difficult situation are rather confusing, but if anything, they resemble most what is expected in a moderately difficult/easy situation, and thus form a pattern almost the opposite of the expected one. Previously, however, the possibility was mentioned that the situation was in fact perceived as a moderately difficult/easy one by most subjects, instead of as intended, i.e. as an extremely/moderately difficult one (cf. pp. 216 f.). If this were the case, as the subjects' own estimates of probability of success may indicate, the pattern of results is not very surprising. In this connection it should not be forgotten that the relationship between each of the variables M_s score and M_f score on the one hand and persistence score on the other changed in the expected direction when subjects with very low probability of success estimates were considered (cf. p. 232, Table 38).

MODERATELY DIFFICULT/EASY SITUATION

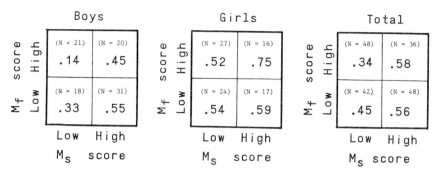

EASY/MODERATELY DIFFICULT SITUATION

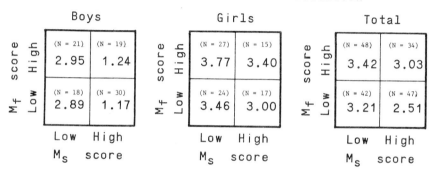

EXTREMELY DIFFICULT/MODERATELY DIFFICULT SITUATION

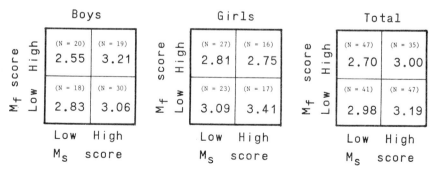

Fig. 34. Mean persistence scores on the initial task in the moderately difficult/easy, easy/moderately difficult, and extremely difficult/moderately difficult situations in relation to motive constellation, for boys, girls, and total sample. (Number of subjects in each motive constellation group in parentheses.)

The above finding that the relationship between motive constellation and persistence at the initial task was different in the moderately difficult/easy and the easy/moderately difficult situation also bears on the circumstance that individuals with the same motive constellation react in different ways to different situations. To concretize and exemplify what this implies, it is recapitulated that a majority of the $M_s > M_f$ subjects had a high persistence score (score 1) in the moderately difficult/easy situation, which, when traced back to the raw data (cf. pp. 175 f.) is seen to mean that they worked at the initial task for as long or almost as long a time as they were allowed to (19 minutes or more). This result is in sharp contrast to that from the easy/moderately difficult situation. Thus, the low mean persistence score for the $M_s > M_f$ group in this situation is due to the fact that close to half, (i.e. 16 out of 38 subjects in this group) had persistence scores of 1 or 2 (cf. p. 203, Fig. 21), which in raw data (p. 200, Fig. 20) means that they worked for less than two minutes at the initial task. Eight of these subjects scored 1 on the persistence variable, i.e. they switched to the alternative task before one minute had passed. In comparison, only one subject in the $M_s < M_f$ group had a persistence score of 1, and only three subjects had persistence scores of 2.

Thus, to sum up, although not all the findings in the present investigation have been equally clear-cut and easily interpretable, the main pattern of results is nevertheless judged to have provided strong support for an interaction-oriented approach to this kind of problem. However, one matter at the heart of the interactional psychological viewpoint on which this study has been based has so far been neglected in this chapter. It will be recalled that in the theoretical part of this work, it was pointed out that the hypotheses formulated about persistence could just as well be derived, albeit for different reasons, from Atkinson's achievement motivation theory as from the revised theory of achievement motivation presented in Chapter 4. Yet the hypotheses were explicitly anchored in the revised theory. This theory stresses the personality by situation interaction principle even more strongly than Atkinson's theory. In the following a closer examination of the explanations of the persistence problems offered by these two theories will be made.

A FINAL CONSIDERATION OF THE THEORETICAL BASIS OF THE STUDY

Strictly speaking, some of the questions to be dealt with below fall outside the area of persistence. Yet, since they may help us in a further evaluation of the theoretical basis for this study, they deserve some attention in this concluding part. Their relatively peripheral connection with the problems of persistence means, however, that they will not be examined in too much detail. Attention will be focused on some of the findings for the motive constellation groups referred to in the summing up section above. But first a recapitulation to clarify the point of departure.

Briefly stated, Atkinson's theory of achievement motivation implies that the $M_s > M_f$ group should be more strongly motivated than the $M_s < M_f$ group for all tasks except those where $P_s = .00$ and those where $P_s = 1.00$, and in neither of these two extreme cases should there be any reversal between the two motive constellation groups in motivation level. The difference in favour of the $M_s > M_f$ group should be most marked at tasks of some moderate difficulty (cf. p. 83, Fig. 4). The latter is also in agreement with the revised theory of achievement motivation. However, in contrast to Atkinson's theory, the revised theory suggests a reversal of the motivation level of these groups when we turn to very easy or very difficult tasks, i.e. $M_s > M_f$ subjects are assumed to have a weaker motivation than $M_s < M_f$ subjects for very easy and very difficult tasks.

Relating these theories to the persistence situations dealt with in this chapter, the following should appear: According to Atkinson's theory the $M_s > M_f$ group should have much stronger motivation than the $M_s < M_f$ group for the initial task in the moderately difficult/easy situation, while there should be hardly any or no difference between the groups in motivation for the alternative task. The former is in accordance with the revised theory, but this theory suggests that there should also be a difference in motivation for the alternative, easy task, with the $M_s < M_f$ group as the one most motivated for this task. According to both positions the $M_s > M_f$ group should be the most persistent one at the initial moderately difficult task. Despite some ambiguity in the pattern of results, this prediction has received considerable support from the data.

As to the easy/moderately difficult situation and the extremely/moderately difficult situation there should, according to Atkinson's theory, be hardly any or no difference between the two motive groups in favour of the $M_s > M_f$ group in motivation for the initial task, while the $M_s > M_f$ group should have a strong positive motivation for the alternative task as compared with a negative motivation for this task on the part of the $M_s < M_f$ group. This should result in less persistence at the initial task among $M_s > M_f$ subjects than among $M_s < M_f$ subjects. The same prediction follows from the revised theory, but here it is based on the assumption of a clear difference in motivation for the initial task as well, the $M_s > M_f$ group being least motivated for this task. The prediction has been verified in the present study as far as the easy/moderately difficult situation is concerned, while it did not receive any clear support in the data from the extremely/moderately difficult situation, possibly because the established situation corresponded badly with that to which the prediction referred.

Are there then any indications in the results arising from this study that the additional assumptions of the revised theory have any merit? Immediately, one springs to mind in the fact that in the easy/moderately difficult situation a considerable number of the $M_s > M_f$ subjects abandoned the initial task before one minute had passed, as compared to only one subject in the $M_s < M_f$ group. This must be evaluated on the basis that the subjects were asked to start with the easy task. Thus, despite the administrator's request to start with the easy task, which is assumed to have created a certain extrinsic motivation for that task, many of the $M_s > M_f$ subjects switched to the alternative task immediately. Yet, no matter how much this may seem to resemble our predicted resistence against working at the easy task, one cannot, of course, exclude the possibility that the low persistence level was due only to a very strong motivation for the alternative, moderately difficult task. But, as far as intuition may be trusted, the latter explanation does not look convincing, and I intuitively favour the former.

There is, however, another way of comparing and contrasting the two theoretical standpoints, which is connected with the fact that there is no one-to-one relationship between time spent at the initial task and the amount of work output. The subject's motivation for a task is assumed to be reflected not only in persistence, but also in efficiency of performance, e.g. in terms of amount of work output. Since time spent at the initial task varied, efficiency had to be understood in the present case as the relationship between work output and time of work.

Let us then return to the two theoretical positions, sticking to a simple assumption of a positive relationship between motivation strength and efficiency of performance (cp. pp. 105 f.). Both positions imply that in the moderately difficult/easy situation the $M_s > M_f$ subjects should work more efficiently at the initial task than the $M_s < M_f$ subjects. Recognizing that Atkinson's theory of achievement motivation implies higher motivation among $M_s > M_f$ subjects for tasks at all perceived difficulty levels except where P_s is 1.00 or .00, the $M_s > M_f$ subjects should, according to this theory, either be more efficient than the $M_s < M_f$ subjects or there should be no difference between these groups as far as efficiency at the initial task in the easy/moderately difficult and extremely/moderately difficult situations is concerned. In contrast, the revised theory assumes that $M_s > M_f$ subjects have lower motivation than $M_s < M_f$ subjects for very easy and very difficult tasks. On this basis we should therefore expect the $M_s < M_f$ subjects to be most efficient at the initial task in easy/moderately difficult and in extremely/moderately difficult situations. According to both positions the $M_s \approx M_f$ groups should in all instances fall between the $M_s > M_f$ and the $M_s < M_f$ group with respect to efficiency.

Thus, by the introduction of the concept of efficiency it should be possible to shed further light on the novel assumptions presented in the revised theory of achievement motivation. Efficiency scores were therefore computed, according to the formula

$$\text{Efficiency} = \frac{\text{Output} \times 10^1}{\text{Time of work}},$$

where in connection with the moderately difficult/easy situation "output" referred to the number of anagrams solved, in connection with the easy/moderately difficult situation to the number of rows of figures drawn, and in connection with the extremely/moderately difficult situation to the number of labyrinths attempted.

Because the efficiency scores obtained in this way were loaded with obvious weaknesses, which will be discussed below, it was found unreasonable to analyse the efficiency results in their original, finely graded form. Instead, subjects were graded as being high or low in efficiency, according to whether their scores were above or below the median for the distribution of efficiency scores.

The efficiency results for the groups which were compared with respect to persistence scores in Fig. 34 are presented in Fig. 35.

As regards the moderately difficult/easy situation the figure shows the expected pattern among boys. Thus, the $M_s > M_f$ group worked most efficiently and the $M_s < M_f$ group worked least efficiently. Applying the χ^2 test, we find the difference in efficiency in favour of the $M_s > M_f$ group to be significant (with Yates' correction because of expected frequencies below 10: $\chi^2 = 2.99$, $\phi = +.24$, df = 1, p < .05, one-tailed test). Moreover, the phi coefficient represents a clear underestimation of the influence of motive constellation on efficiency, due to a weakness connected with the efficiency scores. This becomes clear when taking into consideration that the anagrams in the initial task set were of increasing difficulty (cf. p. 172). Subjects working for a long time at the initial task should then, on the average, work out more difficult anagrams than those working for a shorter time. Hence, their chance of getting a high efficiency score should be reduced. Any exhaustion during work should have the same effect. Recalling now from Fig. 34 that the $M_s > M_f$ group worked for a longer

----

1. The output scores were multiplied by 10 to avoid decimals. Since the original time scores referred to whole minutes only, and time score 1 therefore implied that the subject worked at the initial task somewhere between 1 and 2 minutes, and time score 2 that he worked between 2 and 3 minutes, the subject's time scores were adjusted to the mid-point of the intervals before the computation.

MODERATELY DIFFICULT/EASY SITUATION

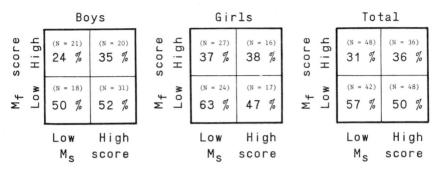

EASY/MODERATELY DIFFICULT SITUATION

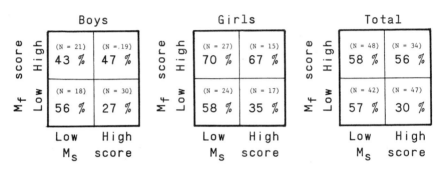

EXTREMELY DIFFICULT/MODERATELY DIFFICULT SITUATION

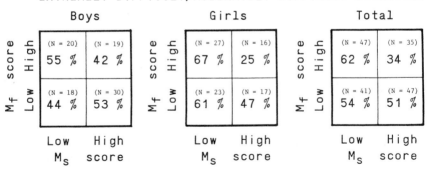

Fig. 35. Percentage of subjects with a high efficiency score on the initial task in the moderately difficult/easy, easy/moderately difficult, and extremely difficult/moderately difficult situations in relation to motive constellation, for boys, girls, and total sample. (Number of subjects in each motive constellation group in parentheses.)

time than the $M_s < M_f$ group at the initial task, the null hypothesis of no effect of motive constellation on persistence implies, if true, that in this particular case the $M_s > M_f$ group should have the lowest percentage of subjects with a high efficiency score. Evaluated against this background the observed difference in the opposite direction indicates a rather strong motive effect on efficiency.

For girls a less clear relationship was observed, but this was also the case in connection with the persistence variable. It is nevertheless of interest to note that here too the difference between the $M_s > M_f$ group and the $M_s < M_f$ group was in the expected direction. Following the reasoning above, the somewhat higher percentage of subjects with a high efficiency score in the low M_s/low M_f group may be understood as being at least partly a reflection of the fact that on the average they worked with somewhat easier tasks than the $M_s > M_f$ group.

Needless to say, the results which have been considered hitherto do not differentiate between the validity of the two positions, since both positions lead to the same predictions for this situation. But what they do do, is to underscore that motivation differences display themselves clearly in differential efficiency of work. Thus, they indicate that in connection with the validity question considerable emphasis should be placed on efficiency results from situations for which the predictions from the two theoretical positions differ. Let us then turn to one such situation, the easy/moderately difficult one.

Although the efficiency index from this situation seems less problematical than that from the moderately difficult/easy situation, there is nevertheless one aspect which should be kept in mind when evaluating the results. That is, it seems reasonable to expect a building up of a certain fatigue in subjects during work. On this basis alone one would expect lower average efficiency among subjects who have worked for a long time at the initial task than among those who have worked for a shorter time.

Returning to the results, we can see from Fig. 35 that as far as girls are concerned the pattern of results is quite in accordance with the revised theory of achievement motivation. The proportion of subjects with a high efficiency score was higher in the $M_s < M_f$ group than in the $M_s > M_f$ group (with Yates' correction because of expected frequencies below 10: $x^2 = 4.01$, $\phi = -.30$, df = 1, $p < .025$, one-tailed test), and the results from the two $M_s \approx M_f$ groups fell between those for these extreme motive constellation groups. Thus, to stress the most interesting aspect of the results, not only did the $M_s < M_f$ group spend most time at the initial task, but it also had the highest productivity per time unit (number of rows of figures drawn), and not only did the $M_s > M_f$ group spend least time at the initial task, but it also worked least efficiently at this task. The result is all the more remarkable when a possible exhaustion factor as indicated above is taken into consideration.

The pattern of results is not equally clear among boys (corrected $\chi^2 = .82$, $\phi = -.04$, $p > .10$, one-tailed test), but here too the direction of the difference between the $M_s < M_f$ and the $M_s > M_f$ group is in accordance with the revised theory. Although it is a weak relationship, it should not, on the basis of the fatigue factor discussed above, be summarily dismissed as negligible. Since the $M_s < M_f$ group was the most persistent one at the initial, easy task and therefore might have become most fatigued, the circumstance that the efficiency results for this group did not exceed those for the $M_s \approx M_f$ groups is not very surprising.

On the whole, then, the pattern of efficiency results from the easy/moderately difficult situation is judged to provide considerable support for the assumption made in the revised theory of achievement motivation, of higher motivation for very easy tasks among $M_s < M_f$ subjects than among $M_s > M_f$ subjects.

Now the results from the extremely/moderately difficult situation remain to be discussed, but these results may be problematical for several reasons. At first glance the efficiency results presented in Fig. 35 may seem to lend a certain support to the assumption of higher motivation among $M_s < M_f$ subjects than among $M_s > M_f$ subjects for very difficult tasks, since we find a somewhat higher percentage of high efficiency subjects in the $M_s < M_f$ than in the $M_s > M_f$ group, for both boys and girls. One should, however, in this connection bear in mind the circumstance mentioned several times previously, that the initial task was not perceived as an extremely difficult one by a majority of the subjects. This means, of course, that the results presented in Fig. 35 are not suited for testing the hypothesis of higher motivation among $M_s < M_f$ subjects than among $M_s > M_f$ subjects for tasks at a very low P_s level. It might then seem natural to concentrate on subjects with very low probability of success estimates, as in the analyses of the persistence data (cf. pp. 222 ff.). However, there is one weakness connected with the efficiency index which is immediately obvious, and which makes such an analysis more or less pointless. That is, it is not self-evident that a high number of attempts at the labyrinth task reflects high effort expenditure. It might equally well mean little concentration and rapid, superficial work at each of the labyrinths. Since it was difficult to know how to interpret the data, no further analyses were undertaken. Thus, no further light can be shed on the question of whether there is a difference between $M_s < M_f$ and $M_s > M_f$ subjects in motivation for tasks at the lower end of the P_s continuum in favor of the former group.

Summing up and conclusion

On the assumption that motivation strength also manifests itself in efficiency of work, the efficiency data substantiated the implication common to the achievement motivation theory as developed by Atkinson and to the revised theory of achievement motivation, that $M_s > M_f$ subjects should work more efficiently than $M_s < M_f$ subjects at tasks of moderate difficulty. Further, through the demonstration of lower efficiency among $M_s > M_f$ subjects than among $M_s < M_f$ subjects at a very easy, routine task, the data have lent considerable support to the alternative viewpoint presented in the revised theory, that $M_s > M_f$ subjects are less motivated than $M_s < M_f$ subjects for easy tasks. According to Atkinson's theory, the difference in efficiency, if any, should be in the opposite direction of that observed here, i. e. the $M_s > M_f$ group should be the most efficient at this easy task too. Finally, there are no data from the present study which make possible a further evaluation of the other novel view in the revised theory, that $M_s > M_f$ subjects are also less motivated than $M_s < M_f$ subjects for tasks perceived to be extremely difficult. The data from the extremely/moderately difficult situation do not provide any guide for future research.

However, the results from the easy/moderately difficult situation along with the validity indications presented in Chapter 4 (pp. 116 ff.) may be sufficient to give grounds for hope of some renewal or redirection of research on the effects of M_s and M_f on the basis of the alternative viewpoints offered by the revised theory of achievement motivation.

A FINAL WORD CONCERNING THE MOTIVE MEASURES

Having examined the empirical results in the light of achievement motivation theory without further regard to the motive measuring instrument used, it now behoves us once more to take up the rather obvious circumstance that the validity of the conclusions presupposes that the instrument measures what it is purported to do. Some indications of instrument validity were considered in Chapter 6 (pp. 146 f.). The results of the present study cannot, of course, be used both as a test of the validity of the theory on which the study is based and as a further test of the validity of the measuring instrument. A main point should nevertheless be emphasized: By means of the Achievement Motive Scale (AMS) we were able to discriminate between groups of individuals who to a considerable extent behaved in accordance with expectations based on the theory, with respect to both persistence and efficiency. More specifically, we were able to discriminate between groups which behaved quite differently in different situations. While on the one hand this encourages the use of the AMS in future achievement motivation studies, on the other hand it throws into focus the importance of sharpening the specifications for how a motive should be expected to affect behaviour. The specifications offered in the revised theory of achievement motivation, as touched upon previously, also have implications for the evaluation of previously used motive tests. That is, the fact that in the findings, relationships between M_s as well as M_f measures and behaviour criteria vary from positive to negative, does not necessarily mean that the tests are invalid.

FINAL SUMMARY AND CONCLUSIONS

This work started out with the assumption that better insight into the phenomenon of persistence is of central importance to all of us who are concerned with problems in the areas of learning and performance. Persistence was assumed to be a key factor in learning and performance situations, and knowledge about the determinators of persistence was expected to help to make possible a better adjustment of such situations to the individuals. Having completed the presentation of empirical results, we shall now briefly return to this, our point of departure.

Needless to say, the achievement motivation theory which has provided the frame of reference for the empirical part of this study is not an all-encompassing theory of motivation, and cannot account for more than a modest part of the variation in persistence. But the data have nevertheless demonstrated that this theory emphasizes some aspects which are of central importance for the understanding of persistence. The basic viewpoint that behaviour results from personality characteristics in interaction with situation or task characteristics, has in this theory found its expression by the bringing into focus of on the one hand the two personality characteristics designated the motive to achieve success (M_s) and the motive to avoid failure (M_f), and on the other hand the perceived difficulty of the task (P_s), which is also assumed to determine the incentive value of the task.

Three different situations have been selected, i.e. where the initial/alternative task was moderately difficult/easy, easy/moderately difficult, and extremely difficult/moderately difficult. The main purpose of the empirical part of this study was to demonstrate the relationship between the motive variables and persistence in each of these situations. The underlying assumption was that if the motives M_s and M_f affected persistence in these three more or less controlled situations, then one could have greater confidence that they also affect persistence in real life situations, such as in school work, in leisure activities, and in occupational life. Within all these areas we are confronted with and have from time to time to choose between tasks varying in difficulty.

What, then, did we find? Unfortunately, the results from the extremely/moderately difficult situation, although to some extent in accordance with the expectations, were so unclear that they cannot provide a basis for any conclusions. But the results from the remaining two persistence settings, although not in all details in accordance with the expectations, are of considerable interest. Apart from the finding of higher persistence among girls than among boys, which is only of peripheral interest here, and the finding of a main effect of type of situation on persistence, clear personality by situation interaction effects were demonstrated. Thus, in the moderately difficult/easy situation the $M_s > M_f$ group was more persistent than the $M_s < M_f$ group, while the opposite was the case in the easy/moderately difficult situation. Furthermore, the $M_s > M_f$ subjects did also work more efficiently than the $M_s < M_f$ subjects at the initial task in the moderately difficult/easy situation, while they worked less efficiently at the banal, simple drawing task which was the initial one in the easy/moderately difficult situation. The former results, those of persistence, may be accounted for, albeit for different reasons, both by the achievement motivation theory as developed by Atkinson and by the revised theory. The efficiency results from the easy/moderately difficult situation lend support to the assumption made in the revised theory that $M_s > M_f$ subjects are less motivated for simple tasks than are $M_s < M_f$ subjects. In sum, the results serve as a relatively clear illustration of the general principle very strongly emphasized by Cronbach (1957, p. 679) that the individual who adapts well in one situation does not necessarily do so in another.

Provided that the motives focused upon here function in similar ways in real-life situations, the results may permit various speculations and conclusions concerning how to arrange performance situations in such a way that the individual finds them attractive, how to arrange learning programs, how to select personnel for routine, repetitive work or for more difficult work, etc. However the present study concludes, not with these implications, but where it started, with one particular aspect which from a pedagogical point of view must be considered a much more fundamental one, i.e. the observation mentioned in the Introduction (pp. 17 f.) that some individuals are more oriented towards mastering the problems with which they are confronted and thus maximize their possibilities of unfolding and developing their resources, while others give up at the first failure and therefore minimize their possibilities of developing greater problem-solving skills. The present study has told us something about who these individuals are, who behave in this way. The M_s-dominated individual is more attracted to a situation where the outcome is uncertain, while he displays more resistance towards a routine, repetitive task than the M_f-dominated individual. The data cannot shed light on the question of whether M_f-dominated personalities are <u>absolutely</u> more or less attracted towards easy tasks than towards moderately difficult tasks. This is due to the fact that the tasks varied not only in difficulty, but also in kind. However, they indicate at least a <u>relatively</u> higher attractiveness to the simple routine situation among M_f-dominated than among M_s-dominated individuals. The cumulative effect of these different modes of reaction implies that the failure-threatened individual is less well off than the mastery-oriented one as far as personality development is concerned. Since the motives are considered as early learning results (cf. pp. 59 f.) this circumstance stresses the importance of early learning environments which promote the development of an individual who does not avoid realistic challenges. In addition, it also raises the question of to what extent it is possible to affect and change the motives of the adult individual. While we have previously pointed out that motives are considered as relatively stable personality characteristics and have primarily emphasized their <u>stability</u>, attention should finally be called to their <u>relative</u> stability and thus their modifiability. Recently McClelland and his associates have directed their research towards this problem and have presented some encouraging results (cf. e.g. McClelland, 1973). There is much room for further research within this area.

249

REFERENCES

Anastasi, Anne. Differential psychology. (3rd. ed.) New York: Macmillan, 1958.

Armitage, P. Statistical methods in medical research. Oxford: Blackwell Scientific Publications, 1971.

Atkinson, J. W. Explorations using imaginative thought to assess the strength of human motives. In M. R. Jones (Ed.), Nebraska symposium on motivation. Lincoln: University of Nebraska Press, 1954. Pp. 56-112.

Atkinson, J. W. Motivational determinants of risk-taking behavior. Psychological Review, 1957, 64, 359-372.

Atkinson, J. W. The social origins of human motives. In J. W. Atkinson (Ed.), Motives in fantasy, action, and society. Princeton: Van Nostrand, 1958. Pp. 435-436.

Atkinson, J. W. Personality dynamics. Annual Review of Psychology, 1960, 11, 255-290.

Atkinson, J. W. An introduction to motivation. Princeton: Van Nostrand, 1964.

Atkinson, J. W. Comments on papers by Crandall and Veroff. In C. P. Smith (Ed.), Achievement-related motives in children. New York: Russel Sage Foundation, 1969. Pp. 200-206.

Atkinson, J. W. & Cartwright, D. Some neglected variables in contemporary conceptions of decision and performance. Psychological Reports, 1964, 14, 575-590.

Atkinson, J. W. & Feather, N. T. (Eds.), A theory of achievement motivation. New York: Wiley & Sons, 1966.

Atkinson, J. W. & Litwin, G. H. Achievement motive and test anxiety conceived as motive to approach success and motive to avoid failure. Journal of Abnormal and Social Psychology, 1960, 60, 52-63.

Atkinson, J. W. & O'Connor, Patricia. Neglected factors in studies of achievement-oriented performance. In J. W. Atkinson & N. T. Feather (Eds.), A Theory of achievement motivation. New York: Wiley & Sons, 1966. Pp. 299-325.

Atkinson, J. W. & Reitman, W. R. Performance as a function of motive strength and expectancy of goal attainment. Journal of Abnormal and Social Psychology, 1956, 53, 361-366.

Baker, B. O., Hardyck, C. D. & Petrinovich, L. F. Weak measurements vs. strong statistics: An empirical critique of S. S. Stevens' proscriptions on statistics. Educational and Psychological Measurement, 1966, 26, 291-309.

Baldwin, A. L. Theories of child development. New York: Wiley & Sons, 1967.

Barker, L. W. An analysis of achievement, motivational, and perceptual variables between students classified on the basis of success and persistence in college. Dissertation Abstracts International, 1968, 29, 1100-A.

Battig, W. F. Paired-associate learning. In T. R. Dixon & D. L. Horton (Eds.), Verbal behavior and general behavior theory. Englewood Cliffs, New Jersey: Prentice-Hall, 1968. Pp. 149-171.

Battle, Esther S. Motivational determinants of academic task persistence. Journal of Personality and Social Psychology, 1965, 2, 209-218.

Berlyne, D. E. Novelty and curiosity as determinants of exploratory behaviour. British Journal of Psychology, 1950, 41, 68-80.

Berlyne, D. E. Conflict, arousal, and curiosity. New York: McGraw-Hill, 1960.

Berlyne, D. E. Motivational problems raised by exploratory and epistemic behavior. In S. Koch (Ed.), Psychology: A study of a science, Vol. 5, The process areas, the person, and some applied fields: Their place in psychology and in science. New York: McGraw-Hill, 1963. Pp. 284-364.

Bexton, W. H., Heron, W. & Scott, T. H. Effects of decreased variation in the sensory environment. Canadian Journal of Psychology, 1954, 8, 70-76.

Bindra, D. Motivation. A systematic reinterpretation. New York: Ronald Press, 1959.

Birch, D. & Veroff, J. Motivation: A study of action. Belmont, California: Brooks /Cole Publishing Company, 1966.

Bitterman, M. E., Feddersen, W. E. & Tyler, D. W. Secondary reinforcement and the discrimination hypothesis. American Journal of Psychology, 1953, 66, 456-464.

Bolles, R. C. The usefulness of the drive concept. In M. R. Jones (Ed.), Nebraska symposium on motivation. Lincoln: University of Nebraska Press, 1958. Pp. 1-33.

Boneau, C. A. The effects of violations of assumptions underlying the t-test. Psychological Bulletin, 1960, 57, 49-64.

Brintnall, A. K. A preliminary study of persistence and ability. Psychological Bulletin, 1940, 37, 585. (Abstract)

Brown, J. S. Problems presented by the concept of acquired drives. In J. S. Brown et al., Current theory and research in motivation: A symposium. Lincoln: University of Nebraska Press, 1953. Pp. 1-21.

Brown, J. S. The motivation of behavior. New York: McGraw-Hill, 1961.

Buxton, C. E. Evaluations of forced-choice and Likert-type tests of motivation to academic achievement. British Journal of Educational Psychology, 1966, 36, 192-201.

Carlson, E. R. & Carlson, Rae. Male and female subjects in personality research. Journal of Abnormal and Social Psychology, 1960, 61, 482-483.

Castaneda, A. Supplementary report: Differential position habits and anxiety in children as determinants of performance in learning. Journal of Experimental Psychology, 1961, 61, 257-258.

Castaneda, A., McCandless, B. R. & Palermo, D. S. The children's form of the manifest anxiety scale. Child Development, 1956, 27, 317-326.

Castaneda, A., Palermo, D. S. & McCandless, B. R. Complex learning and performance as a function of anxiety in children and task difficulty. Child Development, 1956, 27, 327-332.

Cochran, W. G. The comparison of percentages in matched samples. Biometrika, 1950, 37, 256-266.

Cochran, W. G. Some methods for strengthening the common X^2 tests. Biometrics, 1954, 10, 417-451.

Cofer, C. N. & Appley, M. H. Motivation: Theory and research. New York: Wiley & Sons, 1964.

Cohen, J. The statistical power of abnormal-social psychological research: A review. Journal of Abnormal and Social Psychology, 1962, 65, 145-153.

Cohen, J. Some statistical issues in psychological research. In B. B. Wolman (Ed.), Handbook of clinical psychology. New York: McGraw-Hill, 1965. Pp. 95-121.

Cohen, J. Multiple regression as a general data-analytic system. Psychological Bulletin, 1968, 70, 426-443.

Cohen, J. Statistical power analysis for the behavioral sciences. New York: Academic Press, 1969.

Crandall, Virginia C. Sex differences in expectancy of intellectual and academic reinforcement. In C. P. Smith (Ed.), Achievement-related motives in children. New York: Russel Sage Foundation, 1969, Pp. 11-45.

Crandall, V. J. Achievement. In H. W. Stevenson, J. Kagan & C. Spiker (Eds.), Child psychology, 62nd N. S. S. E. yearbook. Chicago: University of Chicago Press, 1963. Pp. 416-459.

Crandall, V. J., Preston, Anne & Rabson, Alice. Maternal reactions and the development of independence and achievement behavior in young children. Child Development, 1960, 31, 243-251.

Crandall, V. J. & Rabson, Alice. Children's repetition choices in an intellectual achievement situation following success and failure. Journal of Genetic Psychology, 1960, 97, 161-168.

Cromwell, R. L. A social learning approach to mental retardation. In N. R. Ellis (Ed.), Handbook of mental deficiency. New York: McGraw-Hill, 1963. Pp. 41-91.

Cronbach, L. J. Coefficient alpha and the internal structure of tests. Psychometrika, 1951, 16, 297-334.

Cronbach, L. J. The two disciplines of scientific psychology. American Psychologist, 1957, 12, 671-684.

Cronbach, L. J., Rajaratnam, Nageswari & Gleser, Goldine C. Theory of generalizability: A liberalization of reliability theory. British Journal of Statistical Psychology, 1963, 16, 137-163.

Crutcher, Roberta. An experimental study of persistence. Journal of Applied Psychology. 1934, 18, 409-417.

Crutchfield, R. S. Conformity and character. American Psychologist, 1955, 10, 191-198.

Cushing, R. A perseverative tendency in pre-school children: A study of personality differences. Archives of Psychology, 1929, 17, No. 108. Cited by D. G. Ryans, The measurement of persistence: An historical review. Psychological Bulletin, 1939, 36. P. 726.

Denny, J. P. Effects of anxiety and intelligence on concept formation. Journal of Experimental Psychology, 1966, 72, 596-602.

Denny, M. R. The role of secondary reinforcement in a partial reinforcement learning situation. Journal of Experimental Psychology, 1946, 36, 373-389.

Diciaula, P. J., Jr. Relationship of persistence to varying success and other relevant variables. Dissertation Abstracts International, 1970, 31, 3688 B.

Diciaula, P. J., Jr., Martin, R. B. & Lotsof, E. J. Persistence and intermittent reinforcement. Psychological Reports, 1968, 23, 739-742.

Diggory, J. C. & Ostroff, Bena. Estimated probability of success as a function of variability in performance. American Journal of Psychology, 1962, 75, 94-101.

Diggory, J. C. , Riley, E. J. & Blumenfeld, Ruth. Estimated probability of success for a fixed goal. American Journal of Psychology, 1960, 73, 41-55.

Draper, N. R. & Smith, H. Applied regression analysis. New York: Wiley & Sons, 1966.

Edmiston, R. W. & Jackson, L. A. The relationship of persistence to achievement. Journal of Educational Psychology, 1949, 40, 47-51.

Edwards, A. L. Edwards Personal Preference Schedule. New York: Psychological Corporation, 1953.

Elam, C. B. , Tyler, D. W. & Bitterman, M. E. A further study of secondary reinforcement and the discrimination hypothesis. Journal of Comparative and Physiological Psychology, 1954, 47, 381-384.

Escalona, Sybille K. The effect of success and failure upon the level of aspiration and behavior in manic-depressive psychoses. University of Iowa Studies in Child Welfare, 1940, 16, 199-302.

Estes, W. K. Comments on Dr. Bolles' paper. In M. R. Jones (Ed.), Nebraska symposium on motivation. Lincoln: University of Nebraska Press, 1958. Pp. 33-34.

Evans, E. D. The effects of achievement motivation and ability upon discovery learning and accompanying incidental learning under two conditions of incentive-set. Journal of Educational Research, 1967, 60, 195-200.

Eysenck, H. J. The structure of human personality. (3rd. ed.) London: Methuen, 1970.

Farber, I. E. & Spence, K. W. Complex learning and conditioning as a function of anxiety. Journal of Experimental Psychology, 1953, 45, 120-125.

Feather, N. T. The relationship of persistence at a task to expectation of success and achievement related motives. Journal of Abnormal and Social Psychology, 1961, 63, 552-561.

Feather, N. T. The study of persistence. Psychological Bulletin, 1962, 59, 94-115.

Feather, N. T. Persistence at a difficult task with alternative task of intermediate difficulty. Journal of Abnormal and Social Psychology, 1963, 66, 604-609.

Feather, N. T. Performance at a difficult task in relation to initial expectation of success, test anxiety, and need achievement. Journal of Personality, 1965, 33, 200-217.

Fehrer, Elizabeth. Effects of amount of reinforcement and of pre- and post reinforcement delays on learning and extinction. Journal of Experimental Psychology, 1956, 52, 167-176.

Feld, Sheila & Smith, C. P. An evaluation of the objectivity of the method of content analysis. In J. W. Atkinson (Ed.), Motives in fantasy, action, and society. Princeton: Van Nostrand, 1958. Pp. 234-241.

Fenichel, O. On the psychology of boredom. In D. Rapaport (Ed.), Organization and pathology of thought. New York: Columbia University Press, 1951.

Ferguson, G. A. Statistical analysis in psychology and education. New York: McGraw-Hill, 1966.

Festinger, L. A theoretical interpretation of shifts in level of aspiration. Psychological Review, 1942, 49, 235-250.

Finger, F. W. Retention and subsequent extinction of a simple running response following varying conditions of reinforcement. Journal of Experimental Psychology. 1942, 31, 120-133.

Fiske, D. W. & Maddi, S. R. A conceptual framework. In D. W. Fiske & S. R. Maddi (Eds.), Functions of varied experience. Homewood, Illinois: Dorsey Press, 1961. Pp. 11-56.

French, Elizabeth G. Development of a measure of complex motivation. In J. W. Atkinson (Ed.), Motives in fantasy, action, and society. Princeton:Van Nostrand, 1958. Pp. 242-248.

French, Elizabeth G. & Thomas, F. H. The relation of achievement motivation to problem-solving effectiveness. Journal of Abnormal and Social Psychology, 1958, 56, 45-48.

French, J. W. The validity of a persistence test. Psychometrika, 1948, 13, 271-277.

Freud, S. Triebe und Triebschicksale. In S. Freud, Gesammelte Werke. Chronologisch geordnet. Vol. 10. Werke aus den Jahren 1913-1917. London: Imago, 1946. Pp. 210-232. [First published in 1915.]

Furst, E. J. Validity of some objective scales of motivation for predicting academic achievement. Educational and Psychological Measurement, 1966, 26, 927-933.

Gaudry, E. & Spielberger, C. D. Anxiety and educational achievement. Sydney: Wiley & Sons - Australasia, 1971.

Gjesme, T. Prestasjonsmotivasjon og skoleprestasjoner. Unpublished cand. paed. thesis, University of Oslo, 1968.

Gjesme, T. Initial study of the achievement motive scale (AMS). Preliminary analyses of the M_S scale. Unpublished manuscript, University of Oslo, 1971. (a)

Gjesme, T. Motive to achieve success and motive to avoid failure in relation to school performance for pupils of different ability levels. Scandinavian Journal of Educational Research, 1971, 15, 81-99. (b)

Gjesme, T. Relationships between achievement-related motives and school performance for girls. Theoretical deductions and empirical analyses. Unpublished manuscript, University of Oslo, 1971. (c)

Gjesme, T. & Nygård, R. Achievement-related motives: Theoretical considerations and construction of a measuring instrument. Unpublished manuscript, University of Oslo, 1970.

Gold, D. Statistical tests and substantive significance. American Sociologist, 1969, 4, 42-46.

Grant, D. A., Riopelle, A. J. & Hake, H. W. Resistance to extinction and the pattern of reinforcement. I. Alternation of reinforcement and the conditioned eyelid response. Journal of Experimental Psychology, 1950, 40, 53-60.

Guilford, J. P. Fundamental statistics in psychology and education. (4th ed.) Tokyo: Kōgakusha Company, 1965.

Haber, R. N. & Alpert, R. The role of situation and picture cues in projective measurement of the achievement motive. In J. W. Atkinson (Ed.), Motives in fantasy, action, and society. Princeton: Van Nostrand, 1958. Pp. 644-663.

Hartshorne, H., May, M. A. & Maller, J. B. Studies in the nature of character: II. Studies in service and self-control. New York: Macmillan, 1929.

Hays, W. L. Statistics for psychologists. New York: Holt, Rinehart & Winston, 1963.

Hebb, D. O. The organization of behavior. New York: Wiley & Sons, 1949.

Hebb, D. O. Drives and the C. N. S. (Conceptual nervous system). Psychological Review, 1955, 62, 243-254.

Heckhausen, H. Hoffnung und Furcht in der Leistungsmotivation. Meisenheim am Glan: Hain, 1963.

Heckhausen, H. The anatomy of achievement motivation. New York: Academic Press, 1967.

Heckhausen, H. Achievement motive research: Current problems and some contributions towards a general theory of motivation. In W. J. Arnold (Ed.), Nebraska symposium on motivation. Lincoln: University of Nebraska Press, 1969. Pp. 103-174.

Helmstadter, G. C. Principles of psychological measurement. London: Methuen, 1966.

Hendrick, I. Instinct and the ego during infancy. Psychoanalytic Quarterly, 1942, 11, 33-58.

Hilgard, E. R., Jones, L. V. & Kaplan, S. J. Conditioned discrimination as related to anxiety. Journal of Experimental Psychology, 1951, 42, 94-99.

Himelstein, P. & Kimbrough, W. W., Jr. Reliability of French's "Test of Insight". Educational and Psychological Measurement, 1960, 20, 737-741.

Howells, T. H. An experimental study of persistence. Journal of Abnormal and Social Psychology, 1933, 28, 14-29.

Hull, C. L. Principles of behavior. New York: Appleton-Century Company, 1943.

Humphreys, L. G. Acquisition and extinction of verbal expectations in a situation analogous to conditioning. Journal of Experimental Psychology, 1939, 25, 294-301. (a)

Humphreys, L. G. The effect of random alternation of reinforcement on the acquisition and extinction of conditioned eyelid reactions. Journal of Experimental Psychology, 1939, 25, 141-158. (b)

Hurley, J. R. The Iowa Picture Interpretation Test: A multiple-choice variation of the TAT. Journal of Consulting Psychology, 1955, 19, 372-376.

James, W. H. & Rotter, J. B. Partial and 100% reinforcement under chance and skill conditions. Journal of Experimental Psychology, 1958, 55, 397-403.

Jenkins, W. O. & Stanley, J. C. Partial reinforcement: A review and critique. Psychological Bulletin, 1950, 47, 193-234.

Jones, M. R. (Ed.) Nebraska symposium on motivation. Lincoln: University of Nebraska Press, 1955.

Kagan, J. & Moss, H. A. Birth to maturity. A study in psychological development. New York: Wiley & Sons, 1962.

Karsten, Anitra. Psychische Sättigung. Psychologische Forschung, 1928, 10, 142-254.

Katahn, M. Interaction of anxiety and ability in complex learning situations. Journal of Personality and Social Psychology, 1966, 3, 475-479.

Klinger, E. Fantasy need achievement as a motivational construct. Psychological Bulletin, 1966, 66, 291-308.

Kounin, J. S. Experimental studies of rigidity. I. The measurement of rigidity in normal and feeble-minded persons. Character and Personality, 1941, 9, 251-272.

Krause, M. S. The construct validity of measuring instruments. Journal of General Psychology, 1967, 77, 277-284.

Krumboltz, J. D. & Farquhar, W. W.   Reliability and validity of the nAchievement test. Journal of Consulting Psychology, 1957, 21, 226-228.

Lester, D. Determinants of resistance to extinction after three training trials: 1. Cronological age and mental age. Psychological Reports, 1966, 19, 970. (a)

Lester, D. Partial reinforcement effect after a small number of training trials. Psychological Reports, 1966, 19, 1335-1336. (b)

Leuba, Clarence. Toward some integration of learning theories: The concept of optimal stimulation. Psychological Reports, 1955, 1, 27-33.

Leuba, Clarence J. Man: A general psychology. New York: Holt, Rinehart & Winston, 1961.

Lewin, K. A dynamic theory of personality. Selected papers. New York: McGraw-Hill, 1935.

Lewin, K. , Dembo, Tamara, Festinger, L. & Sears, Pauline S. Level of aspiration. In J. McV. Hunt (Ed.), Personality and the behavior disorders. Vol.1. New York: Ronald Press, 1944. Pp. 333-378.

Lewis, D. J. Partial reinforcement: A selective review of the literature since 1950. Psychological Bulletin, 1960, 57, 1-28.

Likert, R. A technique for the measurement of attitudes. Archives of Psychology, 1932, No. 140.

Lilly, J. C. Mental effects of reduction of ordinary levels of physical stimuli on intact, healthy persons. Psychiatric Research Reports, 1956, 5, 1-9.

Lindquist, E. F. Statistical analysis in educational research. Boston: Houghton Mifflin, 1940.

Lindquist, E. F. Design and analysis of experiments in psychology and education. Boston: Houghton Mifflin, 1953.

Littig, L. W. Effects of motivation on probability preferences. Journal of Personality, 1963, 31, 417-427.

Litwin, G. H. Achievement motivation, expectancy of success, and risk-taking behavior. In J. W. Atkinson & N. T. Feather (Eds.), A theory of achievement motivation. New York: Wiley & Sons, 1966. Pp. 103-115.

Longenecker, E. D. , Krauskopf, J. & Bitterman, M. E. Extinction following alternating and random partial reinforcement. American Journal of Psychology, 1952, 65, 580-587.

Lowell, E. L. The effect of need for achievement on learning and speed of performance. Journal of Psychology, 1952, 33, 31-40.

MacArthur, R. S. An experimental investigation of persistence in secondary school boys. Canadian Journal of Psychology, 1955, 9, 42-54.

McCandless, B. R. , Bilous, Carylon B. & Bennett, Hannah L. Peer popularity and dependence on adults in preschool-age socialization. Child Development, 1961, 32, 511-518.

McClelland, D. C. Personality. New York: Dryden Press, 1951.

McClelland, D. C. Methods of measuring human motivation. In J. W. Atkinson (Ed.), Motives in fantasy, action, and society. Princeton: Van Nostrand, 1958. Pp. 7-42.

McClelland, D. C. What is the effect of achievement motivation training in the schools? In D. C. McClelland & R. S. Steele (Eds.), Human motivation. A book of readings. Morristown, New Jersey: General Learning Press, 1973. Pp. 492-509.

McClelland, D. C., Atkinson, J. W., Clark, R. A. & Lowell, E. L. The achievement motive. New York: Appleton-Century-Crofts, 1953.

McClelland, D. C. & Liberman, A. M. The effect of need for achievement on recognition of need-related words. Journal of Personality, 1949, 18, 236-251.

Mahone, C. H. Fear of failure and unrealistic vocational aspiration. Journal of Abnormal and Social Psychology, 1960, 60, 253-261.

Mandler, G. & Sarason, S. B. A study of anxiety and learning. Journal of Abnormal and Social Psychology, 1952, 47, 166-173.

Mandler, G. & Watson, D. L. Anxiety and the interruption of behavior. In C. D. Spielberger (Ed.), Anxiety and behavior. New York: Academic Press, 1966. Pp. 263-288.

Miles, G. H. Achievement drive and habitual modes of task approach as factors in skill transfer. Journal of Experimental Psychology, 1958, 55, 156-162.

Miller, N. E. & Dollard, J. Social learning and imitation. New Haven: Yale University Press, 1941.

Moss, H. A. & Kagan, J. Stability of achievement and recognition seeking behaviors from early childhood through adulthood. Journal of Abnormal and Social Psychology, 1961, 62, 504-513.

Moulton, R. W. Effects of success and failure on level of aspiration as related to achievement motives. Journal of Personality and Social Psychology, 1965, 1, 399-406.

Mowrer, O. H. Learning theory and behavior. New York: Wiley & Sons, 1960.

Mowrer, O. H. & Jones, Helen. Habit strength as a function of the pattern of reinforcement. Journal of Experimental Psychology, 1945, 35, 293-311.

Murray, H. A. Explorations in personality. New York: Oxford University Press, 1938.

Myers, A. E. Risk taking and academic success and their relation to an objective measure of achievement motivation. Educational and Psychological Measurement, 1965, 25, 355-363.

Myers, A. K. & Miller, N. E. Failure to find a learned drive based on hunger; evidence for learning motivated by "exploration". Journal of Comparative and Physiological Psychology, 1954, 47, 428-436.

Norton, D. W. An empirical investigation of some effects of non-normality and heterogenity on the F-distribution. Unpublished doctoral dissertation, State University of Iowa, 1952. Cited by E. F. Lindquist, Design and analysis of experiments in psychology and education. Boston: Houghton Mifflin, 1953. Pp. 78-86.

Nunnally, J. C. Psychometric theory. New York: McGraw-Hill, 1967.

Nygård, R. Prestasjonsmotiv hos elever med ulik sosial bakgrunn. En undersøkelse blant gutter i 7. og 8. klasse. Unpublished cand.paed.thesis, University of Oslo, 1967.

Nygård, R. Prestasjonsmotiv hos elever med ulik sosial bakgrunn. En undersøkelse blant jenter i 7. og 8. klasse. Unpublished manuscript, University of Oslo, 1968.

Nygård, R. Motive to approach success and motive to avoid failure in boys from different social groups. Scandinavian Journal of Educational Research, 1969, 13, 222-232.

Nygård, R. Measuring achievement-related motives. The motive to approach success. Unpublished manuscript, University of Oslo, 1970.

Nygård, R. The achievement motive scale (AMS). Initial studies of the M_f scale. Unpublished manuscript, University of Oslo, 1971.

Nygård, R. & Gjesme, T. Analyses of the achievement motive scale (AMS). Reliability and validity. Unpublished manuscript, University of Oslo, 1972.

Nygård, R. & Gjesme, T. Assessment of achievement motives: Comments and suggestions. Scandinavian Journal of Educational Research, 1973, 17, 39-46.

O'Connor, Patricia, Atkinson, J. W. & Horner, Matina. Motivational implications of ability grouping in schools. In J. W. Atkinson & N. T. Feather (Eds.), A theory of achievement motivation. New York: Wiley & Sons, 1966. Pp. 231-248.

Ovsiankina, Maria. Die Wiederaufnahme unterbrochener Handlungen. Psychologische Forschung, 1928, 11, 302-379.

Patterson, G. R. & Anderson, D. Peers as social reinforcers. Child Development, 1964, 35, 915-960.

Peaker, G. F. Sampling. In D. K. Whitla (Ed.), Handbook of measurement and assessment in behavioral sciences. Reading, Massachusetts: Addison-Wesley, 1968.

Piaget, J. The origin of intelligence in the child. (2nd ed.) London: Routledge & Kegan Paul, 1966. [La naissance de l'intelligence chez l'enfant. Neuchâtel: Delachaux & Niestlé 1936.]

Piaget, J. Six psychological studies. London: University of London Press, 1968.

Porter, J. P. A comparative study of some measures of persistence. Psychological Bulletin, 1933, 30, 664. (Abstract)

Preston, M. & Baratta, P. An experimental study of the auction-value of an uncertain outcome. American Journal of Psychology, 1948, 61, 183-193.

Rand, P. Anxiety in connection with school performance: III. Try-out of a Norwegian translation of the Test Anxiety Questionnaire for Children. Pedagogisk Forskning, 1960, 4, 178-199.

Rand, P. Achievement motivation and school performance. Oslo: Universitetsforlaget, 1965.

Rand, P. Curvilinear relationship between motive strength and performance. A possible explanation based on J. W. Atkinson's model. Scandinavian Journal of Educational Research, 1973, 17, 83-94.

Raynor, J. O. & Rubin, Ira S. Effects of achievement motivation and future orientation on level of performance. Journal of Personality and Social Psychology, 1971, 17, 36-41.

Resnick, J. H. Reversals in the superiority of high- and low-anxious Ss in verbal conditioning. Journal of Personality, 1965, 33, 218-233.

Rethlingshafer, Dorothy. Relationship of tests of persistence to other measures of continuance of activities. Journal of Abnormal and Social Psychology, 1942, 37, 71-82.

Rethlingshafer, Dorothy. Motivation as related to personality. New York: McGraw-Hill, 1963.

Retterstøl, N. Paranoid and paranoiac psychoses. Oslo: Universitetsforlaget, 1966.

Rosen, B. C. The achievement syndrome: A psychocultural dimension of social stratification. American Sociological Review, 1956, 21, 203-211.

Rotter, J. B. Social learning and clinical psychology. New York: Prentice-Hall, 1954.

Rotter, J. B. Generalized expectancies for internal versus external control of reinforcement. Psychological Monographs, 1966, 80, No. 1 (Whole No. 609)

Rotter, J. B., Fitzgerald, B. J. & Joyce, J. N. A comparison of some objective measures of expectancy. Journal of Abnormal and Social Psychology, 1954, 49, 111-114.

Rotter, J. B., Liverant, S. & Crowne, D. P. The growth and extinction of expectancies in chance controlled and skilled tasks. Journal of Psychology, 1961, 52, 161-177.

Ruebush, B. K. Anxiety. In H. W. Stevenson, J. Kagan & C. Spiker (Eds.), Child Psychology, 62nd N. S. S. E. yearbook. Chicago: University of Chicago Press, 1963. Pp. 460-516.

Ryans, D. G. An experimental attempt to analyze persistent behavior: I. Measuring traits presumed to involve "persistence". Journal of General Psychology, 1938, 19, 333-353. (a)

Ryans, D. G. An experimental attempt to analyze persistent behavior: II. A persistence test. Journal of General Psychology, 1938, 19, 355-371. (b)

Ryans, D. G. The meaning of persistence. Journal of General Psychology, 1938, 19, 79-96. (c)

Ryans, D. G. A note on variations in "persistence" test score with sex, age, and academic level. Journal of Social Psychology, 1939, 10, 259-264. (a)

Ryans, D. G. The measurement of persistence: An historical review. Psychological Bulletin, 1939, 36, 715-739. (b)

Sarason, I. G. Intelligence and personality correlates of test anxiety. Journal of Abnormal and Social Psychology, 1959, 59, 272-275.

Sarason, I. G. Characteristics of three measures of anxiety. Journal of Clinical Psychology, 1961, 17, 196-197.

Sarason, S. B., Davidson, K., Lighthall, F. & Waite, R. A test anxiety scale for children. Child Development, 1958, 29, 105-113.

Sarason, S. B., Davidson, K. S., Lighthall, F. F., Waite, R. R. & Ruebush, B. K. Anxiety in elementary school children. New York: Wiley & Sons, 1960.

Sarason, S. B. & Mandler, G. Some correlates of test anxiety. Journal of Abnormal and Social Psychology, 1952, 47, 810-817.

Sarason, S. B., Mandler, G. & Craighill, P. G. The effect of differential instructions on anxiety and learning. Journal of Abnormal and Social Psychology, 1952, 47, 561-565.

Saunders, D. R. Moderator variables in prediction. Educational and Psychological Measurement, 1956, 16, 209-222.

Schofield, W. An attempt to measure 'persistence' in its relationship to scholastic achievement. Journal of Experimental Psychology, 1943, 33, 440-445.

Smith, C. P. Relationships between achievement-related motives and intelligence, performance level, and persistence. Journal of Abnormal and Social Psychology, 1964, 68, 523-532.

Smith, C. P. The influence of testing conditions on need for achievement scores and their relationship to performance scores. In J. W. Atkinson & N. T. Feather (Eds.), A theory of achievement motivation. New York: Wiley & Sons, 1966. Pp. 277-297.

Smith, S. & Myers, T. I. Stimulation seeking during sensory deprivation. Perceptual and Motor Skills, 1966, 23, 1151-1163.

Smith, S. , Myers, T. I. & Johnson, E. Stimulation seeking throughout seven days of sensory deprivation. Perceptual and Motor Skills, 1967, 25, 261-271.

Spence, K. W. Behavior theory and conditioning. New Haven: Yale University Press, 1956.

Spence, K. W. & Farber, I. E. Conditioning and extinction as a function of anxiety. Journal of Experimental Psychology, 1953, 45, 116-119.

Spence, K. W. , Farber, I. E. & McFann, H. H. The relation of anxiety (drive) level to performance in competitional and noncompetitional paired-associates learning. Journal of Experimental Psychology, 1956, 52, 296-310.

Spence, K. W. & Spence, Janet T. The motivational components of manifest anxiety: Drive and drive stimuli. In C. D. Spielberger (Ed.), Anxiety and behavior. New York: Academic Press, 1966. Pp. 291-326.

Spence, K. W., Taylor J. & Ketchel, Rhoda. Anxiety (drive) level and degree of competition in paired-associates learning. Journal of Experimental Psychology, 1956, 52, 306-310.

Spielberger, C. D. The effects of anxiety on complex learning and academic achievement. In C. D. Spielberger (Ed.), Anxiety and behavior. New York: Academic Press, 1966. Pp. 361-398.

Spielberger, C. D. & Weitz, H. Improving the academic performance of anxious college freshmen: A group-counseling approach to the prevention of underachievement. Psychological Monographs, 1964, 78, No. 13 (Whole No. 590).

Spitz, H. H. Field theory in mental deficiency. In N. R. Ellis (Ed.), Handbook of mental deficiency. New York: McGraw-Hill, 1963. Pp. 11-40.

Taylor, Janet A. The relationship of anxiety to the conditioned eyelid response. Journal of Experimental Psychology, 1951, 41, 81-92.

Taylor, Janet A. A personality scale of manifest anxiety. Journal of Abnormal and Social Psychology, 1953, 48, 285-290.

Taylor, Janet A. Drive theory and manifest anxiety. Psychological Bulletin, 1956, 53, 303-320.

Taylor, Janet A. & Chapman, J. P. Anxiety and the learning of paired-associates. American Journal of Psychology, 1955, 68, 671.

Thomas, F. H. Visualization, experience, and motivation as related to feedback in problem solving. American Psychologist, 1956, 11, 444-445. (Abstract)

Thornton, G. R. A factor analysis of tests designed to measure persistence. Psychological Monographs, 1939, 51, No. 3 (Whole No. 229).

Thornton, G. R. How general is the factor of "persistence"? A reexamination and evaluation of Ryans' results. Journal of General Psychology, 1940, 23, 185-189.

Thornton, G. R. The use of tests of persistence in the prediction of scholastic achievement. Journal of Educational Psychology, 1941, 32, 266-274.

Tryon, R. C. Reliability and behavior domain validity: Reformulation and historical critique. Psychological Bulletin, 1957, 54, 229-249.

Vernon, P. E. The structure of human abilities. (2nd ed.) London: Methuen, 1961.

Vislie, Lise. Stimulus research in projective techniques. Oslo: Universitetsforlaget, 1972.

Vogel, W. , Baker, R. W. , & Lazarus, R. S. The role of motivation in psychological stress. Journal of Abnormal and Social Psychology, 1958, 56, 105-112.

Vroom, V. H. Work and motivation. New York: Wiley & Sons, 1964.

Vukovich, A. , Heckhausen, H. & von Hatzfeld, Anette. Konstruktion eines Fragebogens zur Leistungsmotivation. Unpublished manuscript, University of Münster, 1964. Cited by H. Heckhausen, The anatomy of achievement motivation. New York: Academic Press, 1967. P. 114.

Weiner, B. The effects of unsatisfied achievement motivation on persistence and subsequent performance. Journal of Personality, 1965, 33, 428-442.

Weiner, B. Role of success and failure in the learning of easy and complex tasks. Journal of Personality and Social Psychology, 1966, 3, 339-344.

Wendt, H. W. Motivation, effort, and performance. In D. C. McClelland (Ed.), Studies in motivation. New York: Appleton- Century-Crofts, 1955. Pp. 448-459.

White, R. W. Motivation reconsidered: The concept of competence. Psychological Review, 1959, 66, 297-333.

Winch, R. F. & Campbell, D. T. Proof? No. Evidence? Yes. The significance of tests of significance. American Sociologist, 1969, 4, 140-143.

Winterbottom, Marian R. The relation of need for achievement to learning experiences in independence and mastery. In J. W. Atkinson (Ed.), Motives in fantasy, action, and society. Princeton: Van Nostrand, 1958. Pp. 453-478.

Woodworth, R. S. Dynamics of behavior. New York: Holt, 1958.

Yerkes, R. M. & Dodson, J. D. The relation of strength of stimulus to rapidity of habit-formation. Journal of Comparative and Neurological Psychology, 1908, 18, 459-482.

Young, P. T. Motivation and emotion. A survey of the determinants of human and animal activity. New York: Wiley & Sons, 1961.

Zeigarnik, Bluma. Über das Behalten von erledigten und unerledigten Handlungen. Psychologische Forschung, 1927, 9, 1-85.

Zigler, E. Social deprivation and rigidity in the performance of feebleminded children. Journal of Abnormal and Social Psychology, 1961, 62, 413-421.

Zigler, E. Rigidity in the feebleminded. In E. P. Trapp & P. Himelstein (Eds.), Readings on the exceptional child. Research and theory. New York: Appleton-Century-Crofts, 1962. Pp. 141-162.

NAME INDEX

SUBJECT INDEX

APPENDIXES

APPENDIX A

Determination of sample size

One important and difficult question to be considered before carrying out an investigation is that of the size of the sample to be used. Other things being equal, the larger the sample, the more precise the information obtained. In other words, the larger the sample, the better the chance that false null hypotheses will be rejected. The problem lies in what degree of insecurity we are willing to accept, or what kind of chance we want to have to reject false null hypotheses.

Any statistical test of a null hypothesis can be regarded as a complex relationship between the following four parameters (Cohen, 1965, p. 96):

1. The power of the test, defined as 1- β. Here β means the probability of not rejecting a null hypothesis when in fact it is false (Type II error). Hence, 1 - β, the power of the test, means the probability of rejecting a false null hypothesis.

2. The region of rejection of the null hypothesis, determined by the α level and whether the test is one- or two-tailed. As α increases, power increases.

3. The sample size, N. As N increases, power increases.

4. The strength of the relationship in the population in question. The stronger the relationship, the greater the power.

These four parameters are so related to each other that when any three of them are fixed, the fourth is determined. This means that if we want to take a certain α risk, i.e. a certain risk of mistakenly rejecting the null hypothesis when it is true, and if we want our test to have a certain power to detect a relationship of a certain strength, then the sample size is given.

As to the first point, that of the α risk, significance of course exists on a continuum, and therefore a decision to regard a result as significant if the α risk does not exceed a certain value has to be regarded as a more or less arbitrary decision. Nevertheless this decision has to be made if one wants to set a desired power value in advance. In the present case there was no reason for deviation from the conventional 5 per cent risk as a limit.

With the regard to the question of the strength of the relationship, not just any non-zero values were being sought in this investigation, i.e. the relationship had to be of a certain strength to be of interest. In connection with this problem, Cohen suggests that in the absence of any basis for specifying an alternative to the null hypothesis, one should, as a convention, look for relationships of medium strength, operationally defined by him as population correlations of .40 (1965, pp. 98 f.). However, previous research within the achievement motivation area has often revealed relationships of a more modest strength (see for example McClelland et al., 1953, Chapter 8).

Accordingly, it was decided to look even for what Cohen characterizes as small relationships, operationally defined by him in terms of population correlations of .20.[1]

The next step then was to decide what the probability should be of rejecting the null hypothesis if the population correlation reached this critical value, i.e. to decide the power value to be sought. As a rule of thumb it is suggested that a value of .80 (β risk equal to .20) be sought when no other basis for selecting a power value is available (Cohen, 1965, pp. 98 f.). This suggestion was followed in the present case.[2]

Given these values, the sample size could be determined easily. Correlation values may be transformed to normally distributed values, z_r (Ferguson, 1966, pp. 185 f.), and since the hypotheses in this investigation are one-sided, the case may be illustrated as in Fig. A-1. The left part of the figure represents the sampling distribution of z_r if the null hypothesis is true, and point C marks the critical point for rejection of the null hypothesis with a 5 per cent α risk. The right part illustrates the sampling distribution of z_r if the population correlation is .20. With C as the critical point, the risk of not rejecting the null hypothesis is 20 per cent, i.e. the power of the test is .80. Further, $r = .00$ corresponds to $z_r = .00$, and $r = .20$ corresponds to $z_r = .20$ (Ferguson, 1966, p. 412).

----

1. In a later work on power analysis for the behavioural sciences Cohen argues that it may be meaningful to seek for even considerably smaller relationships, and therefore he has changed the operational definition of "small" relationships to population correlations of only .10 (Cohen, 1969, p. 76).

2. If this seems to be a low value, it should be noted that it is far higher than has been the case in most psychological investigations. Thus, of the studies reported in the Journal of Abnormal and Social Psychology, 1960, volume 61, not one had a power as high as .50 to detect "small" effects (Cohen, 1962, p. 150).

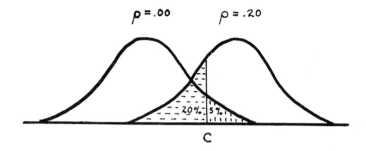

$$\rho = .00 \qquad \rho = .20$$

C

Fig. A-1. Sampling distribution of z_r in relation to critical point of rejection of the null hypothesis when the population correlation is .00 and .20.

Given the standard error of z_r,

$$\sigma_{z_r} = \frac{1}{\sqrt{N-3}} \qquad \text{(Ferguson, 1966, p. 186)}$$

the critical point C can be expressed in two different ways.

Referring to the left curve:

$$C = .000 + 1.65 \, \sigma_{z_r} = \frac{1.65}{\sqrt{N-3}}$$

Referring to the right curve:

$$C = .20 - .85 \, \sigma_{z_r} = .20 - \frac{.85}{\sqrt{N-3}}$$

This means that

$$\frac{1.65}{\sqrt{N-3}} = .20 - \frac{.85}{\sqrt{N-3}}$$

$$N \approx 153$$

So far only the case of the relationship between two variables has been discussed. The investigation was, however, concerned with two main predictor variables, the motives M_s and M_f, and with how persistence was related to these two variables simultaneously. This and other similar questions were to be analysed by multiple analysis of regression. However, the inclusion of more variables in the analyses had no practical consequences for the sample size to be aimed at in the present case. This is due to the fact that the degrees of freedom for the denominator, representing the estimate of error, in the F-test of regression are reduced by one only for each new variable included in the analysis. Consequently, the power of the test remains almost the same unless the number of variables added is very large, which it would not be in the present case, or the sample is a very small one (cf. a related problem discussed by Cohen, 1969, p. 373).

Finally, it may be argued that the values referred to above are more or less arbitrarily selected, which indeed they are. The rejection or acceptance of a hypothesis is of course in itself a cognitive process, a question of degree of be-lieving or disbelieving. Therefore, the important thing is not the set of selected critical values itself, but that such a set of values provides a frame of reference within which the results may be evaluated and interpreted.

INSTRUCTIONS FOR THE MODERATELY DIFFICULT/EASY PERSISTENCE
SITUATION (translated from the Norwegian)

We shall spend the rest of this session working at some tasks. I'll first pass round
a booklet and an envelope to each of you. Don't open the booklet until you are told
to do so. (Pass round the booklets and envelopes.)
    Now write your name on the front page of the booklet. (Short pause.)
    Now listen very carefully. The envelope you have received contains a booklet
with tasks which are very, very easy, so easy that all the pupils usually manage
them.
    The booklet you have written your name on contains tasks which are moderately
difficult, that is, so difficult that only about half of the pupils usually manage them.
We shall start with these moderately difficult tasks. But before we start on the tasks
themselves, we shall look at an example which will show us what to do.
    Turn to the next page, where "example" is written at the top. The task consists
of putting together the letters you can see there to make a word. (These letters,
T Y H E T, are written on the blackboard.) You can use the space under the letters
for trials. When you have found what the word is, you are to write it on the line to
the right of the letters.
    Has anybody found out what it is? (Whether or not they have found the solution,
the word, HYTTE, the Norwegian word for cottage, is written on the blackboard.)
Now, write the word HYTTE on the line to the right.
    You can see that there are many similar tasks on the next pages, where you are
to put letters together to make quite common Norwegian words. As I told you before,
these tasks are moderately difficult, that is, so difficult that only about half of the
pupils usually manage them. But before you start on the tasks, we would like to
know what you yourself think of your chances of solving them. From the figure at
the bottom of the page (a row of twenty small squares) you can see that the answers
may vary from "Quite sure I'll manage them" to "Quite sure I won't manage them"
If you mark a square far to the left it means that you are almost sure that you can
manage the tasks. A mark far to the right means that you are almost sure that
you can't manage the tasks, while a mark near the middle should mean that you
are very uncertain whether you'll manage them or not. Now, place a mark in the
square which is most appropriate for you.

    (Pause.)

    Now you must listen very carefully. In a moment you can get on with the tasks.
You are free to make as many trials as you want to, and if you fail at a task you
may skip it and turn to the next one. But, and this is very important, you may
also leave this task set and turn to the one in the envelope whenever you wish.
When you want to change task set, you just put the booklet you have now into the
envelope. So you may work for as long a time as you wish at the first, moderately
difficult task set, and turn to the other, very easy set, whenever you want to. But
do remember that when you have changed task set, you cannot go back to the first
set again.

    Since what I have said now is very important, I'll say it once more.

    The latter section of the instructions is then repeated, and after that the sub-

jects are told to start working. The time before each subject switches over to the

alternative task set is noted.

INSTRUCTIONS FOR THE EASY/MODERATELY DIFFICULT PERSISTENCE
SITUATION (translated from the Norwegian)

Today we are going to work at tasks which are rather different from those we had
last time. This time, too, I'm going to pass round an envelope and a booklet. Don't
open the booklet or the envelope yet. (Pass round the booklets and the envelopes.)
Now write your name on the front page of the booklet. (Short pause.)
Now you must listen very carefully. The envelope you have received contains a
set of tasks which are moderately difficult, that is, so difficult that only about half
of the pupils usually manage them. The booklet contains a task which is very, very
easy, that is, so easy that all of you will manage it. We shall start with this very
easy task.
Turn to the next page. At the top of the page you can see a row of simple
figures. Now you are to draw the same row of figures on the next line. Do
that. (Pause.)
The task now consists of filling in the rest of the lines down the page with the same
row of figures. When you have filled in the first page, you can go on with the next
one. You may keep on doing this task for as long as you wish, but you may also leave
it and switch over to the moderately difficult task set in the envelope whenever you
want to. But do remember that when you have changed task sets, you cannot go back
to the first booklet again. When you change task sets, put the booklet you have now
into the envelope.

The latter section of the instructions is then repeated, and after that the subjects
are asked to start working. The time before each subject switches over to the alternative task set is registered.

INSTRUCTIONS FOR THE EXTREMELY DIFFICULT/MODERATELY DIFFICULT
PERSISTENCE SITUATION (translated from the Norwegian)

Today we are going to work at tasks which are rather different from those we had
last time. This time, too, I'm going to pass round one envelope and one booklet.
The envelope is to remain closed for the moment. (Pass round the booklets and
the envelopes.)
   Now write your name on the front page of the booklet. (Short pause.)
   Now you must listen very carefully. The envelope you have received contains a
set of tasks which are moderately difficult, that is, so difficult that only about half
of the pupils are usually able to solve them. The booklet you have written your name
on, contains a task which is very, very difficult, so difficult that hardly more than
one out of a hundred pupils manages it. We shall start with this very difficult task.
But before we start with the task itself, we shall take an example which shows what
to do.
   Turn to the next page. There you can see a labyrinth, and you can also see the
route which the man in the figure has followed in order to pass through all the paths
in the labyrinth. Notice that he has passed only once through each of the paths and
that the routes do not cross at any point.
   You are now to try to solve a similar task, which as you heard me say is very,
very difficult, so difficult that the chances are very small that any of you will manage
it. Turn to the next page. You must now try to trace a line through all the paths in
the labyrinth you see there in such a way that the routes do not cross at any point.
But before you start on the task, we would like to know, as we did the first time,
what you yourself think of your chances of solving the task. You can show this by
marking a square in the figure at the top of the page (a row of twenty small squares).
You can see that the answers, like the first time, may vary from "Quite sure I'll
manage the task" to "Quite sure I won't manage the task". If you mark a square
far to the left, it means that you are almost sure you will manage the task. A mark
far to the right means that you are almost sure you won't manage the task, while a
mark near the middle means that you are very uncertain whether you'll manage it
or not. Now, put a mark in the square you think is most appropriate for you.
   (Pause.)
   Now you must listen very hard again. In a moment you can get on with the task.
Remember then that when you have failed in a labyrinth, you can go on with the next
one. All the labyrinths are equal. You are free to make as many trials as you want
to at this task, but you may also turn to the moderately difficult tasks in the envelope
whenever you wish. When you want to change task set, you just put the booklet you
have now into the envelope. So you may work at this first, very difficult task set for
as long as you wish, and turn to the other, moderately difficult set whenever you
want to. But do remember that when you have changed task sets, you cannot return
to the first set again.
   Since what I have said now is very important, I'll repeat it.

The latter section of the instructions is then repeated, after which the subjects
are asked to start working. The time before each subject switches to the alternative
task set is registered.

0534